Tried-and-True Recipes Make Entertaining Fun and Easy

IF YOU'VE EVER offered to host a special holiday dinner with family or a casual get-together with friends, you might have become panic-stricken when it actually came down to planning the menu. But those dread-filled days are over!

That's because *Taste of Home's Holiday & Celebrations 2006* is packed with 260 recipes to make Christmas, Thanksgiving, Easter and any other celebration throughout the year simple for the hostess. We provide menu options, timetables and family-tested recipes…so entertaining is easy!

'Tis the Season. The Christmas season is a flurry of activity. Take the worry out of every holiday happening with this chapter's merry array of 114 recipes, such as Crab-Stuffed Mushrooms, Pepper-Crusted Sirloin Roast, Butter Brickle Biscotti and Cashew Tossed Salad. Don't forget to check out the 17 dazzling chocolate desserts, including Dark Chocolate Souffle, Black Forest Tart and Mocha Latte Parfaits. We even offer menu ideas for an authentic Italian Christmas Eve seafood celebration, a Christmas Day dinner and a family-style St. Nick Party.

Giving Thanks. Are you looking to add a tasty twist to the Thanksgiving table but think your family will resist? We guarantee they'll fall for Citrus-Scented Brined Turkey, Cranberry Pear Stuffing, Curried Squash Soup and Apple-Sweet Potato Bake. In addition to your favorite pumpkin pie, try awesome autumn desserts like Cranberry Creme Brulee, Four-Fruit Pie and Honey-Pecan Tart. Plus, there are 13 delicious ideas for dressing up ordinary Thanksgiving leftovers!

Easter Gatherings. Early day dining is a snap with a bounty of brunch recipes, including Asparagus Strudel, Potato Sausage Frittata and Citrus Scones. Or invite six guests for an Easter dinner that features succulent chicken. Don't forget to round out your springtime meals with an assortment of oven-fresh breads.

Special Celebrations. You'll also find 76 family-favorite recipes for a host of other gatherings throughout the year. On Valentine's Day, prepare a romantic dinner for two. Southern comfort is in the spotlight at a Kentucky Derby bash, while on Memorial Day, a patriotic picnic is perfect. Have a teen turning Sweet 16? Plan a Mexican fiesta! Celebrate summer with recipes showcasing sweet, juicy berries or with a fun-filled hoedown. Then on Halloween, host a mad scientist "spooktacular!"

Can-Do Decorating Ideas. There are dozens of ideas for stunning table-toppers (such as the Fall Floral Centerpiece on page 117), eye-catching napkins (see page 159 for the Bunny Napkin Fold) and fun food crafts (like the Halloween Shrunken Apple Heads on page 245).

With perfect party menus, unforgettable fare and simple decorating ideas, *Taste of Home's Holiday & Celebrations Cookbook 2006* will help you make magical memories throughout the year!

WOULD YOU like to see one of your family-favorite recipes featured in a future edition of this timeless treasury? See page 256 for details!

Taste of Home's
HOLIDAY & Celebrations
COOKBOOK
2006

Executive Editor, Books: Heidi Reuter Lloyd
Senior Book Editor: Mark Hagen
Project Editor: Julie Schnittka
Senior Layout Designer: Julie Wagner
Associate Art Director: Linda Dzik
Craft Editor: Jane Craig
Editorial Assistant: Barb Czysz
Proofreaders: Linne Bruskewitz, Jean Steiner

Taste of Home Test Kitchens
Assistant Food Editor: Karen Scales
Senior Recipe Editor: Sue A. Jurack
Recipe Editor: Mary King
Contributing Copy Editor: Kristine Krueger
Test Kitchen Home Economists: Ann Liebergen, Annie Rose
Contributing Home Economists: Anne Addesso,
Susan Guenther, Dot Vartan

Taste of Home Photo Studio
Senior Food Photographer: Rob Hagen
Food Photographers: Dan Roberts, Jim Wieland
Associate Food Photographer: Lori Foy
Set Stylists: Julie Ferron, Stephanie Marchese,
Sue Myers, Jennifer Bradley Vent
Assistant Set Stylist: Melissa Haberman
Senior Food Stylist: Joylyn Trickel
Food Stylist: Sarah Thompson
Photo Studio Coordinator: Suzanne Kern

Reiman Media Group, Inc.
Creative Director: Ardyth Cope
Senior Vice President, Editor in Chief: Catherine Cassidy
President: Barbara Newton
Founder: Roy Reiman

Taste of Home Books
©2006 Reiman Media Group, Inc.
5400 S. 60th St., Greendale WI 53129
International Standard Book Number: 0-89821-511-0
International Standard Serial Number: 1535-2781
All rights reserved.
Printed in U.S.A.

Photo Credits: Furniture shown on pages 6-13 courtesy of Leath
Furniture. Furniture shown on pages 130-139 courtesy of Ashley
Furniture Homestores. Dishes and table linens shown on pages
168-177 courtesy of Belongings, Lake Geneva, Wisconsin. Photos on
pages 226-235 shot at Trimborn Farm, Greendale, Wisconsin.

For additional copies of this book, write *Taste of Home* Books,
P.O. Box 908, Greendale WI 53129. Or to order by credit card,
call toll-free 1-800/344-2560 or visit our Web site at
www.reimanpub.com.

PICTURED ON THE COVER: Citrus-Scented Brined Turkey (p. 112).

'TIS THE *Season*

The Christmas season provides ample opportunities to get together with family and friends. We offer two sit-down dinner choices—one formal affair with Individual Beef Wellingtons and one authentic Italian Christmas Eve feast, featuring assorted seafood dishes. Perhaps hosting a party with a table decked out in hors d'oeuvres or decadent chocolate desserts works better with your busy schedule. We have all of your holiday happenings covered with a merry array of recipes. We even offer ideas for making (and creatively packaging!) gifts from the kitchen.

'Tis the Season

Italian Christmas Eve Feast

IN OLD-TIME Italian tradition, Christmas Eve is a major celebration and features the Feast of the Seven Fishes.

Traditionally, this seafood supper is served after midnight mass and includes seven kinds of fish. (The number symbolizes Catholicism's seven sacraments.)

"My family has adhered to this custom for years," says Weda Mosellie of Phillipsburg, New Jersey. "I'm pleased to share the following six dishes with you."

You'll net compliments with Classic Antipasto Platter, Tomato Clam Chowder and Angel Hair Pasta with Tuna. (All recipes pictured at right.)

Round out the meal with Weda's Crabmeat Spread, Sicilian Fig Pastries and Tender Italian Sugar Cookies.

FROM-THE-SEA CELEBRATION

(Top to bottom)

Tomato Clam Chowder (p. 9)

Classic Antipasto Platter (p. 8)

Angel Hair Pasta with Tuna (p. 8)

Angel Hair Pasta with Tuna

(Pictured on page 7)

When my summer garden is in full bloom, I'll make homemade puree with fresh tomatoes.
Instead of tuna steaks, you can use two 10-ounce cans of chunk white tuna.

4 garlic cloves, minced
2 tablespoons olive oil
2 cans (29 ounces *each*) tomato
   puree
1/2 cup dry red wine *or* chicken
   broth
2 tablespoons minced fresh
   basil
1 to 1-1/2 teaspoons crushed
   red pepper flakes
1 teaspoon salt
2 to 2-1/2 pounds tuna steaks
2 packages (16 ounces *each*)
   angel hair pasta
1/2 cup grated Parmesan cheese

In a large saucepan, saute garlic in oil for 2-3 minutes or until tender. Stir in the tomato puree, wine or broth, basil, pepper flakes and salt. Bring to a boil. Reduce heat; simmer, uncovered, for 35-45 minutes or until flavors are blended.

In a large skillet coated with nonstick cooking spray, cook tuna over medium-high heat for 6-8 minutes on each side or until fish flakes easily with a fork. Flake tuna into large chunks; add to sauce. Cook pasta according to package directions; drain. Top with sauce; sprinkle with Parmesan cheese. **Yield:** 12 servings.

Classic Antipasto Platter

(Pictured on page 6)

This is a real favorite on our Christmas Eve buffet table.
The large platter of fish, cheese, olives and vegetables disappears quickly.

1 pound fresh mozzarella
   cheese, sliced
1 jar (16 ounces) pickled
   pepper rings, drained
1 jar (10 ounces) colossal
   Sicilian olives, drained
4 large tomatoes, cut into
   wedges
6 hard-cooked eggs, sliced
1 medium cucumber, sliced
1 medium sweet red pepper,
   julienned

1 can (3-3/4 ounces) sardines, drained
1 can (2 ounces) anchovy fillets, drained
1/4 cup olive oil
1 teaspoon grated Parmesan cheese
1 teaspoon minced fresh oregano
1/8 teaspoon salt
1/8 teaspoon pepper

On a large serving platter, arrange the first nine ingredients. In a small bowl, combine oil, Parmesan cheese, oregano, salt and pepper; drizzle over antipasto. **Yield:** 14-16 servings.

Tomato Clam Chowder

(Pictured at right and on page 7)

Steaming bowls of this Manhattan-style clam chowder really warm guests when they come in from the cold on Christmas Eve.

5 to 6 medium potatoes, peeled
  and diced
6 bacon strips, diced
1 small onion, finely chopped
2 celery ribs, chopped
1 garlic clove, minced
2 cans (6 ounces *each*) minced
  clams
2 cups water
1 can (15 ounces) tomato sauce
1 can (14-1/2 ounces) diced
  tomatoes, undrained
1/2 to 1 teaspoon pepper
1/4 teaspoon salt
2 teaspoons minced fresh
  parsley

Place the potatoes in a soup kettle or Dutch oven and cover with water. Bring to a boil. Reduce heat; cover and cook for 10-15 minutes or until tender.

Meanwhile, in a large skillet, cook bacon over medium heat until crisp. Using a slotted spoon, remove to paper towels; drain, reserving 2 tablespoons drippings. In the drippings, saute the onion, celery and garlic until tender.

Drain clams, reserving liquid; set clams aside. Drain potatoes and return to the pan. Add onion mixture, bacon and reserved clam liquid. Stir in the water, tomato sauce, tomatoes, pepper and salt. Bring to a boil. Reduce heat; simmer, uncovered, for 30-35 minutes or until heated through. Add clams and parsley; simmer 5 minutes longer. **Yield:** 11 servings (2-3/4 quarts).

Sicilian Fig Pastries

(Pictured at far right, bottom)

*These fig-filled desserts have true European flavor. They add just
the right amount of sweetness to the buffet table.*

    4 cups all-purpose flour
  3/4 cup shortening
  1/4 teaspoon salt
  1/3 cup sugar
  1/2 cup warm water
    1 egg, beaten
  1/4 teaspoon vanilla extract
FILLING:
  1/2 pound dried figs, chopped
  2/3 cup chopped walnuts
    1 tablespoon water
    1 tablespoon grape jelly
  1/2 teaspoon grated orange peel
  1/8 teaspoon ground cinnamon
    1 egg, beaten
    2 tablespoons sugar

In a food processor, combine the flour, shortening and salt; cover and process until mixture resembles coarse crumbs. In a bowl, dissolve sugar in warm water; stir in egg and vanilla. Gradually add to crumb mixture; pulse until dough forms a ball. Cover and let rest for 10 minutes.

In a food processor, combine the figs, walnuts, water, grape jelly, orange peel and cinnamon; cover and process until blended. Set aside.

Separate dough into six portions. On a lightly floured surface, roll each portion into a 12-in. x 8-in. rectangle (dough will be very thin). Cut into 4-in. x 2-in. rectangles. Place a teaspoon of fig mixture on one short side of each rectangle; fold dough over filling. Press edges with a fork to seal.

Place 1 in. apart on ungreased baking sheets. Brush with egg and sprinkle with sugar. Bake at 375° for 15-17 minutes or until golden brown. Remove from pans to wire racks. **Yield:** 3 dozen.

Crabmeat Spread

This versatile crab spread can be served warm or cold. Either way, it's delicious!

  1/4 cup mayonnaise
    2 tablespoons sour cream
    1 tablespoon sweet pickle relish
    1 teaspoon lemon juice
    1 pound canned crabmeat,
      drained, flaked and cartilage
      removed
    1 small onion, finely chopped
    1 celery rib, finely chopped
Paprika and pimiento-stuffed
  olives, optional
Assorted crackers *or* Italian bread
  slices

In a bowl, whisk the mayonnaise, sour cream, pickle relish and lemon juice until blended. Stir in the crab, onion and celery. Transfer to a serving bowl. Garnish with paprika and olives if desired. Serve with crackers.

Or spread on slices of bread. Place on a baking sheet; broil 4-6 in. from the heat for 1-2 minutes or until heated through. **Yield:** 3 cups.

Tender Italian Sugar Cookies

(Pictured at right, top)

These traditional cookies are moist and tender. To tie into the colors of the Italian flag, you could tint the icing red, green and white.

3/4 cup shortening
3/4 cup sugar
  3 eggs
  1 teaspoon vanilla extract
  3 cups all-purpose flour
  3 teaspoons baking powder
1/8 teaspoon salt
ICING:
  1/4 cup milk
    2 tablespoons butter, melted
  1/2 teaspoon vanilla extract
2-1/2 cups confectioners' sugar
Food coloring and colored sugar,
    optional

In a large mixing bowl, cream shortening and sugar. Beat in eggs and vanilla. Combine the flour, baking powder and salt; gradually add to creamed mixture and mix well.

Shape dough into 1-1/2-in. balls. Place 1 in. apart on ungreased baking sheets. Bake at 400° for 8-10 minutes or until lightly browned. Remove to wire racks to cool.

For icing, in a small bowl, combine the milk, butter, vanilla and confectioners' sugar until smooth. Tint with food coloring if desired. Dip the tops of cookies in icing. Sprinkle with colored sugar if desired. Place on waxed paper until set. **Yield:** 3 dozen.

CHRISTMAS EVE TIMELINE

A Few Weeks Before:

- Prepare two grocery lists—one for non-perishable items to purchase now and one for perishable items to purchase a few days before Christmas Eve.
- Purchase any items for Dressed-Up Dishes (opposite page).
- Bake Sicilian Fig Pastries and Tender Italian Sugar Cookies (don't ice the sugar cookies). Freeze.

Two Days Before:

- Buy remaining grocery items.
- Assemble Dressed-Up Dishes and set the table.
- Make the Crabmeat Spread; cover and chill.
- Prepare Tomato Clam Chowder; cover and refrigerate.
- Hard boil the eggs for the Classic Antipasto Platter; chill.

The Day Before:

- For Angel Hair Pasta with Tuna, make the marinara sauce. Cook and flake the tuna. Store sauce and tuna in separate containers; chill.
- Thaw the Sicilian Fig Pastries and Tender Italian Sugar Cookies at room temperature. Ice the sugar cookies.

Christmas Eve:

- Early in the day, assemble the Classic Antipasto Platter; refrigerate.
- For Angel Hair Pasta with Tuna, reheat marinara sauce; add tuna and heat through. Cook pasta; serve with sauce.
- Reheat the Tomato Clam Chowder. If desired, use a slow cooker.
- Set out the Classic Antipasto Platter.
- Make Crabmeat Spread canapes or serve cold.
- For dessert, serve Sicilian Fig Pastries and Tender Italian Sugar Cookies.

Dressed-Up Dishes

(Pictured above)

CHRISTMAS GUESTS will ask you to take a bow for presenting these pretty place settings!

First, set a dinner plate on a charger of your choice. (Options include gold, silver, wicker and colored.) Make sure the dinner plate fits in the indentation of the charger. Top with a coordinating salad plate.

Unwrap your creativity and tie a wide ribbon around the stack. Then make a bow. (Or attach a purchased, pre-made bow.)

This place setting cleverly ties into the gift-giving season.

EMBOSSED PLACE CARD

ADD even more elegance to your tabletop by making embossed place cards (as shown in the photo above).

Stop at your local craft store for plain place cards, a rubber stamp in the design of your choice, embossing ink, an embossing pen and embossing powder.

Stamp the front of the card with embossing ink. While still wet, sprinkle the stamped area with embossing powder. Tap to remove any excess powder. Heat with a heat gun until the embossing powder melts; let cool.

Use the embossing pen to write guests' names on each place card. Sprinkle with the embossing powder; heat and cool as directed above.

Merry Christmas Menu

WHEN gathering with a small group on Christmas Day, treat them to an elegant, sit-down dinner.

Welcome guests in from the outdoor winter wonderland with a hot, hearty appetizer like Stuffed Butterflied Shrimp.

Family and friends will sing your praises when you serve Individual Beef Wellingtons! These golden bundles feature a flaky crust, juicy beef tenderloin and a savory mushroom-wine sauce.

Surefire sides include Garlic Roasted Green Beans, Dilly Onion Dinner Rolls and Mushroom Spinach Salad.

Then wrap up the dinner for six with impressive White Chocolate Torte.

JOYFUL FARE
(Pictured above)

Individual Beef Wellingtons (p. 18)

Garlic Roasted Green Beans (p. 19)

Dilly Onion Dinner Rolls (p. 20)

Merry Christmas *Menu*

CHRISTMAS DAY AGENDA

A Few Weeks Before:
- Prepare two grocery lists—one for non-perishable items to purchase now and one for perishable items to purchase a few days before Christmas Day.
- From your butcher, order beef tenderloin steaks for the Individual Beef Wellingtons.
- Bake Dilly Onion Dinner Rolls; cool. Freeze in a single layer in large, heavy-duty resealable plastic bags.
- Make the Snowflake Table Runner and Napkin Wraps on page 21. Order a centerpiece from your florist.

Two Days Before:
- Set the table.
- Buy remaining grocery items, including the tenderloin steaks you ordered.

Christmas Eve:
- Bake the White Chocolate Torte; cool and frost as directed. Cover; chill.
- For Garlic Roasted Green Beans, clean and trim beans. Store in a plastic bag in your refrigerator's crisper drawer.

- Toast pine nuts; store in a covered container at room temperature.
- Make the dressing for Mushroom Spinach Salad; cover and chill.
- Pick up the centerpiece you ordered.

Christmas Day:
- In the morning, assemble the Individual Beef Wellingtons; cover with a damp paper towel and refrigerate. Prepare the mushroom-wine sauce; cover and chill.
- Assemble Stuffed Butterflied Shrimp; cover and refrigerate.
- Thaw the Dilly Onion Dinner Rolls at room temperature.
- As guests arrive, bake and serve the shrimp.
- Bake the beef wellingtons and reheat the mushroom-wine sauce.
- Make Garlic Roasted Green Beans as directed.
- If desired, wrap the rolls in foil and reheat in a 350° oven for 15-20 minutes. Set out the rolls with butter.
- Pour dressing over the Mushroom Spinach Salad; toss and serve.
- For dessert, slice White Chocolate Torte.

White Chocolate Torte

(Pictured at right)

Looking for a change from heavy, chocolate desserts? Try this white chocolate cake! It's wonderfully moist and slices well.
—Norma Van Devander, Calais, Maine

1 cup butter, softened
2 cups sugar
4 squares (1 ounce *each*) white baking chocolate, melted and cooled
4 eggs
1-1/2 teaspoons clear vanilla extract
3 cups all-purpose flour
1 teaspoon baking soda
1 cup buttermilk
1/2 cup water
1/2 cup chopped pecans, toasted

FROSTING:
2 packages (one 8 ounces, one 3 ounces) cream cheese, softened
1/3 cup butter, softened
4 squares (1 ounce *each*) white baking chocolate, melted and cooled
1-1/2 teaspoons clear vanilla extract
6-1/2 cups confectioners' sugar
White chocolate curls

Line three greased 9-in. round baking pans with waxed paper and grease the paper; set aside. In a large mixing bowl, cream butter and sugar. Add chocolate; mix well. Add eggs, one at a time, beating well after each. Beat in vanilla. Combine flour and baking soda; add to creamed mixture alternately with buttermilk and water. Fold in pecans. Pour batter into prepared pans.

Bake at 350° for 23-27 minutes or until a toothpick inserted near the center comes out clean. Cool for 10 minutes before removing from pans to wire racks; discard waxed paper.

For frosting, in a large mixing bowl, beat cream cheese and butter until smooth. Add chocolate and vanilla; mix well. Gradually add confectioners' sugar, beating until light and fluffy. Spread frosting between layers and over top and sides of cake. Garnish with chocolate curls. Store in the refrigerator. **Yield:** 14-16 servings.

Individual Beef Wellingtons

(Pictured on page 14)

A savory mushroom-wine sauce is draped over the golden pastry in this recipe from our Test Kitchen. The elegant entree is perfect to present to guests on Christmas.

6 beef tenderloin steaks (1-1/2 to 2 inches thick and 8 ounces *each*)
4 tablespoons butter, *divided*
3 sheets frozen puff pastry, thawed
1 egg, lightly beaten
1/2 pound sliced fresh mushrooms
1/4 cup chopped shallots
2 tablespoons all-purpose flour
1 can (10-1/2 ounces) condensed beef consomme, undiluted
3 tablespoons port wine
2 teaspoons minced fresh thyme

In a large skillet, brown steaks in 2 tablespoons butter for 2-3 minutes on each side. Remove and keep warm.

On a lightly floured surface, roll each puff pastry sheet into a 14-in. x 9-1/2-in. rectangle. Cut into two 7-in. squares (discard scraps). Place a steak in the center of each square. Lightly brush pastry edges with water. Bring opposite corners of pastry over steak; pinch seams to seal tightly. Cut four small slits in top of pastry.

Place in a greased 15-in. x 10-in. x 1-in. baking pan. Brush with egg. Bake at 400° for 25-30 minutes or until pastry is golden brown and meat reaches desired doneness (for medium-rare, a meat thermometer should read 145°; medium, 160°; well-done, 170°).

Meanwhile, in the same skillet, saute mushrooms and shallots in remaining butter for 3-5 minutes or until tender. Combine flour and consomme until smooth; stir into mushroom mixture. Bring to a boil; cook and stir for 2 minutes or until thickened. Stir in wine and thyme. Cook and stir 2 minutes longer. Serve with beef. **Yield:** 6 servings.

Mushroom Spinach Salad

A simple salad like this one is all you need to round out holiday dinners.
The unique dressing is delicious with oil, vinegar and soy sauce.
—Delma Braley, Lewiston, Maine

1 package (10 ounces) fresh baby spinach
1-1/2 cups sliced fresh mushrooms
3/4 cup sliced peeled cucumber
3 tablespoons olive oil
3 tablespoons white wine vinegar
4-1/2 teaspoons soy sauce
3/4 to 1-1/2 teaspoons minced garlic

1/4 teaspoon pepper
3/4 cup salad croutons

In a large salad bowl, combine the spinach and mushrooms. In a blender or food processor, combine the cucumber, oil, vinegar, soy sauce, garlic and pepper; cover and process until smooth. Pour over salad and toss to coat. Sprinkle with croutons. Serve immediately. **Yield:** 6 servings.

Stuffed Butterflied Shrimp

(Pictured at right)

These flavorful, baked shrimp can be an appetizer or entree. I've handed out this recipe to many friends and family.
—Joan Elliott, Deep River, Connecticut

24 uncooked unpeeled large
   shrimp
1 cup Italian salad dressing
1-1/2 cups seasoned bread crumbs
1 can (6-1/2 ounces) chopped
   clams, drained and minced
6 tablespoons butter, melted
1-1/2 teaspoons minced fresh parsley

Peel shrimp, leaving tail section on. Make a deep cut along the top of each shrimp (do not cut all the way through); remove the vein. Place shrimp in a shallow dish; add salad dressing. Set aside for 20 minutes.

Meanwhile, in a bowl, combine the bread crumbs, clams, butter and parsley. Drain and discard salad dressing. Arrange shrimp in a greased 13-in. x 9-in. x 2-in. baking dish. Open shrimp and press flat; fill each with 1 tablespoon of crumb mixture. Bake, uncovered, at 350° for 20-25 minutes or until shrimp turn pink. **Yield:** 2 dozen.

Garlic Roasted Green Beans

(Pictured on page 15)

This easy recipe is a family favorite throughout the year. It can be served warm or at room temperature, making it a great take-along dish.
—Laura Stahl, Two Harbors, Minnesota

2 tablespoons olive oil
1-1/2 pounds fresh green beans,
   trimmed
1 cup thinly sliced onion
12 garlic cloves, peeled and
   halved
1/4 to 1/2 teaspoon salt
1/8 teaspoon pepper
2 tablespoons balsamic vinegar
1/3 cup pine nuts, toasted

Brush a 15-in. x 10-in. x 1-in. baking pan with the oil. Place the green beans, onion and garlic in a single layer in pan. Sprinkle with salt and pepper. Bake, uncovered, at 400° for 25-30 minutes or until crisp-tender, stirring twice.

Transfer to a serving bowl. Drizzle with vinegar and toss to coat. Sprinkle with pine nuts. **Yield:** 6 servings.

Dilly Onion Dinner Rolls

(Pictured on page 14)

These light, golden rolls are packed with the flavors of onion and dill.
The dough can also be rolled out and cut with a biscuit cutter.
—Carol Faulkner, Sunman, Indiana

    1 package (1/4 ounce) active
       dry yeast
1/4 cup warm water (110° to 115°)
    1 cup (8 ounces) small-curd
       cottage cheese
    1 egg
    2 tablespoons sugar
    2 tablespoons dried minced
       onion
    3 tablespoons butter, softened,
       divided
    3 teaspoons dill seed, *divided*
    1 teaspoon salt
2-1/4 to 2-1/2 cups all-purpose flour

In a large mixing bowl, dissolve yeast in warm water. In a small saucepan, heat cottage cheese to 110°-115°. Add the cottage cheese, egg, sugar, onion, 1 tablespoon butter, 2 teaspoons dill seed, salt and 1 cup flour to yeast mixture; beat until well combined. Stir in enough remaining flour to form a stiff dough.

Turn onto a floured surface; knead until smooth and elastic, about 6-8 minutes. Place in a greased bowl, turning once to grease top. Cover and let rise in a warm place until doubled, about 1 hour.

Punch dough down. Turn onto a lightly floured surface; divide dough in half. Roll each portion into a 14-in. x 6-in. rectangle. Spread with 1 tablespoon butter.

With the dull edge of a table knife, score dough widthwise at 2-in. intervals. Using those marks as a guideline, make score marks widthwise across dough. Fold dough accordion-style, back and forth along creased lines. Cut folded dough into 1-in. pieces. Place each piece cut side down in a greased muffin cup.

Melt remaining butter; brush over dough. Sprinkle with remaining dill seed. Cover and let rise until doubled, about 30 minutes. Bake at 375° for 15-17 minutes or until golden brown. Remove from pan to a wire rack. **Yield:** 1 dozen.

Snowflake Table Runner And Napkin Wraps

(Pictured at right)

For a touch of class on the Christmas table, make a velvet table runner and six napkin wraps embossed with a simple snowflake design. Snowflake place card holders and a purchased flocked centerpiece further add to the snowy scene.

1/2 yard of velvet (rayon, not polyester) for runner and one 8-inch square of same velvet for each napkin wrap in color of your choice

All-purpose thread matching velvet

Flat metal snowflake ornament *or* snowflake rubber stamp

Press cloth

Iron

Quilter's marking pen *or* pencil

Double stick tape

For Velvet Napkin Wraps:

Cut an 8-inch square of velvet for each napkin wrap.

Place metal snowflake ornament or rubber stamp (stamp side up) on a hard, flat ironing surface. Center velvet right side down on top of ornament or stamp. Cover with damp press cloth. Press with iron and hold in place without moving it for about 10 seconds or until nap has been flattened. Carefully remove iron and press cloth. Let fabric cool before handling it.

Fold fabric with right sides together and opposite edges matching. Sew opposite edges together with a 1/2-inch seam to make a tube. Turn right side out and center design on the front.

Turn raw edges on one end under. Slip opposite end of tube inside folded edge. Hand-sew ends together. Center design on the front again and slip napkin inside.

For Velvet Table Runner:

Cut a 16-inch x 44-inch piece of velvet, trimming both ends to a point if desired.

Use quilter's marking pen or pencil to mark the position of the snowflakes on the back of the runner.

Emboss the snowflakes using the same technique as for the napkin wraps.

Apply double stick tape to wrong side of runner around all outside edges. Fold velvet to back to hem. Or turn raw edges 1/2 inch to the wrong side and sew hem in place with matching thread.

'TIS THE *Season*

Delightful Holiday Hors d'oeuvres

THERE'S no better way to welcome friends and neighbors into your holiday home than with a lovely table decked out in appealing appetizers!

For merry munching, offer an assortment of hot appetizers (such as Veggie Wonton Quiches and Peach-Glazed Meatballs) as well as cold choices (Beef Canapes with Cucumber Sauce, fruit and cheese, for instance).

A refreshing beverage like Fruity Rum Punch rounds out the evening. (All recipes are shown at right.)

To cater to a large number of people, use a buffet-style setup. Guests can easily help themselves, leaving you lots of time to meet and greet all those who've gathered.

SEASONAL SNACKING
(Pictured above)

Beef Canapes with Cucumber Sauce (p. 25)

Veggie Wonton Quiches (p. 24)

Peach-Glazed Meatballs (p. 24)

Fruity Rum Punch (p. 26)

Veggie Wonton Quiches

(Pictured on page 23)

*With green broccoli and red pepper, these mini quiches from our home economists are
a fitting finger food for Christmas. Crispy wonton cups make a tasty "crust."*

24 wonton wrappers
1 cup finely chopped fresh
   broccoli
3/4 cup diced fresh mushrooms
1/2 cup diced sweet red pepper
1/4 cup finely chopped onion
3 eggs
1 tablespoon water
2 teaspoons dried parsley flakes
1/4 teaspoon salt
1/4 teaspoon dried thyme
1/4 teaspoon white pepper
Dash cayenne pepper
3/4 cup shredded cheddar cheese

Gently press wonton wrappers into miniature muffin cups coated with nonstick cooking spray. Lightly coat wontons with nonstick cooking spray. Bake at 350° for 5 minutes. Remove wontons from cups; place upside down on baking sheets. Lightly coat with nonstick cooking spray. Bake 5 minutes longer or until light golden brown.

Meanwhile, in a nonstick skillet, cook the broccoli, mushrooms, red pepper and onion over medium heat for 4-5 minutes or until crisp-tender. In a bowl, whisk eggs and water; stir in the parsley, salt, thyme, white pepper and cayenne. Add to vegetable mixture; cook over medium heat for 4-5 minutes or until eggs are completely set.

Remove from the heat; stir in cheese. Spoon about 1 tablespoonful into each wonton cup. Bake for 5 minutes or until filling is heated through. Serve warm. **Yield:** 2 dozen.

Peach-Glazed Meatballs

(Pictured on page 23)

*When my daughter and her husband come to visit over the holidays, we enjoy nibbling on these
mouth-watering meatballs while playing games. Water chestnuts add a bit of crunch.*
— Christine Martin, Durham, North Carolina

2 eggs, lightly beaten
1 can (8 ounces) water chestnuts,
   drained and chopped
3/4 cup dry bread crumbs
1 tablespoon beef bouillon
   granules
1-1/2 pounds ground beef
1 jar (16 ounces) peach preserves
1 bottle (12 ounces) chili sauce
1 envelope onion soup mix

In a large bowl, combine the eggs, water chestnuts, bread crumbs and bouillon. Crumble beef over mixture and mix well. Shape into 1-in. balls. In a large skillet, cook meatballs in batches until no longer pink; drain. Return all to the skillet.

In a small saucepan, combine the preserves, chili sauce and soup mix. Cook over medium-low heat for 5 minutes. Pour over meatballs. Simmer, uncovered, for 10 minutes or until heated through. **Yield:** about 4-1/2 dozen.

Beef Canapes With Cucumber Sauce

(Pictured at right and on page 22)

A homemade cucumber yogurt sauce complements tender slices of beef in this recipe from our Test Kitchen. Both the meat and sauce are conveniently made in advance.

- 4 cups (32 ounces) plain yogurt
- 1 whole beef tenderloin (1-1/2 pounds)
- 2 tablespoons olive oil, *divided*
- 1 teaspoon salt, *divided*
- 1/4 teaspoon plus 1/8 teaspoon white pepper, *divided*
- 1 medium cucumber, peeled, seeded and diced
- 1 tablespoon finely chopped onion
- 1 garlic clove, minced
- 1 tablespoon white vinegar
- 1 French bread baguette, cut into 36 thin slices
- 1 cup fresh arugula

Line a fine mesh strainer with two layers of cheesecloth; place over a bowl. Place yogurt in strainer. Cover and refrigerate for at least 4 hours or overnight.

Rub tenderloin with 1 tablespoon oil. Sprinkle with 1/2 teaspoon salt and 1/4 teaspoon white pepper. In a large skillet, cook tenderloin over medium-high heat until browned on all sides. Transfer to a shallow roasting pan. Bake at 400° for 25-30 minutes or until a meat thermometer reads 145°. Cool on a wire rack for 1 hour. Cover and refrigerate.

Transfer yogurt from strainer to another bowl (discard yogurt liquid). Add the cucumber, onion, garlic and remaining salt and white pepper. In a small bowl, whisk the vinegar and remaining oil; stir into yogurt mixture.

Thinly slice the tenderloin. Spread yogurt mixture over bread slices; top with beef and arugula. Serve immediately or cover and refrigerate until serving. **Yield:** 3 dozen.

Fruity Rum Punch

(Pictured on page 23)

Our Test Kitchen home economists stirred together this sweet punch by combining four kinds of juice. Feel free to omit the rum for a kid-friendly option.

2 cups unsweetened apple juice
1-1/2 cups unsweetened pineapple juice
1 can (12 ounces) frozen cranberry juice concentrate, thawed
1 can (6 ounces) frozen orange juice concentrate, thawed
1 cup gold rum
4 cups club soda, chilled
Ice cubes

In a pitcher or punch bowl, combine the apple juice, pineapple juice, cranberry juice concentrate, orange juice concentrate and rum. Refrigerate until chilled. Just before serving, add club soda. Serve over ice. **Yield:** 10 servings (2-1/2 quarts).

Olive-Onion Cheese Squares

This rich appetizer goes a long way so it's perfect for potlucks and parties. I've relied on this recipe for more than 20 years, and it hasn't failed me yet!
—Sharon Ambrose, Mason, Michigan

1 package (16 ounces) hot roll mix
1 cup warm water (120° to 130°)
2 tablespoons butter, softened
1 egg, beaten
1 tablespoon minced chives
4 cups (16 ounces) shredded part-skim mozzarella cheese
1 cup mayonnaise
1/2 cup chopped green onions
1/4 cup chopped pimiento-stuffed olives
Grated Parmesan cheese

In a large bowl, combine the contents of hot roll mix and yeast packet. Stir in the warm water, butter, egg and chives until dough pulls away from sides of bowl. Turn onto a lightly floured surface; knead until smooth and elastic, about 5 minutes. Place in a greased bowl, turning once to grease top. Cover and let rest for 5 minutes.

Turn dough onto a lightly floured surface. Roll into a 15-in. x 10-in. rectangle. Transfer to a greased 15-in. x 10-in. x 1-in. baking pan.

In a large bowl, combine the mozzarella cheese, mayonnaise, onions and olives; spread over dough to within 1/2 in. of edges. Sprinkle with Parmesan cheese. Bake at 375° for 25-30 minutes or until lightly browned. Cut into 1-1/4-in. squares; serve warm. **Yield:** 8 dozen.

Chicken Satay

(Pictured at right)

Our home economists came up with this Asian-style dish featuring a simple-to-prepare peanut sauce. It's a hearty addition to an appetizer buffet.

2 pounds boneless skinless chicken breasts
1/3 cup soy sauce
1 green onion, sliced
2 tablespoons sesame oil
1 tablespoon brown sugar
1 tablespoon honey
2 garlic cloves, minced
1/2 teaspoon ground ginger

PEANUT SAUCE:
1/2 cup salted peanuts
1/4 cup chopped green onions
1 garlic clove, minced
3 tablespoons chicken broth
3 tablespoons butter, melted
2 tablespoons soy sauce
1 tablespoon lemon juice
1 tablespoon honey
1/2 teaspoon ground ginger
1/4 to 1/2 teaspoon crushed red pepper flakes

Flatten chicken to 1/4-in. thickness; cut lengthwise into 1-in.-wide strips. In a large resealable plastic bag, combine the soy sauce, onion, sesame oil, brown sugar, honey, garlic and ginger; add chicken. Seal bag and turn to coat; refrigerate for 4 hours.

In a food processor or blender, combine the peanuts, onions and garlic; cover and process until mixture forms a paste. Add the broth, butter, soy sauce, lemon juice, honey, ginger and pepper flakes; cover and process until smooth. Transfer to a bowl. Refrigerate until serving.

Drain and discard marinade. Thread chicken strips onto soaked wooden skewers. Broil 6 in. from the heat for 2-4 minutes on each side or until chicken is no longer pink. Serve with peanut sauce. **Yield:** 10-12 servings.

GET CREATIVE WITH CREAM CHEESE!

THE CHRISTMAS SEASON often includes spur-of-the-moment gatherings with friends and neighbors. You'll eagerly open your door to drop-in guests with these made-in-minutes munchies that start with convenient cream cheese and other items you can keep on hand.

1. Confetti Cheese Balls. Beat a 3-ounce package of softened cream cheese with 1 cup finely shredded cheddar cheese. Stir in 2 to 3 tablespoons each of chopped ripe olives, chopped pimiento and chopped green pepper. Shape mixture into 1-in. balls; roll half in chopped pecans and the other half in fresh minced parsley. Serve with crackers or breadsticks.

2. Pesto-Cream Cheese Spread. Cut an 8-ounce package of cream cheese in half diagonally. Turn one piece around and arrange both pieces with long sides touching to form a triangular "tree." Place a piece of a cinnamon stick at the base for the trunk. Spoon 1/2 cup of prepared pesto sauce over the cream cheese. Cut a 1-in. star out of red pepper and place it at the top of the tree. Serve with assorted crackers.

3. Hot Pizza Dip. Spread 8 ounces of softened cream cheese in a 9-in. pie plate. Top with 1/2 cup pizza sauce, shredded mozzarella cheese and pizza toppings like chopped onion, chopped green pepper, sliced ripe olives, sliced mushrooms and chopped pepperoni. Bake at 350° for 15-20 minutes. Serve with soft or hard breadsticks.

4. Speedy Taco Spread. Pour salsa over an 8-ounce block of cream cheese. (If desired, first cut the block into four sections and stagger on the plate.) Sprinkle with your favorite taco toppings such as shredded cheddar cheese, sliced green onion, chopped tomato and sliced ripe olives. Serve with corn or tortilla chips.

Shrimp Salad On Endive

(Pictured at right)

Our home economists make a simple-to-prepare shrimp salad and serve it on endive leaves for a from-the-sea version of lettuce wraps.

1/3 cup mayonnaise
1/2 teaspoon lemon juice
1/4 teaspoon dill weed
1/4 teaspoon seafood seasoning
1/8 teaspoon salt
1/8 teaspoon pepper
1/2 pound cooked shrimp, chopped
1 green onion, sliced
2 tablespoons chopped celery
1 tablespoon diced pimientos
2 heads Belgian endive, separated into leaves

In a small bowl, combine the first six ingredients. Stir in the shrimp, onion, celery and pimientos. Spoon 1 tablespoonful onto each endive leaf; arrange on a platter. Refrigerate until serving. **Yield:** about 1-1/2 dozen.

Crab-Stuffed Mushrooms

I've tried a variety of recipes for stuffed mushrooms. But when I make these seafood "shrooms," they seem to disappear before I can put them on a platter!
— Paula Cummings, Whitefish Bay, Wisconsin

2 pounds large fresh mushrooms
6 green onions, finely chopped
1/3 cup butter, cubed
1 can (6 ounces) lump crabmeat, drained
1 cup seasoned bread crumbs
2 tablespoons blue cheese
2 teaspoons minced fresh parsley
1/8 teaspoon salt

Remove mushroom stems and finely chop; set caps aside. In a large skillet, saute chopped mushrooms and onions in butter for 5-7 minutes or until tender. Remove from the heat. Stir in the crab, bread crumbs, blue cheese, parsley and salt. Spoon into mushroom caps.

Place on an ungreased baking sheet. Bake at 450° for 8-10 minutes or until heated through. **Yield:** about 2 dozen.

Santa Fe Chicken Pate

I love to cook, and appetizers are my specialty. My husband, son and I
have enjoyed this hearty spread for years. Hot pepper sauce adds some zest.
—Robin Lautenschleger, Wayland, Michigan

1 teaspoon vegetable oil
1 pound ground chicken
1/2 cup chopped onion
2 tablespoons chopped seeded
   jalapeno pepper
1 garlic clove, minced
3/4 cup mayonnaise
1/4 cup minced fresh cilantro
2 tablespoons lime juice
1 teaspoon ground cumin
1 teaspoon chili powder
1 teaspoon grated lime peel
1/4 teaspoon salt
1/4 teaspoon pepper
1/4 teaspoon hot pepper sauce,
   optional
Assorted crackers

In a large skillet over medium heat, heat oil. Add the chicken, onion, jalapeno and garlic. Cook until chicken is no longer pink, stirring to crumble. Drain; place in a food processor.

Add the mayonnaise, cilantro, lime juice, cumin, chili powder, lime peel, salt, pepper and hot pepper sauce if desired; cover and process until smooth. Transfer to a bowl. Refrigerate until serving. Serve with crackers. **Yield:** 2-1/4 cups.

Editor's Note: When cutting or seeding hot peppers, use rubber or plastic gloves to protect your hands. Avoid touching your face.

Sweet Spiced Tea

Welcome guests in from the cold at Christmas with this honey-laden hot tea from our Test Kitchen.
If you don't have orange-flavored tea, regular tea can be used with equally good results.

3 cinnamon sticks (3 inches)
2 orange peel strips (1 to 3
   inches)
12 whole cloves
12 whole allspice
3 quarts water
12 bags orange-flavored
   black tea
2/3 cup honey
1 tablespoon lemon juice
Orange slices, optional

Place the cinnamon sticks, orange peel, cloves and allspice on a double thickness of cheesecloth. Bring up corners of cloth; tie with string to form a bag. Place water and spice bag in a large kettle or Dutch oven; bring to a boil. Remove from the heat. Add tea bags; cover and steep for 5 minutes. Discard tea bags.

Add honey and lemon juice to tea; bring to a boil. Discard spice bag. Serve tea in mugs. Garnish with orange slices if desired. **Yield:** 3 quarts.

Hot Artichoke Spinach Dip

(Pictured at right)

This hot dip is favored by family and friends so it always appears on my party menus. To avoid last-minute fuss, I assemble it the night before and bake it when I need it the next day.
—Candy Jensen, Marrero, Louisiana

1/2 cup chopped green onions
2 tablespoons butter
4 ounces cream cheese, softened
2 packages (10 ounces *each*) frozen creamed spinach, thawed
1 can (14 ounces) water-packed artichoke hearts, rinsed, drained and chopped
1 cup (4 ounces) shredded Monterey Jack cheese
1 cup (4 ounces) shredded Swiss cheese
1 tablespoon Worcestershire sauce
1/2 teaspoon Cajun seasoning
1/2 teaspoon minced fresh thyme
1/2 teaspoon hot pepper sauce
1 garlic clove, minced
1/4 cup grated Parmesan cheese
Toasted baguette slices *or* pita chips

In a small skillet, cook onions in butter until tender; set aside. In a large mixing bowl, beat cream cheese until smooth. Stir in the onion mixture, spinach, artichokes, Monterey Jack and Swiss cheeses, Worcestershire sauce, Cajun seasoning, thyme, hot pepper sauce and garlic.

Transfer to a greased 1-1/2-qt. baking dish. Bake, uncovered, at 350° for 25-30 minutes or until bubbly around the edges.

Top with Parmesan cheese. Broil 4-6 in. from the heat for 3-5 minutes or until golden brown. Serve warm with baguette slices or pita chips. Refrigerate leftovers. **Yield:** 5 cups.

Jalapeno Poppers

*After sampling similar poppers at a wedding reception, I went home to
create my own recipe. The creamy filling pairs well with the crunchy, spicy peppers.*
—*James Brophy, Feasterville Trevose, Pennsylvania*

2 jars (11-1/2 ounces *each*)
  jalapeno peppers
1 package (8 ounces) cream
  cheese, softened
1 cup (4 ounces) shredded
  cheddar cheese
1/4 cup grated Parmesan cheese
1 tablespoon dried parsley flakes
2 teaspoons garlic salt
2 teaspoons paprika
1/4 cup all-purpose flour
3 eggs
1 cup crushed cornflakes
1/2 cup dry bread crumbs
Oil for frying
SAUCE:
1/4 cup mayonnaise
1/4 cup Russian salad dressing
1 teaspoon prepared horseradish
1 teaspoon dried parsley flakes
1/2 teaspoon pepper
1/4 teaspoon salt
Dash Louisiana-style hot sauce

Select 12-16 large jalapenos from jars; pat dry with paper towels (refrigerate any remaining jalapenos for another use). Remove stems from jalapenos; cut a lengthwise slit on one side. Discard seeds. In a small mixing bowl, combine the cheeses, parsley, garlic salt and paprika. Pipe or stuff into each pepper.

Place flour in a shallow bowl. In another shallow bowl, lightly beat the eggs. In a separate bowl, combine cornflakes and bread crumbs. Roll jalapenos in flour, dip in eggs, then roll in crumbs. Dip again in eggs, then roll in crumbs to completely coat.

In an electric skillet, heat 1/4 in. of oil to 375°. Fry peppers, a few at a time, for 30-60 seconds or until lightly browned. Drain on paper towels. In a small bowl, combine sauce ingredients. Serve with warm peppers. **Yield:** 12-16 appetizers.

Editor's Note: When cutting or seeding hot peppers, use rubber or plastic gloves to protect your hands. Avoid touching your face.

PREPARING JALAPENO POPPERS

TO SAVE TIME when making Jalapeno Poppers, fill them with the cream cheese mixture in the morning. Cover with plastic wrap and refrigerate. Just before guests arrive, fry the peppers as directed. Keep them warm in a 200° oven for up to 45 minutes.

Mozzarella Tomato Tartlets

(Pictured at right)

Convenient frozen phyllo shells add to this impressive appetizer's easy preparation. Although I make them year-round, they're especially tasty with garden-fresh tomatoes.
—Amy Golden, East Aurora, New York

1 garlic clove, minced
1 tablespoon olive oil
1-1/2 cups seeded chopped tomatoes
3/4 cup shredded part-skim
    mozzarella cheese
1/2 teaspoon dried basil
Pepper to taste
24 frozen miniature phyllo tart
    shells
6 pitted ripe olives, quartered
Grated Parmesan cheese

In a small skillet, saute garlic in oil for 1 minute. Add the tomatoes; cook until liquid has evaporated. Remove from the heat; stir in the mozzarella cheese, basil and pepper.

Spoon 1 teaspoonful into each tart shell. Top each with a piece of olive; sprinkle with Parmesan cheese. Place on an ungreased baking sheet. Bake at 450° for 5-8 minutes or until bubbly. **Yield:** 2 dozen.

Nutty Pimiento-Olive Spread

When my husband was a school bus driver, he received a jar of this special spread as a Christmas gift from a student. Now I like to share it with others.
—Marvel Gregerson, Baldwin, Wisconsin

2 packages (3 ounces *each*)
    cream cheese, softened
1/2 cup mayonnaise
1 cup chopped pimiento-stuffed
    olives
1/2 cup chopped pecans
Assorted crackers

In a small mixing bowl, beat cream cheese and mayonnaise until smooth. Stir in the olives and pecans. Cover and refrigerate overnight. Serve with crackers. **Yield:** 2 cups.

Blue Cheese Cheesecake

(Pictured at far right, bottom)

Whenever I set out this savory cheese spread, guests can't seem to stop eating it!
—*Niki Trapp, Cudahy, Wisconsin*

1 cup crushed butter-flavored
   crackers
3 tablespoons butter, melted
12 ounces cream cheese, softened
2 packages (4.4 ounces *each*)
   crumbled blue cheese
1 carton (6-1/2 ounces) garlic-
   herb cheese spread
1 cup (8 ounces) sour cream
3 eggs, lightly beaten
1/3 cup milk
1/4 cup sherry
1/4 teaspoon coarsely ground
   pepper
Assorted crackers

In a small bowl, combine cracker crumbs and butter; press onto the bottom of an ungreased 9-in. springform pan. Bake at 350° for 5 minutes or until lightly browned.

In a blender or food processor, combine the next eight ingredients; cover and process until blended. Pour over crust. Place pan in a large baking pan; add 1 in. of hot water to larger pan.

Bake for 50-55 minutes or until center is almost set. Remove springform pan from water bath. Cool on a wire rack for 10 minutes. Carefully run a knife around edge of pan to loosen. Refrigerate overnight. Remove sides of pan. Serve with crackers. **Yield:** 20 servings.

FREEZE SOME CHEESE

IF YOU'RE hosting a smaller gathering, you may want to cut the Blue Cheese Cheesecake into four wedges after refrigerating overnight.

Set aside one wedge for serving. Wrap the remaining pieces in plastic wrap. Place in a heavy-duty resealable plastic bag; seal bag and freeze for future use. To use, thaw completely in the refrigerator.

Cappuccino Punch

I first had this coffee-flavored punch at my baby shower, and it's been my favorite ever since. The beverage rivals any coffeehouse variety.
—*Angela Schwartz, Marietta, Georgia*

3-1/2 quarts water
2-1/3 cups sugar
3/4 cup instant coffee granules
1/2 cup chocolate syrup
1 gallon vanilla ice cream
1 pint coffee ice cream

In a large kettle, bring water to a boil. Remove from the heat. Stir in the sugar, coffee and chocolate syrup until sugar is dissolved. Cool to room temperature. Transfer to four half-gallon containers. Cover and refrigerate for 4 hours or overnight.

Just before serving, pour coffee mixture into a punch bowl. Add scoops of vanilla and coffee ice cream; stir until partially melted. **Yield:** about 2 gallons.

A Tasteful Cheese Tray

(Pictured above)

WHEN trying to decide on a cold option for your appetizer buffet, consider an easy-yet-elegant cheese tray. Guests can always find a cheese that pleases their palates. They also have a chance to discover some newfound favorites.

Here's a slice of advice for asembling an attractive cheese tray:

- Plan on about 2 ounces of cheese per person and use four to five kinds. Offer a blend of hard and soft cheeses, as well as sharp- and mellow-flavored varieties.
- Hard and semi-hard cheeses include Asiago, Parmesan, cheddar, Swiss, Gruyere, Edam, Gouda, Colby, Monterey Jack, Havarti, provolone and Jarlsburg.
- For semisoft cheese, we suggest blue, brick, Gorgonzola, Muenster, mozzarella and Roquefort.
- Brie, camembert, feta and goat cheese are some soft ripened cheese selections.
- Cheese will cut better when cold but tastes best at room temperature. Remove cheese from the refrigerator about an hour before serving. Cover and let stand at room temperature.
- Set out cheese knives for cutting and spreading wedges. Also have forks or picks for serving slices and cubes.
- Enhance the cheese tray with both sweet accompaniments (like grapes, strawberries, pears, apples and kiwi) and savory items (such as nuts, olives, salami and roasted red peppers).
- Offer a host of breadsticks, crackers and sliced bread on the side.
- As the finishing touch, garnish the trays with fresh herbs.
- Consider labeling the cheeses for your guests to reference.

'TIS THE *Season*

Festive Main Courses

SELECTING the all-important entree to showcase on your Christmas table can be a daunting task.

Whether you're hosting a casual buffet or a formal sit-down dinner, you can say good-bye to ho-hum holiday dinners by turning to the merry array of recipes on the following pages.

For elegant entrees, excellent options include Pork Loin with Peppers (pictured at right), Crab-Stuffed Beef Tenderloin and Chicken Breasts Grecian-Style.

Or chart a new course at a buffet with classy, casual fare like Apricot Ham Balls, Special Manicotti and Artichoke Spinach Lasagna.

With such enticing foods adorning the table, your holidays are sure to be happy!

PERFECT PORK
(Pictured above)

Pork Loin with Peppers (p. 38)

Parmesan Risotto (p. 120)

Pork Loin with Peppers

(Pictured on page 36)

A sweet and zesty sauce perfectly flavors pork and peppers in this
mouth-watering main course. The aroma while baking is unbeatable.
—*Jean Ecos, Hartland, Wisconsin*

1/3 cup Dijon mustard
3 tablespoons brown sugar
3 tablespoons horseradish
1 teaspoon minced fresh dill
1 boneless rolled pork loin
   roast (4-1/2 pounds)
2 medium green peppers, cut
   into 3-inch strips
2 medium sweet red peppers,
   cut into 3-inch strips
1/2 pound sliced fresh
   mushrooms
1-1/4 cups dry red wine, cranberry
   juice *or* grape juice
4-1/2 teaspoons lemon juice

In a small bowl, combine the mustard, brown sugar, horse-radish and dill; spread over roast. Place in a shallow roasting pan. Bake, uncovered, at 350° for 1 hour.

Arrange peppers and mushrooms around roast. Combine wine or juice and lemon juice; pour over vegetables. Bake 30 minutes longer or until a meat thermometer reads 160° and vegetables are tender.

Remove vegetables and keep warm. Broil roast 4-6 in. from the heat for 5-7 minutes or until a crust forms. Let stand for 10 minutes before slicing. Serve with vegetables. **Yield:** 12 servings.

Chicken Breasts Grecian-Style

When my husband and I have guests for dinner, we try to make the meal impressive as well as tasty.
These chicken breasts stuffed with a flavorful feta cheese and spinach mixture fit the bill.
—*Dorothy Johnson, Punta Gorda, Florida*

1 package (10 ounces) frozen
   chopped spinach, thawed and
   squeezed dry
2 packages (4 ounces *each*)
   crumbled feta cheese
1/2 cup mayonnaise
1/4 cup all-purpose flour
6 to 8 boneless skinless chicken
   breast halves
Pinch pepper
6 to 8 bacon strips

In a bowl, combine the spinach, feta cheese, mayonnaise and flour; set aside. Cut a 2-in.-deep pocket in the side of each chicken breast half. Lightly fill each pocket with spinach mixture. Sprinkle with pepper.

Wrap a strip of bacon around each piece of chicken; spoon 1 tablespoon of spinach mixture on top of each. Place in a greased 13-in. x 9-in. x 2-in. baking dish. Bake, uncovered, at 325° for 50-60 minutes or until juices run clear. **Yield:** 6-8 servings.

Herbed Roast Turkey Breast

(Pictured at right)

I made this turkey breast for my first formal dinner party as a newlywed. It was such a success that it's become a standby on all of my entertaining menus.
—Lisa Mahon Fluegeman
Cincinnati, Ohio

5 teaspoons lemon juice
1 tablespoon olive oil
1 to 2 teaspoons pepper
1 teaspoon dried rosemary, crushed
1 teaspoon dried thyme
1 teaspoon garlic salt
1 bone-in turkey breast (6 to 7 pounds)
1 medium onion, cut into wedges
1 celery rib, cut into 2-inch pieces
1/2 cup white wine *or* chicken broth

In a small bowl, combine the lemon juice and oil. In another bowl, combine the pepper, rosemary, thyme and garlic salt. With fingers, carefully loosen the skin from both sides of turkey breast. Brush oil mixture under the skin; rub with herb mixture.

Arrange onion and celery in a 3-qt. baking dish. Place turkey breast, skin side up, on top of vegetables. Pour wine or broth into the dish.

Bake, uncovered, at 325° for 2 to 2-1/2 hours or until a meat thermometer reads 170°, basting every 30 minutes with pan drippings. (Cover loosely with foil if turkey browns too quickly.) Cover and let stand for 15 minutes before carving. **Yield:** 6 servings.

Individual Seafood Casseroles

*My husband can't get enough of these mini casseroles and is disappointed when
there aren't leftovers. This dish is a mainstay on my holiday menus.*
—*Jaelynne Smigel, Vancouver, British Columbia*

1/3 cup chopped onion
1/3 cup butter
1/3 cup all-purpose flour
1/2 teaspoon salt
1/2 teaspoon white pepper
1-1/2 cups milk
1 cup heavy whipping cream

3 tablespoons *each* finely chopped sweet red and green pepper
2 teaspoons curry powder
1 teaspoon ground mustard
1/4 teaspoon dried thyme
1/4 teaspoon *each* ground ginger and turmeric
1/2 teaspoon lemon juice
3 to 5 drops hot pepper sauce
3 cans (6 ounces *each*) crabmeat, drained, flaked and cartilage removed
1 can (6 ounces) tuna, drained and flaked
1/4 pound cooked medium shrimp, peeled and deveined
2 hard-cooked eggs, chopped

TOPPING:
1/2 cup shredded cheddar cheese
1/4 cup dry bread crumbs
1/4 teaspoon garlic powder
1 tablespoon *each* chopped sweet red and green pepper

In a large saucepan, saute onion in butter until tender. Stir in flour, salt and pepper until blended. Gradually whisk in milk and cream. Bring to a boil; cook and stir for 2 minutes or until thickened and bubbly. Stir in the peppers, seasonings, lemon juice and hot pepper sauce until blended.

Remove from the heat; add the crab, tuna, shrimp and eggs. Transfer to six greased ovenproof 10-oz. dishes.

In a small bowl, combine the cheese, bread crumbs and garlic powder. Sprinkle over seafood mixture. Bake, uncovered, at 350° for 15 minutes. Sprinkle with peppers. Bake 5-8 minutes longer or until heated through and edges are bubbly. **Yield:** 6 servings.

Editor's Note: This casserole can also be baked in a greased 2-quart baking dish for 25 to 30 minutes.

Crab-Stuffed Beef Tenderloin

(Pictured at right)

Here's a deliciously different way to serve surf and turf. It's an elegant entree that often appears on my Christmas dinner table.
—*Gloria Warczak, Cedarburg, Wisconsin*

8 bacon strips
1 beef tenderloin (3 pounds)
3 pouches (6 ounces *each*) lump crabmeat
1 cup water, *divided*
1/2 cup burgundy wine *or* beef broth
2 teaspoons lemon juice
2 tablespoons minced green onion
1 tablespoon butter
1 tablespoon steak sauce
1 teaspoon soy sauce
1 teaspoon browning sauce, optional
1 teaspoon sugar
1-1/2 teaspoons minced fresh parsley *or* 1/2 teaspoon dried parsley flakes

In a large skillet, cook bacon over medium heat until cooked but not crisp. Remove to paper towels to drain.

Make a lengthwise slit down the center of tenderloin to within 1/2 in. of bottom. Open meat so it lies flat. Mound crab over the center. Close tenderloin; tie at 2-in. intervals with kitchen string. Place on a rack in a shallow roasting pan. Wrap bacon around meat. Combine 1/2 cup water, wine or broth and lemon juice; pour over beef.

Bake, uncovered, at 425° for 45-60 minutes or until meat reaches desired doneness (for medium-rare, a meat thermometer should read 145°; medium, 160°; well-done, 170°). Remove meat to a serving platter. Cover and let stand for 10 minutes.

Pour pan drippings and loosened brown bits into a saucepan. Skim fat. Stir in the onion, butter, steak sauce, soy sauce, browning sauce if desired, sugar and remaining water. Bring to a boil. Reduce heat; simmer, uncovered, for 5 minutes. Stir in parsley. Slice tenderloin; serve with sauce. **Yield:** 10 servings.

VEGETABLE RIBBONS

IN ADDITION to serving Crab-Stuffed Beef Tenderloin with mashed potatoes, make vegetable ribbons like the ones pictured above.

With a vegetable peeler or metal cheese slicer, cut a very thin slice down the length of 5 small yellow summer squash and 5 small zucchini, making long ribbons. Place in a steamer basket in a saucepan over 1 in. of boiling water. Cover and steam for 2-3 minutes or until tender. Transfer to a bowl; season with melted butter, salt and pepper.

Apricot Ham Balls

My family requests these ham balls for our annual Christmas Eve open house.
—Loretta Walker, Great Falls, Montana

3 eggs
1-3/4 cups apricot nectar, *divided*
1 cup dry bread crumbs
1/4 cup chopped onion
1-1/2 pounds ground fully cooked ham
1 pound bulk pork sausage
1 cup packed brown sugar
1/4 cup vinegar
2 tablespoons all-purpose flour
1 teaspoon ground mustard
1/2 teaspoon ground allspice
1/2 teaspoon Worcestershire sauce

In a large bowl, whisk eggs and 3/4 cup apricot nectar. Stir in bread crumbs and onion. Crumble ham and sausage over mixture and mix well. Shape into 2-in. balls. Place in an ungreased 13-in. x 9-in. x 2-in. baking dish.

In a bowl, combine the brown sugar, vinegar, flour, mustard, allspice, Worcestershire sauce and remaining apricot nectar. Pour over ham balls. Bake, uncovered, at 325° for 45-50 minutes or until meat is no longer pink. **Yield:** 8 servings.

APPETIZER APRICOT HAM BALLS

APRICOT Ham Balls can also be served as an appetizer. Shape meat mixture into 1-in. balls; place in an ungreased 13-in. x 9-in. x 2-in. baking dish. Combine sauce ingredients; pour over top. Bake at 325° for 25-30 minutes or until meat is no longer pink.

Serve immediately. Or cool and refrigerate overnight. Reheat in a slow cooker before guests arrive.

Pepper-Crusted Sirloin Roast

Guests will be surprised to hear this festive entree only calls for
five ingredients. It's the perfect choice when feeding a large group.
—Mary Ann Griffin, Saginaw, Michigan

1 boneless beef sirloin tip roast (4 pounds)
2 tablespoons Dijon mustard
1 tablespoon coarsely ground pepper
1 tablespoon minced fresh rosemary *or* 1 teaspoon dried rosemary, crushed
1 tablespoon minced fresh mint *or* 1 teaspoon dried mint

Place roast, fat side up, on a rack in a shallow roasting pan; spread with mustard. Combine the pepper, rosemary and mint; press into mustard.

Bake, uncovered, at 350° for 2-1/4 to 3 hours or until meat reaches desired doneness (for medium-rare, a meat thermometer should read 145°; medium, 160°; well-done, 170°). Cover and let stand for 10-15 minutes before slicing. **Yield:** 12-16 servings.

Cranberry Catch of the Day

(Pictured at right)

Most folks may not think of serving fish for Christmas. But a colorful cranberry sauce and pleasant pecan dressing make this entree elegant.
—Linda Patrick, Houston, Texas

1-1/2 cups chopped celery
1/2 cup chopped onion
9 tablespoons butter, *divided*
6 cups cubed bread
3/4 cup chopped pecans
1/3 cup orange juice
1-1/2 teaspoons grated orange peel
1 teaspoon salt, *divided*
6 haddock, cod *or* halibut fillets
(6 ounces *each*)

ORANGE-CRANBERRY SAUCE:
1/2 cup sugar
2 teaspoons cornstarch
1/2 cup water
1/2 cup orange juice
1 cup fresh *or* frozen cranberries
2 teaspoons grated orange peel

In a large skillet over medium heat, cook and stir celery and onion in 6 tablespoons butter until tender. Stir in the bread cubes, pecans, orange juice, orange peel and 1/2 teaspoon salt. Transfer to a greased 13-in. x 9-in. x 2-in. baking dish. Arrange fillets over stuffing.

Melt remaining butter; drizzle over fillets. Sprinkle with remaining salt. Bake, uncovered, at 350° for 25-28 minutes or until fish flakes easily with a fork.

In a small saucepan, combine sugar and cornstarch; whisk in water and orange juice until smooth. Bring to a boil, stirring constantly. Add cranberries; cook for 5 minutes or until berries pop. Stir in orange peel. Serve with fish and stuffing. **Yield:** 6 servings.

Special Manicotti

*This classic casserole is terrific to serve at more casual Christmas gatherings.
It's so special because it features both a white and red sauce.*
—*Karen Hanger, Keizer, Oregon*

2 cups water
1 can (6 ounces) tomato paste
1 tablespoon sugar
1 tablespoon Worcestershire sauce
MANICOTTI:
1 pound ground beef *or* bulk Italian sausage
1 garlic clove, minced
1 package (10 ounces) fresh spinach
3 tablespoons grated Parmesan cheese
2 tablespoons half-and-half cream
1 egg, lightly beaten
1 tablespoon dried parsley flakes
Salt and pepper to taste
1 package (8 ounces) manicotti shells, cooked and drained
WHITE SAUCE:
1/4 cup butter
1/4 cup all-purpose flour
1/2 teaspoon salt
2 cups milk

In a saucepan, combine the water, tomato paste, sugar and Worcestershire sauce. Bring to a boil. Reduce heat; cover and simmer for 30 minutes. Meanwhile, in a large skillet, cook beef and garlic over medium heat until meat is no longer pink; drain and set aside.

Place spinach in a steamer basket; place in a saucepan over 1 in. of water. Bring to a boil; cover and steam for 2-3 minutes or until wilted. Drain on paper towels; finely chop. Add to beef. Stir in the Parmesan cheese, cream, egg, parsley, salt and pepper. Stuff into manicotti shells. Spread 1 cup of the tomato sauce in a greased 13-in. x 9-in. x 2-in. baking dish. Place manicotti over sauce.

For white sauce, melt butter in a small saucepan. Stir in flour until smooth; gradually add milk. Bring to a boil; cook and stir for 1-2 minutes or until thickened. Pour over manicotti. Top with remaining tomato sauce.

Cover and bake at 350° for 30 minutes. Uncover; bake 15 minutes longer or until heated through. Let stand for 5 minutes before serving. **Yield:** 6 servings.

FILLING MANICOTTI SHELLS

TO save time and effort when filling manicotti shells, use this simple technique.

Place the filling in a heavy-duty resealable plastic bag. Cut a 1/2-inch hole in one corner. Holding a noodle in one hand, pipe the filling into one end; turn the noodle around and fill the other end.

Artichoke Spinach Lasagna

(Pictured at right)

We were served this meatless entree while visiting friends in Maryland. We took the recipe with us when we left and have since added a few more ingredients which make it even better.

—Carole Rago, Altoona, Pennsylvania

1/2 cup chopped onion
  4 garlic cloves, minced
  1 tablespoon olive oil
  1 can (14-1/2 ounces) vegetable *or* chicken broth
  1 teaspoon dried rosemary, crushed
1/4 teaspoon ground nutmeg
1/4 teaspoon pepper
  1 can (14 ounces) water-packed artichoke hearts, rinsed and drained
  1 package (10 ounces) frozen chopped spinach, thawed and squeezed dry
1/2 cup sliced fresh mushrooms
  1 jar (16 ounces) roasted garlic Alfredo *or* Parmesan and mozzarella pasta sauce
12 no-cook lasagna noodles
  3 cups (12 ounces) shredded part-skim mozzarella cheese, *divided*
  1 cup crumbled tomato and basil feta cheese *or* feta cheese
1/8 teaspoon garlic powder
1/8 teaspoon *each* dried oregano, parsley flakes and basil

In a large saucepan, saute onion and garlic in oil for 2-3 minutes or until tender. Stir in the broth, rosemary, nutmeg and pepper. Bring to a boil. Add artichokes, spinach and mushrooms. Reduce heat; cover and simmer for 5 minutes. Stir in pasta sauce.

Spread 1 cup sauce mixture into a greased 13-in. x 9-in. x 2-in. baking dish. Top with three noodles and 3/4 cup mozzarella cheese. Repeat layers three times. Top with remaining sauce mixture and mozzarella cheese. Sprinkle with feta cheese, garlic powder, oregano, parsley and basil.

Cover and bake at 350° for 40 minutes. Uncover; bake 15 minutes longer or until heated through. Let stand for 10 minutes before cutting. **Yield:** 12 servings.

'TIS THE Season

Dazzling Chocolate Desserts

JUST say the word "chocolate" and people's mouths water in eager anticipation of sweet and satisfying delicacies!

Before the time for New Year's resolutions arises, why not indulge in one—or several—of the chocolate concoctions in this chapter?

For a marvelous make-ahead recipe designed for hurried, holiday cooks, give Mocha Almond Dessert a try.

Looking to impress guests? Irresistibly rich Dark Chocolate Souffle fits the bill.

And a yummy Yuletide treat like Chocolate Pecan Torte will elicit countless compliments (and recipe requests) for the hostess. (All recipes shown at right.)

CHOICE CHOCOLATE
(Clockwise from the bottom)

Mocha Almond Dessert (p. 50)

Dark Chocolate Souffle (p. 52)

Chocolate Pecan Torte (p. 48)

Chocolate Pecan Torte

(Pictured on page 47)

This impressive dessert looks lovely on a buffet table. It requires
several steps but is worth the effort for special occasions.
—Lois Schlickau, Haven, Kansas

8 eggs, *separated*
1-1/2 cups sugar, *divided*
1-1/2 cups ground pecans
  2/3 cup all-purpose flour
  2/3 cup baking cocoa
   1 teaspoon baking soda
1/2 teaspoon salt
1/2 cup water
   2 teaspoons vanilla extract
CHOCOLATE FROSTING:
   3 cups heavy whipping cream
   1 cup confectioners' sugar
1/2 cup baking cocoa
   2 teaspoons vanilla extract
CHOCOLATE GLAZE:
   2 tablespoons baking cocoa
   2 tablespoons water
   1 tablespoon butter
   1 cup confectioners' sugar
1/4 teaspoon vanilla extract

Let eggs stand at room temperature for 30 minutes. In a large mixing bowl, beat egg yolks. Gradually add 1 cup sugar, beating until thick and lemon-colored. Combine pecans, flour, cocoa, baking soda and salt; add to yolk mixture alternately with water. Stir in vanilla.

In another mixing bowl, beat egg whites until foamy. Gradually add remaining sugar, beating until stiff peaks form; fold into batter. Spoon into two greased and floured 9-in. round baking pans. Bake at 375° for 20-22 minutes or until cake springs back when lightly touched. Cool for 10 minutes before removing from pans to wire racks to cool completely.

For frosting, in a large mixing bowl, beat cream until soft peaks form. Beat in confectioners' sugar, cocoa and vanilla until stiff peaks form. Split each cake into two horizontal layers. Spread about 1 cup frosting between each layer.

For glaze, in a small saucepan, combine cocoa, water and butter. Cook and stir over medium heat until butter is melted. Remove from the heat; stir in confectioners' sugar and vanilla until smooth. Spread over top cake layer. Spread remaining frosting over sides of cake. Store in the refrigerator. **Yield:** 12-16 servings.

LESSONS IN CHOCOLATE

- Chocolate will stay fresh for about a year if kept in a cool, dry place. Dark chocolate can be stored even longer.
- Sometimes chocolate develops white or gray "blooms" on its surface. This just means that the cocoa butter has separated. While it doesn't look pretty, the chocolate is still fine to use.
- Chocolate can scorch over high heat (generally above 115°). It's better to melt chocolate slowly in the microwave or over low heat in a double boiler.
- When microwaving chocolate, keep in mind that chips and chunks may still appear formed and unmelted after heating but will become fluid upon stirring.
- Water can make chocolate seize so always use dry utensils and pans.

Black Forest Tart

(Pictured at right)

Cherry pie filling and a melted chocolate drizzle tastefully top a rich, fudgy cake in this elegant dessert from our home economists.

1-1/4 cups chocolate wafer crumbs
  1/4 cup sugar
  1/4 cup butter, melted

FILLING:
  1/2 cup butter
    6 squares (1 ounce *each*) semisweet chocolate, chopped
    3 eggs
  2/3 cup sugar
    1 teaspoon vanilla extract
  1/4 teaspoon salt
  2/3 cup all-purpose flour

TOPPING:
    1 can (21 ounces) cherry pie filling
    2 squares (1 ounce *each*) semisweet chocolate, chopped
    1 tablespoon heavy whipping cream

In a small bowl, combine wafer crumbs and sugar; stir in butter. Press onto the bottom and up the sides of a lightly greased 11-in. tart pan with removable bottom. Place pan on a baking sheet. Bake at 350° for 8-10 minutes or until lightly browned. Cool on a wire rack.

In a microwave-safe bowl, melt butter and chocolate; stir until smooth. Cool for 10 minutes. In a large mixing bowl, beat the eggs, sugar, vanilla and salt until thickened, about 4 minutes. Blend in chocolate mixture. Add the flour and mix well.

Pour into crust; spread evenly. Bake at 350° for 25-30 minutes or until a toothpick inserted near the center comes out clean. Cool completely on a wire rack.

Spread pie filling over the top. In a small microwave-safe bowl, combine chocolate and cream. Microwave on high for 20-30 seconds or until chocolate is melted; stir until smooth. Cool for 5 minutes, stirring occasionally. Drizzle over tart. Chill until set. **Yield:** 12 servings.

Editor's Note: This recipe was tested in a 1,100-watt microwave. This tart is best served the day it is prepared.

Mocha Almond Dessert

(Pictured on page 46)

For an easy, make-ahead dessert that's elegant and luscious, try this recipe from our Test Kitchen.
The perfect blend of mocha and chocolate is in each cool, refreshing slice.

1 cup cream-filled chocolate
   sandwich cookie crumbs
1/4 cup sugar
1/4 cup butter, melted
1 package (8 ounces) cream
   cheese, softened
1 can (14 ounces) sweetened
   condensed milk
2/3 cup chocolate syrup
1/2 teaspoon vanilla extract
2 tablespoons instant coffee
   granules
1 tablespoon hot water
1 cup whipped topping
1/3 cup chopped almonds, toasted
Chocolate-covered coffee beans,
  optional

In a small bowl, combine the cookie crumbs, sugar and butter. Press onto the bottom and 1 in. up the sides of a greased 9-in. springform pan; set aside.

In a large mixing bowl, beat cream cheese, milk, chocolate syrup and vanilla until smooth. Dissolve coffee granules in hot water; beat into cream cheese mixture. Fold in whipped topping and almonds. Pour over crust. Cover and freeze for 8 hours or overnight.

Remove from the freezer 10-15 minutes before serving. Carefully run a knife around edge of pan to loosen. Remove sides of pan. Garnish with coffee beans if desired. **Yield:** 10-12 servings.

Chocolate Cheese Pie

The creamy chocolate filling pairs well with the crisp coconut crust in this pleasing pie.
—Lorraine Caland, Thunder Bay, Ontario

2-1/2 cups flaked coconut, toasted
1/3 cup butter, melted
Dash ground cinnamon, optional
FILLING:
1 package (8 ounces) cream
   cheese, softened
1/2 cup packed brown sugar
1 teaspoon vanilla extract
Dash salt

1 cup (6 ounces) semisweet chocolate chips, melted
  and cooled
1 cup heavy whipping cream, whipped

In a small bowl, combine the coconut, butter and cinnamon if desired. Press onto the bottom and up the sides of a greased 9-in. pie plate. Refrigerate for at least 30 minutes or until firm.

In a large mixing bowl, beat the cream cheese, brown sugar, vanilla and salt until smooth. Add chocolate; mix well. Fold in whipped cream. Pour into crust. Cover and refrigerate overnight. **Yield:** 8 servings.

Chocolate Crepes

(Pictured at right)

If you think crepes are merely breakfast fare, our home economists insist you try these cream-filled chocolate crepes for dessert!

1-1/2 cups milk
   3 eggs
   3 tablespoons water
   2 tablespoons vegetable oil
1-1/2 teaspoons vanilla extract
1-1/2 cups all-purpose flour
  1/4 cup sugar
  1/4 cup baking cocoa
  1/8 teaspoon salt
FILLING:
   1 package (8 ounces) cream
     cheese, softened
  1/4 cup sugar
  1/2 cup sour cream
  1/2 teaspoon vanilla extract
  1/3 cup creme de cacao
   1 carton (8 ounces) frozen
     whipped topping, thawed
FUDGE SAUCE:
  3/4 cup semisweet chocolate chips
  1/4 cup butter
  1/2 cup sugar
  2/3 cup half-and-half cream
  10 mint Andes candies, chopped,
     optional

For batter, place the first nine ingredients in a blender or food processor. Cover and process until smooth. Refrigerate for 1 hour.

Meanwhile, in a large mixing bowl, beat cream cheese and sugar until light and fluffy. Beat in sour cream and vanilla. Fold in creme de cacao and whipped topping. Cover and refrigerate for at least 1 hour.

For the fudge sauce, in a large saucepan, melt chocolate chips and butter over low heat. Stir in sugar and cream. Bring to a boil. Reduce heat; simmer, uncovered, for 10 minutes. Set aside and keep warm.

Heat a lightly greased 8-in. nonstick skillet; pour 2 tablespoons of batter into center of skillet. Lift and tilt pan to evenly coat bottom. Cook until top appears dry; turn and cook 15-20 seconds longer. Remove to a wire rack. Repeat with remaining batter, greasing skillet as needed. When cool, stack the crepes with waxed paper or paper towels in between.

Spoon 1/4 cup filling down the center of each crepe; roll up. Top with fudge sauce. Sprinkle with mint candies if desired. **Yield:** 10 servings.

CHOCOLATE MINT CREPES

IF YOU want Chocolate Crepes to have a more refreshing flavor, replace the creme de cacao with creme de menthe and be sure to use the chopped Andes candies in the fudge sauce.

Dark Chocolate Souffle

(Pictured on page 46)

Chocolate lovers won't be able to resist this rich souffle from our Test Kitchen home economists.
The addition of a little orange extract provides a perfect complement.

1 teaspoon plus 3 tablespoons
  butter, *divided*
1 tablespoon plus 1/2 cup sugar,
  divided
1/4 cup all-purpose flour
1/4 teaspoon salt
1 cup milk
4 ounces dark chocolate,
  chopped
4 eggs, *separated*
1/2 teaspoon orange extract,
  optional
1/2 teaspoon vanilla extract
1/4 teaspoon cream of tartar
TOPPING:
1/4 cup confectioners' sugar
2 tablespoons baking cocoa
1/2 teaspoon vanilla *or* orange
  extract
1 cup heavy whipping cream

Grease a 1-1/2-qt. souffle dish with 1 teaspoon butter. Sprinkle 1 tablespoon of sugar into the dish and turn to coat thoroughly; tap out excess sugar and discard.

In a saucepan, combine 1/4 cup sugar, flour and salt. Stir in milk until smooth. Bring to a boil over medium heat; cook and stir for 2 minutes or until thickened. Reduce heat to low; add chocolate and remaining butter. Cook and stir until chocolate is melted; remove from the heat.

In a small bowl, beat egg yolks. Stir a small amount of hot filling into yolks; return all to the pan, stirring constantly. Stir in vanilla; transfer to a large bowl.

In a mixing bowl with clean beaters, beat egg whites and cream of tartar on medium speed until foamy. Gradually beat in remaining sugar on high until stiff peaks form. With a spatula, stir a fourth of the egg white mixture into chocolate batter until blended. Fold in remaining egg white mixture until no white streaks remain.

Pour into prepared dish. Bake, uncovered, at 350° for 50-55 minutes or until a knife inserted near the center comes out clean.

For topping, in a small chilled mixing bowl, combine the confectioners' sugar, cocoa and vanilla. Gradually add cream. Beat on high until stiff peaks form. Serve souffle immediately with a dollop of topping. **Yield:** 6 servings.

Mocha Latte Parfaits

(Pictured at right)

When hosting a small dinner party, our home economists suggest you serve these pretty parfaits. Assemble them earlier in the day for a no-fuss dessert!

    1 cup (6 ounces) semisweet chocolate chips, *divided*
  1/2 teaspoon shortening
Chocolate jimmies
    3 tablespoons half-and-half cream
    1 teaspoon instant coffee granules
    2 egg yolks, beaten
    2 teaspoons vanilla extract
LATTE CREAM:
    2 teaspoons instant coffee granules
1-1/2 cups heavy whipping cream, *divided*
  1/3 cup confectioners' sugar

In a microwave-safe bowl, melt 1/2 cup chocolate chips with shortening; stir until smooth. Dip rims of four parfait glasses in chocolate; sprinkle with jimmies. Let stand until set.

In a small saucepan, heat the half-and-half, coffee granules and remaining chocolate chips over low heat; stir until smooth. Stir a small amount of hot mixture into egg yolks; return all to the pan, stirring constantly. Cook and stir for 2 minutes or until mixture is thickened and reaches at least 160°. Remove from the heat; stir in vanilla. Cool, stirring several times.

In a small mixing bowl, dissolve coffee granules in 1 tablespoon whipping cream. Add remaining cream; beat until mixture begins to thicken. Add confectioners' sugar; beat until soft peaks form. Fold 1-1/2 cups of cream mixture into cooled chocolate mixture.

Spoon about 1/4 cup chocolate mousse into each parfait glass; spoon or pipe about 1/4 cup cream mixture over mousse. Repeat layers. Refrigerate for at least 2 hours. **Yield:** 4 servings.

CHOCOLATE PARFAIT GLASSES

1. Melt chocolate chips and shortening in a microwave-safe bowl. Stir until smooth. Dip rims of parfait glasses into melted chocolate.

2. Holding the glass upside down over a plate, sprinkle chocolate jimmies over the melted chocolate. Stand glasses upright; set aside until chocolate hardens.

Caramel Chocolate Fondue

This dessert created in our Test Kitchen is fast yet fancy.
Keep the ingredients on hand for last-minute entertaining.

2 packages (6 ounces *each*)
   Riesen's chewy chocolate-
   covered caramels
1/2 cup heavy whipping cream
1 teaspoon rum extract
Cubed pound cake, sliced bananas
   and fresh strawberries
1 cup nut topping

In a heavy saucepan, melt caramels in cream over low heat until smooth, stirring frequently. Remove from the heat. Stir in extract. Transfer to a small fondue pot; keep warm. Dip cake and fruit into fondue, then dip into nut topping. **Yield:** 1-1/2 cups.

CHOCOLATE FONDUE TIPS

- Be creative when picking dippers for chocolate fondue. Consider cubed angel food cake, shortbread cookies, biscotti, marshmallows and pretzels. Other fruit options include dried apricots, cantaloupe chunks, orange segments and drained pineapple chunks.
- Before serving, you may want to brush fresh cut fruit with lemon juice to prevent browning.
- If you don't have fondue forks, use ordinary household forks or wooden skewers. You can avoid confusion by adhering a different colored tape for every guest at the end of each utensil.

Milk Chocolate Ice Cream

I've relied on this dessert for more than 30 years. It's a delicious ice cream for chocolate lovers.
—Florine Bruns, Fredericksburg, Texas

3 cups half-and-half cream
1/2 cup sugar
1/4 teaspoon salt
3 eggs, beaten
4 cups heavy whipping cream
3 teaspoons vanilla extract
2 jars (11-3/4 ounces *each*) hot
   fudge ice cream topping

In a large saucepan, heat half-and-half to 175°; stir in the sugar and salt until dissolved. Whisk a small amount of hot cream into eggs. Return all to the pan, whisking constantly. Cook and stir over low heat until mixture reaches at least 160° and coats the back of a metal spoon.

Remove from the heat. Cool quickly by placing pan in a bowl of ice water; stir for 2 minutes. Stir in whipping cream and vanilla. Transfer to a bowl. Press plastic wrap onto surface of custard. Refrigerate for several hours or overnight.

Remove lids from jars of fudge topping. Microwave on high for 30-45 seconds or until warmed; whisk into cream mixture.

Fill cylinder of ice cream freezer two-thirds full; freeze according to manufacturer's directions. Refrigerate remaining mixture until ready to freeze; stir before transferring to ice cream cylinder. Transfer ice cream to a freezer container; freeze for 2-4 hours before serving. **Yield:** about 2 quarts.

Chocolate-Marbled Cheesecake Dessert

(Pictured at right)

This recipe features three kinds of chocolate—baking cocoa, hot fudge topping and chocolate chips! A small piece is all you need to round out a holiday dinner.
—Marjorie Runyan
Middleburg, Pennsylvania

1/2 cup butter, softened
1 cup sugar, *divided*
1 cup all-purpose flour
1/4 cup baking cocoa
1/4 teaspoon salt
2 packages (8 ounces *each*) cream cheese, softened
2 eggs, lightly beaten
1 teaspoon vanilla extract
1/2 cup hot fudge ice cream topping
1/4 cup semisweet chocolate chips, melted
Milk chocolate *or* striped chocolate kisses, optional

In a small mixing bowl, cream butter and 1/2 cup sugar. Combine the flour, cocoa and salt; gradually add to the creamed mixture and mix well. Press into a greased 8-in. square baking dish; set aside.

In a large mixing bowl, beat cream cheese and remaining sugar until smooth. Add eggs and vanilla; beat on low speed just until combined. Remove 1 cup to a small mixing bowl; beat in fudge topping. Spread 1 cup over crust; spread with remaining cream cheese mixture.

Stir melted chips into remaining fudge mixture; drop by teaspoonfuls over cream cheese layer. Cut through batter with a knife to swirl. Bake at 350° for 40-45 minutes or until a toothpick inserted near the center comes out clean. Cool on a wire rack. Garnish with kisses if desired. Store in the refrigerator. **Yield:** 12-16 servings.

Hazelnut Chocolate Cake Roll

Don't be intimidated to prepare this dramatic dessert from our Test Kitchen!
It's actually quite easy to make. Plus, it can be assembled the day before serving.

4 eggs, *separated*
3/4 cup sugar, *divided*
2 tablespoons water
1 teaspoon vanilla extract
1/2 cup all-purpose flour
1/3 cup baking cocoa
1 teaspoon baking powder
1/4 teaspoon salt
FILLING:
1 cup heavy whipping cream
3 tablespoons confectioners' sugar
1/2 teaspoon vanilla extract
1/2 cup chopped hazelnuts, toasted
1 square (1 ounce) semisweet chocolate, grated
Additional confectioners' sugar

Let eggs stand at room temperature for 30 minutes. Line a greased 15-in. x 10-in. x 1-in. baking pan with waxed paper; grease the paper and set aside.

In a large mixing bowl, beat egg yolks until slightly thickened. Gradually add 1/2 cup sugar, beating until thick and lemon-colored. Beat in water and vanilla. Combine the flour, cocoa, baking powder and salt; gradually add to yolk mixture and mix well.

In a small mixing bowl with clean beaters, beat egg whites on medium speed until soft peaks form. Gradually beat in remaining sugar, 1 tablespoon at a time, on high until stiff peaks form. Gradually fold into batter. Spread evenly into prepared pan.

Bake at 375° for 12-15 minutes or until cake springs back when lightly touched. Cool for 5 minutes. Turn cake onto a kitchen towel dusted with baking cocoa. Gently peel off waxed paper. Roll up cake in the towel jelly-roll style, starting with a short side. Cool completely on a wire rack.

For filling, in a small mixing bowl, beat cream and confectioners' sugar until stiff peaks form. Beat in vanilla. Fold in hazelnuts and chocolate. Unroll cake; spread filling evenly over cake to within 1/2 in. of edges. Roll up again. Place seam side down on a serving platter. Cover and refrigerate for 1 hour. Just before serving, dust with confectioners' sugar. Refrigerate leftovers. **Yield:** 10 servings.

Chocolate-Almond Sacher Torte

(Pictured at right)

Guests will be surprised to hear this dessert from our Test Kitchen starts with a convenient cake mix. Each bite features chocolate, almonds and apricots.

1/2 cup chopped dried apricots
1/2 cup amaretto
  1 package (18-1/4 ounces) devil's food cake mix
3/4 cup water
1/3 cup vegetable oil
  3 eggs

APRICOT FILLING:
2/3 cup apricot preserves
  1 tablespoon amaretto

FROSTING:
4-1/2 cups confectioners' sugar
3/4 cup baking cocoa
1/2 cup butter, cubed
1/3 cup boiling water
  1 tablespoon amaretto
  1 cup sliced almonds, toasted

In a small bowl, combine apricots and amaretto; let stand for 15 minutes. In a large mixing bowl, combine cake mix, water, oil, eggs and apricots. Beat on low speed for 30 seconds; beat on medium for 2 minutes.

Pour into two greased and floured 9-in. round baking pans. Bake at 350° for 25-30 minutes or until a toothpick inserted near the center comes out clean. Cool for 10 minutes before removing from pans to wire racks to cool completely.

For filling, in a small saucepan, heat apricot preserves and amaretto on low until preserves are melted, stirring occasionally; set aside. For frosting, in a large mixing bowl, combine confectioners' sugar and cocoa. Add butter, water and amaretto. Beat on low until combined. Beat on medium for 1 minute or until frosting achieves a spreading consistency.

To assemble, split each cake into two horizontal layers. Place a bottom layer on a serving plate; spread with half of the filling. Top with another cake layer; spread with 2/3 cup frosting. Top with third layer and remaining filling. Top with remaining cake layer. Frost top and sides of cake with remaining frosting. Gently press almonds into the sides. Cover and refrigerate for several hours before slicing. **Yield:** 12-16 servings.

Milk Chocolate Bundt Cake

I like to make time to prepare this cake for my husband on special occasions. It stays moist for days.
—Dolores Hambrick, Vinita, Oklahoma

1 can (16 ounces) chocolate
  syrup
1 milk chocolate candy bar (6
  ounces), broken into chunks
1 cup butter, softened
2 cups sugar
4 eggs
2 teaspoons vanilla extract
2-1/4 cups all-purpose flour
1/2 teaspoon baking soda
1 cup buttermilk
1 cup chopped pecans
FROSTING:
  1/4 cup butter, cubed
  2 tablespoons baking cocoa
  3 tablespoons milk
  2 cups confectioners' sugar

1/2 teaspoon vanilla extract
1/4 cup chopped pecans

In a saucepan over low heat, stir chocolate syrup and candy bar until candy bar is melted; cool. In a large mixing bowl, cream butter and sugar. Add eggs, one at a time, beating well after each addition. Add chocolate mixture and vanilla; mix well. Combine flour and baking soda; add to creamed mixture alternately with buttermilk. Fold in pecans.

Pour into a greased and floured 10-in. fluted tube pan. Bake at 350° for 70-75 minutes or until a toothpick inserted near the center comes out clean. Cool for 10 minutes before removing from pan to a wire rack to cool completely.

For frosting, in a saucepan, melt butter. Stir in cocoa until smooth. Add milk. Bring to a boil. Remove from the heat. Stir in the confectioners' sugar and vanilla until smooth. Spread over cake. Sprinkle with pecans. **Yield:** 12-16 servings.

Caramel Pecan Brownies

These rich and gooey brownies are so good, I make them year-round.
—Char Letavish, Woodhaven, Michigan

1 package (18-1/4 ounces)
  German chocolate cake mix
3/4 cup butter, melted
1 can (5 ounces) evaporated
  milk, *divided*
75 caramels
1 cup chopped pecans
1 cup (6 ounces) semisweet
  chocolate chips

In a large bowl, combine the cake mix, butter and 1/3 cup milk. Spread half of the mixture into a greased 13-in. x 9-

in. x 2-in. baking pan. Bake at 350° for 15 minutes.

Meanwhile, in a large microwave-safe bowl, combine caramels and remaining milk. Microwave, uncovered, on high for 2-3 minutes or until caramels are melted; stir until smooth. Pour over crust. Sprinkle with pecans and chocolate chips. Drop reserved cake mixture by tablespoonfuls over the top.

Bake for 10 minutes; remove from the oven and smooth top. Bake 10-15 minutes longer or until top appears dry and is lightly browned. Cool completely on a wire rack. Cut into bars. **Yield:** 4 dozen.

Editor's Note: This recipe was tested in a 1,100-watt microwave.

Mud Pie

(Pictured at right)

We enjoyed this pie while on a trip to California more than 20 years ago. I came home and developed my own recipe. It's always a hit!
—Sandra Ashcraft, Pueblo, Colorado

1-1/2 cups chocolate wafer crumbs
1/3 cup butter, melted
  1 quart chocolate ice cream, softened
  1 quart coffee ice cream, softened
CHOCOLATE SAUCE:
  2 tablespoons butter
  2 squares (1 ounce *each*) unsweetened chocolate
  1 cup sugar
1/4 teaspoon salt
  1 can (5 ounces) evaporated milk
1/2 teaspoon vanilla extract
WHIPPED CREAM:
  1 cup heavy whipping cream
  1 tablespoon sugar

In a small bowl, combine wafer crumbs and butter. Press onto the bottom and up the sides of an ungreased 9-in. deep-dish pie plate. Bake at 350° for 10 minutes. Cool on a wire rack. In a large mixing bowl, beat chocolate ice cream and coffee ice cream. Spoon into crust. Cover and freeze for 8 hours or overnight.

For chocolate sauce, in a small saucepan, melt butter and chocolate over low heat; stir until smooth. Stir in the sugar, salt and evaporated milk. Bring to a boil, stirring constantly. Remove from the heat; stir in vanilla. Set aside.

Remove pie from the freezer 15 minutes before serving. In a small mixing bowl, beat cream until it begins to thicken. Add sugar; beat until soft peaks form. Top each slice with whipped cream and serve chocolate sauce. **Yield:** 8 servings.

CHOCOLATE-LACED WHIPPED CREAM

INSTEAD of simply topping pieces of Mud Pie with sweetened whipped cream, try the "pinstripe" look as shown in the photo above. Here's how:

Drizzle three stripes of some of the recipe's chocolate sauce into a pastry bag. Carefully add the whipped cream. Pipe on top of each slice.

Orange Chocolate Torte

(Pictured at right)

This eye-catching dessert takes the cake at any holiday gathering. Chocolate truffles on top are a fantastic finishing touch.
—Georgiana Hagman
Louisville, Kentucky

2 cups (12 ounces) semisweet chocolate chips
6 tablespoons butter, cubed
4 egg yolks
6 tablespoons confectioners' sugar
1/4 cup chocolate sprinkles *or* ground pecans

CAKE:
1 cup butter, softened
2-1/2 cups sugar
4 eggs
1-1/2 teaspoons orange extract
2-1/4 cups all-purpose flour
1 cup baking cocoa
2 teaspoons baking powder
1/2 teaspoon baking soda
1/2 teaspoon salt
2 cups water

FROSTING:
1 cup butter, cubed
1 cup (6 ounces) semisweet chocolate chips
1/3 cup plus 7 to 8 tablespoons milk, *divided*
1 teaspoon orange extract
2-3/4 cups sifted confectioners' sugar
Chocolate sprinkles

In a small heavy saucepan over medium-low heat, stir chocolate chips and butter until melted. In a small mixing bowl, beat egg yolks until lemon-colored. Gradually stir in warm chocolate mixture; return all to the pan. Cook and stir over medium heat until mixture reaches 160°.

Remove from the heat. Stir in confectioners' sugar until blended. Place 1/2 cup in a small bowl; pour remaining chocolate mixture into a small mixing bowl for filling. Cover each bowl with a paper towel. Let stand for up to 1 hour or until soft-set.

For truffles, roll the 1/2-cup portion into 12 balls. Roll in sprinkles or pecans. Cover and refrigerate until serving.

In a large mixing bowl, cream butter and sugar. Add eggs, one at a time, beating well after each addition. Beat in extract. Combine flour, cocoa, baking powder, baking soda and salt; add to creamed mixture alternately with water. Pour into three greased and floured 9-in. round baking pans. Bake at 350° for 25-30 minutes or until a toothpick inserted near the center comes out clean. Cool for 10 minutes;

remove from pans to wire racks to cool completely.

For frosting, in a microwave-safe bowl, combine the butter, chocolate chips and 1/3 cup milk; microwave until melted. Whisk in extract until smooth. Gradually whisk in confectioners' sugar. Transfer to a mixing bowl. Place in a bowl of ice water. With a portable mixer, beat on medium speed until stiff peaks form, about 7 minutes; set aside.

For filling, gradually add enough of the remaining milk to reserved chocolate mixture, beating until it achieves spreading consistency.

Place one cake layer on a serving plate; spread with half of the filling. Repeat layers. Spread 2-2/3 cups frosting over top and sides of cake. Using a #195 star tip, pipe the remaining frosting into 12 rosettes on top of cake. Place a truffle on each rosette. Press chocolate sprinkles onto sides of cake. Store in the refrigerator. **Yield:** 12 servings.

Mousse-Topped Lime Cheesecake

I created this mouth-watering cheesecake by combining a few different dessert ideas. Chocolate pairs well with the tropical flavors of lime and coconut.
—Jessie Covey, Pikeville, Tennessee

1-1/2 cups crushed chocolate graham crackers
1/2 cup flaked coconut, toasted
2 tablespoons sugar
1/3 cup butter, melted
FILLING:
2 packages (8 ounces *each*) cream cheese, softened
3/4 cup sugar
3 tablespoons all-purpose flour
2 eggs, *separated*
1/4 cup lime juice
1 tablespoon grated lime peel
1 teaspoon vanilla extract
2 drops green food coloring, optional
TOPPING:
1 cup (6 ounces) semisweet chocolate chips
5 tablespoons butter, cubed
4 egg yolks
1/4 cup confectioners' sugar
2 tablespoons hot brewed coffee
1 teaspoon vanilla extract
1/2 cup heavy whipping cream

In a bowl, combine the cracker crumbs, coconut and sugar; stir in butter. Press onto the bottom and 1 in. up the sides of a greased 9-in. springform pan. Place on a baking sheet. Bake at 350° for 7-9 minutes. Place pan on a wire rack. Reduce heat to 325°.

For filling, in a large mixing bowl, beat cream cheese and sugar until smooth. Add flour. Add egg yolks; beat on low speed just until combined. Stir in the lime juice, peel, vanilla and food coloring if desired just until blended.

In a small mixing bowl, beat egg whites until stiff peaks form; fold into filling. Pour into crust. Return pan to baking sheet. Bake for 30-35 minutes or until center is almost set. Cool on a wire rack for 10 minutes. Carefully run a knife around edge of pan to loosen. Cool 1 hour longer. Refrigerate overnight.

For topping, in a microwave-safe bowl, melt chocolate chips and butter; stir until smooth. Set aside. In a heavy saucepan, whisk egg yolks, confectioners' sugar and coffee. Cook and stir over low heat until mixture is thickened and reaches at least 160°. Remove from the heat. Whisk in chocolate mixture and vanilla. Cool completely.

Beat whipping cream until soft peaks form; fold into topping. Spread over cheesecake. Refrigerate for at least 2 hours or until set. Remove sides of pan. **Yield:** 12 servings.

'TIS THE *Season*

Christmas Cookies & Candies

THE JOLLY JOB of making homemade cookies and candies can begin weeks before Christmas. And the wonderful aroma of these assorted confections often signals the much-anticipated start of the holiday season.

Head to the kitchen and create mouth-watering memories by preparing any number of this chapter's tasty treats.

Peppermint Stars and Jeweled Coconut Cookies are two Yuletide yummies guaranteed to please any palate.

Fans of chocolate will certainly favor deliciously rich Buttery Walnut Toffee. (All recipes pictured at right.)

Then on the night before Christmas, set out a few sweets and a glass of milk for Santa. (Don't forget carrots and sugar cubes for the reindeer!)

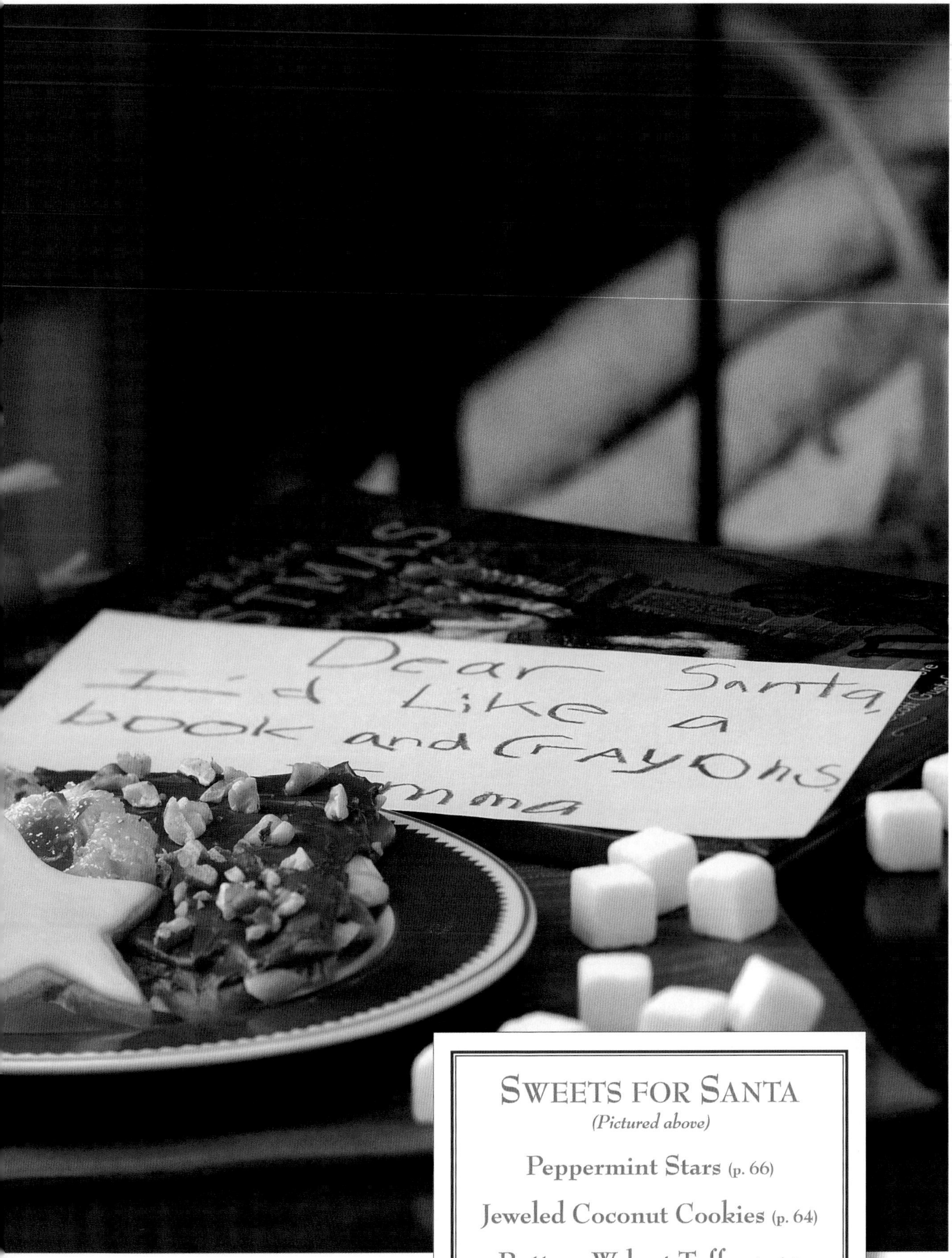

Dear Santa,
I'd Like a
book and crayons
Emma

Buttery Walnut Toffee

(Pictured on page 62)

I've been making this tasty toffee for more than 15 years, and everyone raves about it. Folks often think I bought it at a gourmet candy store!
—Michele Larson, Barre, Vermont

1 tablespoon plus 1 cup butter, softened, *divided*
1 cup whole unblanched almonds, coarsely chopped
1 cup sugar
1/4 teaspoon salt
1/2 teaspoon vanilla extract
1 cup milk chocolate chips, melted
1/2 cup chopped walnuts

Line an 11-in. x 7-in. x 2-in. pan with foil and grease the foil with 1 tablespoon butter. Arrange almonds evenly in pan; set aside.

In a heavy saucepan, combine the sugar, salt and remaining butter. Bring to a boil, stirring constantly. Cook and stir until mixture is caramel-colored and a candy thermometer reads 300° (hard-crack stage). Remove from the heat; stir in vanilla. Immediately pour over almonds. Cool completely.

Spread melted chocolate over toffee; sprinkle with walnuts. Let stand until set. Break into pieces. Store in an airtight container. **Yield:** about 1-1/2 pounds.

Editor's Note: We recommend that you test your candy thermometer before each use by bringing water to a boil; the thermometer should read 212°. Adjust your recipe temperature up or down based on your test.

Jeweled Coconut Cookies

(Pictured on page 62)

I often bake these bite-sized cookies with two flavors of preserves for special occasions.
—Lynn Reynolds, Brookfield, Wisconsin

1/2 cup butter, softened
1/3 cup sugar
1 egg, *separated*
1/4 teaspoon vanilla extract
1 cup all-purpose flour
1/4 teaspoon salt
3/4 cup flaked coconut
1/4 cup *each* apricot and peach preserves
Confectioners' sugar

In a small mixing bowl, cream butter and sugar. Beat in egg yolk and vanilla. Combine the flour and salt; gradually add to creamed mixture. Cover and refrigerate for 1 hour or until easy to handle.

In a small bowl, beat egg white. Place coconut in another bowl. Roll dough into 1-in. balls; roll in egg white and coconut. Place 2 in. apart on ungreased baking sheets. Using the end of a wooden spoon handle, make an indentation in the center of each.

Bake at 325° for 19-22 minutes or until lightly browned. Remove to wire racks. Spoon 1 rounded teaspoon of preserves into each warm cookie. Dust with confectioners' sugar. Cool completely. **Yield:** about 2 dozen.

Mocha Sandwich Cookies

(Pictured at right)

No Christmas cookie tray is complete without these melt-in-your-mouth treats. The buttery shortbread cookie really complements the mocha filling.
—Anna Sylvester, Sylvania, Ohio

3/4 cup butter, softened
1/2 cup confectioners' sugar
1 teaspoon vanilla extract
1 cup all-purpose flour
1/2 cup cornstarch
FILLING:
2 tablespoons butter, softened
2/3 cup confectioners' sugar
1-1/2 teaspoons heavy whipping cream
1/4 teaspoon almond extract
2 tablespoons baking cocoa
1/2 teaspoon instant coffee granules
1 to 2 tablespoons boiling water
2 tablespoons sliced almonds, toasted and finely chopped

In a large mixing bowl, cream butter and confectioners' sugar. Beat in vanilla. Combine flour and cornstarch; gradually add to creamed mixture and mix well. Cover and refrigerate for 1 hour.

Shape dough into 3/4-in. balls; press lightly to flatten. Place 1 in. apart on ungreased baking sheets. Bake at 375° for 10-12 minutes. Cool on wire racks.

For filling, in a small mixing bowl, cream butter and confectioners' sugar. Beat in cream and extract. In a small bowl, combine the cocoa, coffee and boiling water; stir to dissolve coffee granules. Add to creamed mixture and mix well. Fold in almonds. Cover and refrigerate for 30 minutes.

Spread filling over the bottom of half of the cookies; top with remaining cookies. Store in the refrigerator. **Yield:** 2 dozen.

Coconut Chocolate Delights

*I enjoy cooking and experimenting with recipes. My husband and friends
really enjoy this coconut candy, which resembles a popular candy bar.*
—Nancy Flower, Central Square, New York

1 package (8 ounces) cream
cheese, softened
1 package (18 ounces)
cream-filled chocolate
sandwich cookies, crushed
1 package (14 ounces) flaked
coconut
2 cups sliced almonds
2 teaspoons vanilla extract
3-1/2 cups semisweet chocolate chips
2 tablespoons plus 1-1/2
teaspoons shortening

In a large mixing bowl, beat cream cheese until smooth. Beat in cookie crumbs. Add the coconut, almonds and vanilla; mix well. Shape into 1-in. balls. Place on baking sheets; cover and refrigerate for at least 1 hour.

In a microwave-safe bowl, combine chocolate chips and shortening. Microwave on high until melted, stirring every 15 seconds; stir until smooth. Dip balls into melted chocolate; shake off excess. Place on waxed paper until set. Store in an airtight container in the refrigerator. **Yield:** about 6-1/2 dozen.

Peppermint Stars

(Pictured on page 62)

*I make these buttery mint cookies each Christmas because they're my
daughter's favorite. Use whatever cookie cutter design you prefer.*
—Lois White, Brookfield, Missouri

3/4 cup butter, softened
1 cup sugar
2 eggs
2-1/2 cups all-purpose flour
1 teaspoon baking powder
1/2 teaspoon salt
3/4 cup peppermint candies (about
25 pieces), finely crushed
GLAZE:
2 cups confectioners' sugar
3 tablespoons milk
1/8 teaspoon peppermint extract
Red *or* green food coloring, optional

In a large mixing bowl, cream butter and sugar. Beat in eggs. Combine flour, baking powder and salt; add to creamed mixture. Stir in crushed candies. Cover and refrigerate for 1 hour.

On a lightly floured surface, roll dough to 1/8-in. thickness. Cut into shapes with a floured 2-1/2-in. star cookie cutter. Place 2 in. apart on greased baking sheets. Bake at 325° for 10-12 minutes or until lightly browned. Remove to wire racks to cool.

For glaze, in a small bowl, combine confectioners' sugar, milk and extract; stir until smooth. Tint with food coloring if desired. Spread over cookies. **Yield:** 4-1/2 dozen.

Butter Brickle Biscotti

(Pictured at right)

These twice-baked toffee cookies are a must with coffee at Christmastime. They also make great gifts from the kitchen.
—Darlene Brenden, Salem, Oregon

1/2 **cup butter, softened**
1/2 **cup sugar**
1/4 **cup packed brown sugar**
  3 **eggs**
  2 **teaspoons vanilla extract**
  3 **cups all-purpose flour**
  2 **teaspoons baking powder**
1/4 **teaspoon salt**
  1 **package (7-1/2 to 8 ounces) English toffee bits** *or* **almond brickle chips**

In a large mixing bowl, cream butter and sugars until light and fluffy. Add eggs, one at a time, beating well after each addition. Beat in vanilla. Combine the flour, baking powder and salt; gradually add to creamed mixture. Stir in toffee bits.

Divide dough in half. On a parchment paper-lined baking sheet, shape each portion into a 10-in. x 2-1/2-in. rectangle. Cover and refrigerate for 30 minutes.

Bake at 350° for 30-35 minutes or until golden brown. Cool for 10 minutes. Transfer to a cutting board; cut diagonally with a serrated knife into 1/2-in. slices.

Place slices cut side down on ungreased baking sheets. Bake for 20-24 minutes or until golden brown, turning once. Remove to wire racks to cool. Store in an airtight container. **Yield:** about 2-1/2 dozen.

CUTTING BISCOTTI

AFTER the rectangular biscotti dough is baked, it needs to be cut into slices, which will be baked longer.

With a serrated knife, cut the cookie diagonally into 1/2- or 3/4-in.-thick slices. Place the sliced cookies cut side down on a baking sheet and bake as directed.

Peppermint Divinity

This light and airy divinity is like a bit of heaven on earth!
It keeps well in an airtight container at room temperature for up to 4 days.
—Edna Hoffman, Hebron, Indiana

2 egg whites
2-1/2 cups sugar
1/2 cup water
1/2 cup light corn syrup
1 teaspoon vanilla extract
1/2 cup crushed peppermint
   candies
2 to 3 drops red food coloring,
   optional

Place egg whites in a large stand mixer bowl; let stand at room temperature for 30 minutes. Meanwhile, line three 15-in. x 10-in. x 1-in. pans with waxed paper; set aside.

In a heavy saucepan, combine sugar, water and corn syrup; cook and stir until sugar is dissolved and mixture comes to a boil. Cook over medium heat, without stirring, until a candy thermometer reads 260° (hard-ball stage). Just before the temperature is reached, beat egg whites on medium speed until stiff peaks form.

Slowly pour hot sugar mixture in a thin stream over egg whites, beating constantly. Add vanilla. Beat until candy loses its gloss and holds its shape, about 2-3 minutes. Immediately stir in crushed candies and food coloring if desired. (Do not overmix, or candy will get stiff and crumbly.)

Quickly drop by heaping tablespoonfuls onto prepared pans. Let stand at room temperature overnight or until dry to the touch. Store in an airtight container at room temperature. **Yield:** 3 dozen.

Editor's Note: We recommend making this candy on a clear day with low humidity. We recommend that you test your candy thermometer before each use by bringing water to a boil; the thermometer should read 212°. Adjust your recipe temperature up or down based on your test.

CANDY MAKING POINTERS

THERE'S NO NEED to shy away from making homemade candy if you follow these simple guidelines.
- Before each use, test your candy thermometer by bringing water to a boil; the thermometer should read 212°. Adjust your recipe temperature up or down based on your test.
- Humidity greatly effects the outcome of candy that is cooked to a specific temperature or that contains egg whites. For best results, make candy on days when the humidity is less than 60%.
- Measure and assemble all ingredients before beginning. Don't substitute or alter the recipe's basic ingredients.
- Use heavy-gauge saucepans that are deep enough to allow the candy mixture to boil freely without boiling over.
- Use wooden spoons with long handles for safe stirring of hot mixtures.
- A candy mixture will cook very slowly when boiling until it reaches 220°, then it will cook quickly. Be sure to closely watch the candy thermometer at this point.
- Store different kinds of homemade candies in separate tightly covered containers unless otherwise noted.

Holiday Lace Cookies

(Pictured at right)

It's hard to stop eating these buttery cookies dotted with pecans and dried cranberries. I cherish this recipe from my mother.
—Mildred Sherrer, Fort Worth, Texas

1 cup butter, softened
2-1/4 cups confectioners' sugar
1/4 cup light corn syrup
1-1/4 cups all-purpose flour
1 cup chopped pecans
1/4 cup dried cranberries

In a large mixing bowl, cream butter and confectioners' sugar. Beat in corn syrup. Gradually beat in flour. Fold in pecans and cranberries. Shape dough into two 6-in. logs; wrap each in plastic wrap. Chill for at least 2 hours or until firm.

Unwrap and cut into 1/4-in. slices. Place 3 in. apart on ungreased foil-lined baking sheets. Bake at 350° for 11-12 minutes or until center and edges are browned and lacy. Allow cookies to cool completely before carefully removing from foil. **Yield:** 3 dozen.

Chunky Nut 'n' Chip Cookies

These bars are packed with oats, peanut butter, chocolate chips and pecans.
—Kristine Conway, Alliance, Ohio

1/2 cup butter, softened
1/3 cup creamy peanut butter
1/2 cup sugar
1/4 cup packed brown sugar
1 egg
1 teaspoon vanilla extract
1 cup all-purpose flour
1 cup old-fashioned oats
1/2 teaspoon baking soda
1 cup (6 ounces) semisweet
   chocolate chips
1 cup chopped pecans

In a large mixing bowl, cream the butter, peanut butter and sugars until blended. Beat in egg and vanilla. Combine the flour, oats and baking soda; gradually add to creamed mixture. Stir in chocolate chips and pecans.

Drop by teaspoonfuls onto greased baking sheets. Bake at 350° for 10-12 minutes or until lightly browned. Remove to wire racks to cool. **Yield:** 3 dozen.

Peanut 'n' Chocolate Graham Bars

I came up with this recipe for my son-in-law, who loves peanut butter and chocolate.
—Beverly Medalen, Willow City, North Dakota

17 whole graham crackers (about 5 inches x 2-1/2 inches), *divided*
1 cup sugar
1/2 cup butter, cubed
1/2 cup milk
1 egg, beaten
1 cup graham cracker crumbs
1 cup flaked coconut
1/2 cup salted peanuts, finely chopped
1 teaspoon vanilla extract
2-1/4 cups peanut butter chips
4 tablespoons shortening, *divided*
2-1/4 cups semisweet chocolate chips

Line a 13-in. x 9-in. x 2-in. pan with heavy-duty foil. Arrange eight whole graham crackers and one half graham cracker in pan; set aside.

In a heavy saucepan, combine the sugar, butter, milk and egg. Bring to a boil over medium heat, stirring constantly. Remove from the heat. Stir in the cracker crumbs, coconut, peanuts and vanilla. Cool for 10 minutes or until thickened. Spread over graham crackers in pan. Top with remaining graham crackers; press down lightly. Cover and refrigerate for 4 hours or until firm.

Using foil, remove from pan. Discard foil. Cut into 2-1/2-in. x 1-in. bars, following score marks on graham crackers.

In a microwave-safe bowl, melt peanut butter chips and 2 tablespoons shortening; stir until smooth. Dip top of bars in peanut butter mixture; let excess drip off. Invert onto a waxed paper-lined pan. Chill for 15 minutes or until set.

Melt chocolate chips and remaining shortening; stir until smooth. Dip uncoated half of bars in chocolate mixture; let excess drip off. Invert onto a waxed paper-lined pan. Chill for 30 minutes or until set. Store in an airtight container. **Yield:** 3 dozen.

Crisp Cherry-Topped Cookies

I make hundreds of cookies each Christmas to share with family and friends.
With red and green candied cherries, these look so lovely on a holiday cookie tray.
—Delores Edgecomb, Atlanta, New York

1 cup butter, softened
2 packages (3 ounces *each*) cream cheese, softened
1 cup sugar
1/2 teaspoon almond extract
2 cups all-purpose flour
3 teaspoons baking powder
1/2 teaspoon salt
3 cups crisp rice cereal, crushed
Red and green candied cherries, halved

In a large mixing bowl, cream butter, cream cheese and sugar. Beat in extract. Combine the flour, baking powder and salt; gradually add to creamed mixture. Cover and refrigerate overnight.

Shape dough into 1-in. balls; roll in cereal. Place 2 in. apart on ungreased baking sheets. Place a cherry half in the center of each. Bake at 350° for 12-15 minutes or until lightly browned. Remove to wire racks to cool. **Yield:** about 5 dozen.

Double Nut Baklava

(Pictured at right)

It may take some time to make this rich, buttery treat, but it's well worth the effort! The blend of coconut, pecans and macadamia nuts is irresistible.
—Kari Caven, Post Falls, Idaho

1-1/4 cups flaked coconut, toasted
1/2 cup finely chopped
    macadamia nuts
1/2 cup finely chopped pecans
1/2 cup packed brown sugar
  1 teaspoon ground allspice
1-1/4 cups butter, melted
  1 package phyllo dough (16
    ounces, 14-inch x 9-inch
    sheet size)
  1 cup sugar
1/2 cup water
1/4 cup honey

In a bowl, combine the first five ingredients; set aside. Brush a 13-in. x 9-in. x 2-in. baking pan with some of the butter. Unroll the sheets of phyllo dough; trim to fit into pan.

Layer 10 sheets of phyllo in prepared pan, brushing each with butter. (Keep remaining dough covered with plastic wrap and a damp towel to prevent it from drying out.) Sprinkle with a third of the nut mixture. Repeat layers twice. Top with five phyllo sheets, brushing each with butter. Brush top sheet of phyllo with butter.

Using a sharp knife, cut into 36 diamond shapes. Bake at 350° for 30-35 minutes or until golden brown. Cool completely on a wire rack.

In a small saucepan, bring the sugar, water and honey to a boil. Reduce heat; simmer for 5 minutes. Pour hot syrup over baklava. Cover and let stand overnight. **Yield:** 3 dozen.

Family Traditions

WHEN I WAS A CHILD, my parents and I would drive around on Christmas Eve looking at the light displays until the candlelight service at church. When we got home, the lights on our Christmas tree were "magically" blinking...a thrilling sign that Santa had visited while we were out!
—Angela Mork, Milwaukee, Wisconsin

Cheesecake Bars

Years ago, I entered these bars in a contest and won first place! Best of all, you can make them a day or two in advance. Or top individual bars with cherry pie filling for Christmas color.
—*Pat Habiger, Spearville, Kansas*

2 cups all-purpose flour
1 cup finely chopped walnuts
2/3 cup packed brown sugar
2/3 cup butter, melted
FILLING:
2 packages (8 ounces *each*) cream cheese, softened
1/2 cup sugar
2 eggs, lightly beaten
1/4 cup milk
2 tablespoons lemon juice
2 teaspoons vanilla extract

In a bowl, combine the flour, walnuts, brown sugar and butter. Set aside 2 cups. Press the remaining mixture into an ungreased 13-in. x 9-in. x 2-in. baking pan. Bake at 350° for 12 minutes.

Meanwhile, in a small mixing bowl, beat cream cheese and sugar until light and fluffy. Beat in the eggs, milk, lemon juice and vanilla just until combined. Pour over crust.

Sprinkle with reserved walnut mixture. Bake for 25-30 minutes or until edges are lightly browned and filling is set. Cool on a wire rack. Cut into squares. Store in the refrigerator. **Yield:** 2 dozen.

Peanut Goody Candies

A small piece of this rich, sweet candy is all you need so one batch goes a long way.
—*Bonnie Frahm, Prior Lake, Minnesota*

1-1/2 teaspoons plus 1/2 cup butter, softened, *divided*
1 cup semisweet chocolate chips
1 cup butterscotch chips
1 cup peanut butter
1 cup dry roasted peanuts
1/4 cup milk
2 tablespoons cook-and-serve vanilla pudding mix
3-1/4 cups confectioners' sugar
1/2 teaspoon maple flavoring

Line a 13-in. x 9-in. x 2-in. pan with foil and grease the foil with 1-1/2 teaspoons butter; set aside.

In a microwave-safe bowl, combine the chips and peanut butter. Microwave, uncovered, on high for 1-2 minutes or until melted; stir until smooth. Spread half of the chocolate mixture into prepared pan; refrigerate. Stir peanuts into remaining chocolate mixture; set aside.

In another microwave-safe bowl, combine milk, pudding mix and remaining butter. Microwave, uncovered, on high for 1-2 minutes or until mixture comes to a boil, stirring once. Gradually stir in confectioners' sugar and maple flavoring. Spread over chocolate. Carefully spread with reserved peanut mixture (may need to reheat in microwave to spread easily). Refrigerate for 4 hours or until firm.

Using foil, lift candy out of pan. Discard foil; cut into 1-in. squares. Store in an airtight container in the refrigerator. Remove from the refrigerator just before serving. **Yield:** 2-3/4 pounds.

Editor's Note: This recipe was tested in a 1,100-watt microwave.

Mint-Mallow Chocolate Cups

(Pictured at right)

These cute filled chocolate cups get gobbled up whenever I set them out. The fluffy mint filling pairs well with the chocolate.
—Stephanie Klym
Belfield, North Dakota

1 cup (6 ounces) semisweet chocolate chips
12 large marshmallows
1/4 cup milk
1/2 teaspoon vanilla extract
1/8 teaspoon peppermint extract
3 drops red *or* green food coloring
Dash salt
1/2 cup heavy whipping cream
3 tablespoons crushed peppermint candy, *divided*

In a microwave or heavy saucepan, melt chocolate chips; stir until smooth. Brush evenly on the inside of 18 foil miniature muffin cup liners. Chill until set. Add a second coat of chocolate; chill until set.

Meanwhile, in a small saucepan, combine marshmallows and milk; cook and stir over medium-low heat until marshmallows are melted. Remove from the heat. Stir in the extracts, food coloring and salt. Cover and refrigerate for 1 hour or until thickened.

Carefully peel liners off the chocolate cups and discard. In a large mixing bowl, beat whipping cream until stiff peaks form. Fold in marshmallow mixture and 2 tablespoons crushed candy. Spoon into chocolate cups. Sprinkle with remaining candy. Store in the refrigerator. **Yield:** 1-1/2 dozen.

MAKING CHOCOLATE CUPS

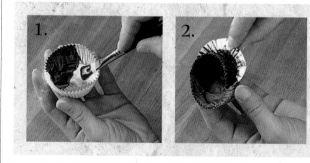

1. With a clean, new paintbrush, evenly brush the melted chocolate inside the foil muffin cup liner. Chill until set; repeat.

2. When the chocolate cups are chilled and set, carefully peel off the foil liner. Avoid handling the chocolate cups too much or they may begin to melt.

Filled Chocolate Spritz

I like to use a cookie disk with an open center so the creamy
mint filling peeks through. A chocolate drizzle on top is a flavorful finishing touch.
—Marilyn Blankschien, Clintonville, Wisconsin

3/4 **cup semisweet chocolate chips**
1/4 **cup butter, cubed**
1/2 **cup packed brown sugar**
2 **eggs, beaten**
1 **teaspoon vanilla extract**
1-1/2 **cups all-purpose flour**
1/8 **teaspoon baking soda**
PEPPERMINT FILLING:
1/4 **cup butter, softened**
3/4 **cup confectioners' sugar**
1 **tablespoon milk**
1/2 **teaspoon peppermint extract**
3 to 4 **drops green food coloring**
GLAZE:
2/3 **cup milk chocolate chips**
1 **teaspoon shortening**

In a large microwave-safe bowl, melt chocolate chips; stir until smooth. Stir in the butter, brown sugar, eggs and vanilla. Add flour and baking soda; mix well. Cover and refrigerate for 30 minutes or until easy to handle.

Using a cookie press filled with a disk that has an open center, press dough 2 in. apart onto ungreased baking sheets. Bake at 375° for 6-8 minutes or until set. Remove to wire racks to cool.

In a bowl, combine filling ingredients; stir until smooth. Spread on the bottom of half of the cookies; top with the remaining cookies.

In a small microwave-safe bowl, melt milk chocolate chips and shortening; stir until blended. Drizzle over cookies. **Yield:** about 2 dozen.

SUCCESS WITH SPRITZ

IT'S EASY to master making spritz cookies with a few helpful hints.

- Before beginning, make sure the butter is softened to room temperature. It's ready to use when you can easily insert the tines of a fork into it.
- Always press the cookies onto a cool baking sheet, otherwise the cookies will spread and bake unevenly.
- Hold the cookie press so that it's upright and touching the baking sheet. Force dough through the press until you see it at the end of the rim of the press. Lift the press straight up when the shape is formed.
- If the design of the cookie is not sharp, the dough is likely too soft and should be refrigerated for a short time. If the dough does not move through the press, the dough is too stiff and should stand at room temperature briefly.

Almond Apricot Dips

(Pictured at right)

My family makes these candied apricots every Christmas. We sometimes dip half of the fruit in white candy coating and the other half in chocolate coating.
—Cathy Childs, Freeland, Michigan

1 package (7 ounces) dried apricots
24 whole almonds, toasted
4 ounces white candy coating

Stuff each apricot with an almond. In a microwave-safe bowl, melt candy coating. Dip each apricot halfway in coating, allowing excess to drip off. Place on a waxed paper-lined baking sheet; refrigerate for 15 minutes or until set. Store in the refrigerator. **Yield: 2 dozen.**

Chocolate Peanut Brittle

Our home economists prepare this brittle in the microwave. So it's easy enough for anyone to make!

1 cup sugar
1/4 cup light corn syrup
2 cups salted peanuts
1 teaspoon butter
1/4 cup baking cocoa
1 teaspoon baking soda
1 teaspoon vanilla extract

Grease a 15-in. x 10-in. x 1-in. baking pan and a metal spatula; set aside. In a 2-qt. microwave-safe bowl, combine sugar and corn syrup. Microwave, uncovered, on high for 4 minutes; stir. Cook 3 minutes longer. Stir in peanuts and butter. Microwave for 30-60 seconds or until mixture turns a light amber color (mixture will be very hot).

Quickly stir in cocoa, baking soda and vanilla until combined. Immediately pour into prepared pan; spread with the metal spatula. Cool before breaking into pieces. Store in an airtight container. **Yield:** about 1-1/4 pounds.

Editor's Note: This recipe was tested in a 1,100-watt microwave.

Eggnog Fudge

(Pictured at far right)

I experimented with many recipes featuring eggnog before coming up with this winning combination.
—*Richell Welch, Buffalo, Texas*

1 tablespoon plus 3/4 cup
  butter, softened, *divided*
3 cups sugar
2/3 cup eggnog
2 tablespoons heavy whipping
  cream
1 package (10 to 12 ounces)
  vanilla *or* white chips
1 cup marshmallow creme
1 cup finely chopped walnuts
2 teaspoons vanilla extract

Line a 13-in. x 9-in. x 2-in. pan with foil and grease the foil with 1 tablespoon butter; set aside.

In a large saucepan, combine sugar, eggnog, cream and remaining butter. Bring to a boil over medium heat, stirring constantly. Reduce heat; cook until a candy thermometer reads 238° (soft-ball stage), stirring occasionally.

Remove from the heat. Stir in chips until melted. Stir in the marshmallow creme, walnuts and vanilla. Spread into prepared pan. Cool to room temperature. Using foil, lift fudge out of pan. Discard foil; cut fudge into 1-in. squares. Store in an airtight container in the refrigerator. **Yield:** about 3-1/4 pounds.

Editor's Note: This recipe was tested with commercially prepared eggnog. We recommend that you test your candy thermometer before each use by bringing water to a boil; the thermometer should read 212°. Adjust your recipe temperature up or down based on your test.

Cherry Chip Cookies

Our family makes these sweets every year for Christmas.
The cake-like cookies have bits of maraschino cherries in every bite.
—*Sarah Brown, Antioch, Illinois*

1 jar (10 ounces) maraschino
  cherries
6 tablespoons butter, softened
1 cup sugar
1 egg
1 teaspoon vanilla extract
2 cups all-purpose flour
1/2 teaspoon baking soda
1/2 teaspoon salt
1/2 cup sour cream
FROSTING:
3-1/2 cups confectioners' sugar
1/2 cup sour cream
Red colored sugar, optional

Drain cherries, reserving 1 tablespoon juice for frosting. Chop cherries and pat dry; set aside. In a large mixing bowl, cream butter and sugar. Beat in egg and vanilla. Combine the flour, baking soda and salt; add to creamed mixture alternately with sour cream. Stir in cherries.

Drop by tablespoonfuls 2 in. apart onto greased baking sheets. Bake at 350° for 12-15 minutes or until lightly browned. Remove to wire racks to cool.

For frosting, in a bowl, combine the confectioners' sugar, sour cream and reserved cherry juice until smooth. Spread over cookies. Sprinkle with colored sugar if desired. **Yield:** 3-1/2 dozen.

Sensational Walnut Fudge

(Pictured at right)

This is the only fudge I make anymore. I receive raves and recipe requests whenever I serve it or give it as gifts.
—Lorrine Kyger, Greeley, Colorado

1-1/2 teaspoons butter, softened
1-1/2 cups semisweet chocolate chips
1-1/2 cups milk chocolate chips
1 can (14 ounces) sweetened condensed milk
1/3 cup confectioners' sugar
1 tablespoon amaretto
Dash salt
1 cup chopped walnuts, *divided*

Line an 8-in. square pan with foil and grease the foil with butter; set aside. In a microwave-safe bowl, melt chips; stir until smooth. Stir in the milk, confec-tioners' sugar, amaretto and salt. Stir in 2/3 cup walnuts. Pour into prepared pan; sprinkle with remaining walnuts. Chill for 2 hours or until firm.

Using foil, lift fudge out of pan. Discard foil; cut fudge in-to 1-in. squares. Store in an airtight container in the refrig-erator. **Yield:** 2-1/4 pounds.

Peanut Butter Logs

This recipe has definitely stood the test of time...my husband has been enjoying it since he was a toddler!
—Micky Faginkrantz, Ft. Bliss, Texas

1/2 cup butter, softened
1 cup chunky peanut butter
1 cup creamy peanut butter
3-3/4 cups confectioners' sugar
6 cups crisp rice cereal
2 cups (12 ounces) semisweet chocolate chips

In a large mixing bowl, cream the butter, peanut butter and confectioners' sugar; stir in cereal. Shape 1/2 cupfuls in-to 1/2-in.-thick logs. Cut logs into 2-in. pieces; place on waxed paper-lined pans.

In a microwave-safe bowl, melt chocolate chips; stir un-til smooth. Drizzle over logs. Chill until set. Store in an airtight container in the refrigerator. **Yield:** about 6 dozen.

'TIS THE *Season*

Gifts from the Kitchen

YOU don't have to spend hours —or lots of money—at the mall to come up with thoughtful holiday gifts for the important people in your life.

Some of the most-treasured tokens are those that are homemade from the heart.

This chapter is packed with Yuletide treats that you can bestow with pride.

Special seasonal snacking is certain with Herbed Popcorn, Glazed Macadamia Nuts and Sweet 'n' Crunchy Snack Mix.

Satisfy a sweet tooth with tasty Gigantic Cinnamon Rolls, Shortbread Ornament Cookies and Raspberry Pastry Twists. (Recipes shown at right.)

We also provide some creative gift containers so you can offer these festive foods in special ways.

YULETIDE TREATS
(Clockwise from top right)

Shortbread Ornament Cookies (p. 80)

Gigantic Cinnamon Rolls (p. 86)

Raspberry Pastry Twists (p. 86)

Herbed Popcorn (p. 82)

Glazed Macadamia Nuts (p. 80)

Sweet 'n' Crunchy Snack Mix (p. 82)

Glazed Macadamia Nuts

(Pictured on page 78)

I came across this recipe years ago, and it's been a hit ever since.
Family and friends can't stop nibbling on the sweet coated nuts.
—Sandy Frano, Polo, Illinois

    3 cups macadamia nuts
1/2 cup sugar, *divided*
    3 tablespoons light corn syrup
    2 teaspoons vegetable oil
1/8 teaspoon salt
    3 tablespoons butter

Spread macadamia nuts in a single layer in a greased 15-in. x 10-in. x 1-in. baking pan. Bake at 250° for 5 minutes; set aside.

In a heavy saucepan, combine 6 tablespoons sugar, corn syrup, oil and salt; bring to a boil, stirring constantly. Boil without stirring until a candy thermometer reads 238° (soft-ball stage).

Remove from the heat; stir in butter until melted. Pour over nuts; stir to coat. Bake for 50-55 minutes or until lightly browned, stirring occasionally. Sprinkle with remaining sugar; toss to coat. Spread on foil to cool. Break apart and store in an airtight container. **Yield:** 5 cups.

Editor's Note: We recommend that you test your candy thermometer before each use by bringing water to a boil; the thermometer should read 212°. Adjust your recipe temperature up or down based on your test.

Shortbread Ornament Cookies

(Pictured on page 79)

These buttery shortbread cookie ornaments from our home economists are almost
too pretty to eat! You can use cookie cutters in shapes of your choice.

    3 cups all-purpose flour
3/4 cup sugar
1/4 teaspoon salt
1-1/2 cups cold butter
    2 tablespoons cold water
1/2 teaspoon rum extract
1/2 teaspoon almond extract
ICING:
    2 cups confectioners' sugar
    2 tablespoons plus 2 teaspoons
      milk
Food coloring of your choice

In a large bowl, combine the flour, sugar and salt; cut in butter until mixture resembles coarse crumbs. Stir in water and extracts until mixture forms a ball.

On a lightly floured surface, roll dough to 1/4-in. thickness. Cut with floured ornament-shaped cookie cutters. Place 1 in. apart on ungreased baking sheets. Cover and refrigerate for 30 minutes.

Bake at 325° for 15-18 minutes or until edges are lightly browned. Cool for 2 minutes before removing to wire racks to cool completely.

For icing, in a bowl, whisk confectioners' sugar and milk. Divide into small bowls; tint with food coloring. Gently spread over cookies. Decorate with other colors of icing if desired. **Yield:** about 3 dozen.

Maraschino Cherry Mini Loaves

(Pictured at right)

I've been making these breads as Christmas gifts for my neighbors for more than 20 years. Each moist slice is dotted with cherries, chocolate and nuts.
—Linda Murch, Litchfield, Minnesota

**1 jar (10 ounces) maraschino
    cherries**
2 cups all-purpose flour
1 cup sugar
2 teaspoons baking powder
1/2 teaspoon salt
3 eggs
1 cup chopped walnuts
**1/2 cup miniature semisweet
    chocolate chips**
1/2 cup chopped dates

Drain cherries, reserving 1/4 cup juice; set aside. In a large bowl, combine the flour, sugar, baking powder and salt. In another bowl, beat eggs and reserved juice; stir into dry ingredients just until moistened. Fold in the walnuts, chocolate chips, dates and cherries.

Spoon into three greased 5-3/4-in. x 3-in. x 2-in. loaf pans. Bake at 325° for 40-45 minutes or until a toothpick inserted near the center comes out clean. Cool for 10 minutes before removing from pans to a wire rack to cool completely. Wrap and store for 24 hours before serving. **Yield:** 3 mini loaves.

Sweet 'n' Crunchy Snack Mix

(Pictured on page 78)

A combination of sweet and savory ingredients gives this treat a fun look and fabulous flavor. The recipe makes a big batch so there's plenty to share...if you can stop your family from eating it!
—Susan Grummert, Plymouth, Nebraska

3 cups Cocoa Puffs
3 cups Rice Chex
1-1/2 cups pretzel twists
1 cup dry roasted peanuts
1 cup packed brown sugar
1/2 cup butter, cubed
1/4 cup light corn syrup
1/4 teaspoon cream of tartar
1/4 teaspoon baking soda
1/2 teaspoon vanilla extract

In a roasting pan, combine the cereals, pretzels and peanuts; set aside. In a heavy saucepan, combine the brown sugar, butter and corn syrup. Cook and stir over low heat until sugar is dissolved. Boil slowly for 4 minutes without stirring.

Remove from the heat; stir in cream of tartar and baking soda. Stir in vanilla. Pour over cereal mixture and stir gently to coat. Bake at 300° for 30 minutes, stirring once. Spread on foil to cool. Store in an airtight container. **Yield:** 12 cups.

Herbed Popcorn

(Pictured on page 78)

This savory popcorn is a nice break from the usual sweet snack mixes.
—Donna Gonda, North Canton, Ohio

8 cups popped popcorn
2 cups potato sticks
1 cup mixed nuts
1/3 cup butter, melted
1 teaspoon dill weed
1 teaspoon lemon-pepper seasoning
1 teaspoon Worcestershire sauce
1/2 teaspoon onion powder
1/2 teaspoon garlic powder

In a large bowl, combine the popcorn, potato sticks and nuts. In a small bowl, combine the remaining ingredients. Drizzle over popcorn mixture and toss to coat.

Spread into two ungreased 15-in. x 10-in. x 1-in. baking pans. Bake, uncovered, at 250° for 25-30 minutes or until lightly browned, stirring twice. Cool on a wire rack. Store in an airtight container. **Yield:** 9 cups.

POPCORN POINTER

TO GET the 8 cups of popped popcorn called for in the Herbed Popcorn recipe (above), start with one cup of unpopped kernels.

Zesty Salt Substitute

(Pictured at right, left)

Folks on a low-sodium diet will fall for this salt substitute. I usually double the recipe because it beautifully seasons a variety of foods.
—Peggy Key, Grant, Alabama

5 teaspoons onion powder
3 teaspoons garlic powder
3 teaspoons ground mustard
3 teaspoons paprika
1/2 teaspoon celery seed
1/2 teaspoon white pepper

In a small bowl, combine all ingredients. Store in an airtight container for up to 6 months. Use to season meats or vegetables. **Yield:** about 1/4 cup.

Curry Seasoning Mix

(Pictured above, right)

I've been making this seasoning blend for many years.
Try sprinkling it on pork chops, seafood, chicken and steak.
—Bonnie Poole, Madison, Wisconsin

3/4 cup salt
2 teaspoons onion powder
2 teaspoons curry powder
2 teaspoons ground mustard
2 teaspoons ground turmeric
2 teaspoons paprika

1-1/2 teaspoons garlic powder
1 teaspoon sugar
1 teaspoon dried thyme

In a small bowl, combine all ingredients. Store in an airtight container for up to 6 months. **Yield:** about 1 cup.

Coffee Vienna

(Pictured at far right)

Don't buy those expensive tins of flavored coffee when it's so easy and inexpensive to make your own. This mix has a hint of cinnamon.
— *Darlene Brenden, Salem, Oregon*

2/3 cup nondairy creamer
2/3 cup sugar
1/2 cup instant coffee granules
1/2 teaspoon ground cinnamon

In an airtight container, combine all ingredients. Store in a cool dry place for up to 2 months.

To make one serving: In a mug, dissolve 2 tablespoons mix in 1 cup boiling water; stir well. **Yield:** 1-1/2 cups mix (12 servings).

Pancake Mix in a Jar

At Christmas, I like to present friends and family with this mix and pure maple syrup. The pancakes are fluffy and fruity.
— *Diane Musil, Lyons, Illinois*

3 cups all-purpose flour
3 tablespoons sugar
2 tablespoons baking powder
4-1/2 teaspoons ground cinnamon
1 teaspoon salt
ADDITIONAL INGREDIENTS
(for each batch):
1 egg
3/4 cup milk
3 tablespoons vegetable oil
1/4 cup chopped dried apples *or* cranberries, optional

In a large bowl, combine the first five ingredients. Transfer to a 1-qt. jar with a tight-fitting lid. Cover and store in a cool dry place for up to 6 months. **Yield:** 2 batches (3 cups total).

To prepare pancakes: Place 1-1/2 cups mix in a bowl. In another bowl, whisk the egg, milk and oil. Stir in dried fruit if desired. Stir into pancake mix just until moistened. Pour batter by 1/4 cupfuls onto a greased hot griddle. Turn when bubbles form on top; cook until second side is golden brown. **Yield:** 2 batches (about 1-1/2 cups per batch).

PREPARING PANCAKES

1. Using a 1/4-cup measure, pour batter onto a hot griddle or skillet, 5-6 in. apart, making sure you leave enough room between pancakes for expansion.

2. Turn pancakes over when edges become dry and bubbles that appear on top begin to pop.

Blueberry Streusel Muffins

(Pictured at right)

A lemon glaze adds a little zest to these mouth-watering muffins. You can substitute raspberries for the blueberries.
—*Jennifer Oller, Springfield, Ohio*

1-1/2 cups all-purpose flour
　1/4 cup sugar
　1/4 cup packed brown sugar
　　2 teaspoons baking powder
　1/2 teaspoon ground cinnamon
　1/4 teaspoon salt
　　1 egg
　1/2 cup plus 2 tablespoons milk
　　2 tablespoons butter, melted
　　1 cup fresh *or* frozen blueberries
　　1 teaspoon grated lemon peel
STREUSEL TOPPING:
　1/4 cup chopped pecans
　1/4 cup packed brown sugar
　　2 tablespoons all-purpose flour
　　1 tablespoon butter, melted
　　1 teaspoon grated lemon peel
　1/2 teaspoon ground cinnamon
GLAZE:
　1/4 cup confectioners' sugar
　　1 tablespoon lemon juice

In a large bowl, combine the flour, sugars, baking powder, cinnamon and salt. In a small bowl, whisk the egg, milk and butter. Stir into dry ingredients just until moistened. Fold in blueberries and lemon peel. Fill greased or paper-lined muffin cups two-thirds full.

Combine topping ingredients; sprinkle over batter. Bake at 350° for 20-25 minutes or until a toothpick comes out clean. Cool for 5 minutes before removing from pan to a wire rack. Combine glaze ingredients until smooth; drizzle over warm muffins. **Yield:** 1 dozen.

Editor's Note: If using frozen blueberries, do not thaw before adding to batter.

Gigantic Cinnamon Rolls

(Pictured on page 79)

These large, luscious cinnamon rolls are always a hit at my parent's Christmas brunch.
The recipe yields two so you can keep one and give the other as a gift.
—Kathy Wells, Brodhead, Wisconsin

1/2 cup sugar
1/2 cup packed brown sugar
2 teaspoons ground cinnamon
2 loaves (1 pound *each*) frozen
bread dough, thawed
1/2 cup butter, melted
1/2 cup chopped pecans
1-1/4 cups confectioners' sugar
6 teaspoons milk
1/2 teaspoon vanilla extract

In a shallow bowl, combine sugars and cinnamon; set aside. On a lightly floured surface, roll each loaf of dough into a 12-in. x 4-in. rectangle. Cut each rectangle lengthwise into four 1-in. strips. Roll each into an 18-in.-long rope. Dip in butter, then roll in sugar mixture.

Coil one rope in the center of a greased 12-in. pizza pan. Add three more ropes, pinching ends together to fill one pan. Repeat with remaining ropes on a second pizza pan. Sprinkle with pecans and remaining cinnamon-sugar. Cover and let rise in a warm place until doubled, about 45 minutes.

Bake at 350° for 20-30 minutes or until golden brown. In a small bowl, combine confectioners' sugar, milk and vanilla until smooth. Drizzle over warm rolls. **Yield:** 2 rolls (6-8 servings each).

Raspberry Pastry Twists

(Pictured on page 78)

Our Test Kitchen home economists give regular round cookies a tasty twist in this recipe.

1 package (8 ounces) cream
cheese, softened
1/2 cup butter, softened
2 egg yolks

2-1/2 cups all-purpose flour
6 tablespoons raspberry filling

In a small mixing bowl, beat cream cheese and butter until fluffy. Beat in egg yolks. Gradually add flour. Cover and refrigerate overnight.

Remove from the refrigerator 1 hour before rolling. Divide the dough in half. Roll each portion into a 12-in. x 8-in. rectangle. Spread raspberry filling widthwise over half of each rectangle. Fold plain portion of dough over filling. Cut each rectangle widthwise into sixteen 1/2-in. strips. Twist each strip three times; pinch open ends to seal.

Place on ungreased baking sheets. Bake at 400° for 13-15 minutes or until golden brown. Immediately remove from pans to wire racks to cool. **Yield:** about 2-1/2 dozen.

Creative Gift Containers

(Pictured above)

THE innovative packaging ideas featured here can be enjoyed long after the homemade goodies inside are gobbled up.

Versatile Vase. On page 78, a metal tussy mussy is blooming with Raspberry Pastry Twists. Recipients can use the vase for a fun, floral arrangement in the future.

Charge It! Stacked silver dinner plate chargers (available at discount department stores) are just the right size for Gigantic Cinnamon Rolls.

Double Dipping. Purchase an inexpensive, sectioned glass chip 'n' dip bowl. Fill with Herbed Popcorn, Glazed Macadamia Nuts and Sweet 'n' Crunchy Snack Mix. Or place a pretty ornament in one of the sections.

Coffee Break. A Blueberry Streusel Muffin shown on a stack of coasters and Coffee Vienna mix in a travel mug (shown on page 85) would be a wonderful seasonal snack for a child's favorite teacher.

Boxed In. Easily impress family and friends by presenting an ornament box decked out in assorted Shortbread Ornament Cookies.

Holiday Holder. For small breads like Maraschino Cherry Mini Loaves, a silver mesh napkin holder is a clever container.

Shake Things Up. Simple salt and pepper shakers (found in the housewares section of a hardware store) are perfect for dispensing Zesty Salt Substitute and Curry Seasoning Mix.

Nuts About Christmas!

COME CHRISTMAS, folks get cracking in the kitchen baking a host of holiday treats. And nuts have long been a staple in seasonal cooking.

From walnuts, almonds and cashews to pistachios, peanuts and more, nuts add rich flavor and crunchy texture to both sweet and savory recipes.

Family and friends will shell out the compliments when they sample Macadamia Nut Pie, Triple-Nut Candy and Buttermilk Nut Bread. (All recipes are shown at right.)

And don't forget to squirrel away a few nuts in unexpected dishes like Chow Mein Sunflower Coleslaw, Pecan Barbecue Sauce and Roasted Peanut Salsa!

Buttermilk Nut Bread

(Pictured on page 88)

*A brown sugar glaze adds a little sweetness to slices of this flavorful quick bread loaded
with toasted walnuts. I often share loaves with friends and neighbors.*
—*Claudia Brown, Breesport, New York*

3-1/2 cups all-purpose flour
  2 cups packed brown sugar
  1 teaspoon baking soda
1/2 teaspoon baking powder
1/2 teaspoon salt
  2 cups buttermilk
  2 eggs
  1 tablespoon butter, melted
  1 cup chopped walnuts, toasted
PENUCHE GLAZE:
1/2 cup packed brown sugar
1/4 cup butter, cubed
  2 tablespoons milk
1/4 teaspoon ground mace
3/4 to 1 cup confectioners' sugar

In a large mixing bowl, combine the flour, brown sugar, baking soda, baking powder and salt. Add buttermilk, eggs and butter; beat just until combined. Fold in walnuts.

Pour into five greased 5-3/4-in. x 3-in. x 2-in. loaf pans. Bake at 350° for 45-55 minutes or until a toothpick inserted near center comes out clean. Cool for 10 minutes before removing from pans to wire racks to cool completely.

For glaze, in a small saucepan, bring brown sugar and butter to a boil. Reduce heat to medium; cook and stir for 2 minutes. Remove from the heat; cool for 5 minutes. Whisk in milk and mace until smooth. Stir in enough confectioners' sugar to achieve desired consistency. Drizzle over loaves. **Yield:** 5 mini loaves.

Hot Pecan Beef Spread

*A friend shared this appetizer with me, and I've made it often over the years.
Leftovers keep well in the refrigerator and can be reheated or served cold.*
—*Harriet Kroeger, Blaine, Minnesota*

1/2 cup chopped pecans
  2 tablespoons butter
  1 package (8 ounces) cream
    cheese, softened
  2 teaspoons milk
1/2 cup sour cream
1/2 teaspoon garlic powder
1/4 teaspoon pepper
  1 package (3 ounces) dried beef,
    finely chopped
  1 small onion, grated

1/4 cup chopped green pepper
Assorted crackers *or* pita chips

In a small skillet, saute pecans in butter until toasted; set aside. In a small mixing bowl, beat cream cheese and milk until smooth. Add the sour cream, garlic powder and pepper; mix well. Stir in the beef, onion and green pepper.

Spoon into a greased shallow 3-cup baking dish. Sprinkle with toasted pecans. Bake, uncovered, at 350° for 15-20 minutes or until heated through. Serve with crackers or pita chips. **Yield:** 2 cups.

Triple-Nut Candy

(Pictured at right and on page 88)

I've been making homemade candy for years. Family and friends look forward to this caramel and nut sweet treat each Christmas.
—*Ardis Gatons Olson*
Brookings, South Dakota

1 cup walnut halves
1 cup pecan halves
1 cup Brazil nuts, halved
1 teaspoon butter
1-1/2 cups sugar
1 cup heavy whipping cream
1/2 cup light corn syrup

Place the walnuts, pecans and Brazil nuts in a single layer on a baking sheet. Bake at 350° for 4-8 minutes or until toasted and golden brown, stirring once. Cool on a wire rack. Line an 8-in. square pan with foil; grease the foil with butter and set aside.

In a heavy saucepan, combine the sugar, cream and corn syrup. Bring to a boil over medium heat, stirring constantly. Stir in the toasted nuts. Cook, without stirring, until a candy thermometer reads 238° (soft-ball stage). Remove from the heat. Stir with a wooden spoon until creamy and thickened. Quickly spread into prepared pan; cool.

Cover and refrigerate for 8 hours or overnight. Using foil, lift candy out of pan; discard foil. Cut candy into squares. Store in an airtight container in the refrigerator. **Yield:** 2 pounds.

Editor's Note: We recommend that you test your candy thermometer before each use by bringing water to a boil; the thermometer should read 212°. Adjust your recipe temperature up or down based on your test.

BRAZIL NUT BASICS

THE BRAZIL NUT shell is very hard. To make it easier to crack, bake the nuts at 400° for 15 minutes. Or place in a saucepan and cover with water. Bring to a boil; boil for 3 minutes. Drain; cover with ice water and let stand for 2 minutes. Drain and crack. One pound of Brazil nuts in the shell yields about 1-1/2 cups of nut meat.

Pecan Barbecue Sauce

*After 18 years, I haven't found anything that this sauce
doesn't taste great on. Pecans are the deliciously different ingredient.*
—Vickie Patterson, Grand Prairie, Texas

1 can (12 ounces) tomato paste
1 cup ground pecans
3/4 cup water
1/3 cup packed brown sugar
1/4 cup cider vinegar
1/4 cup chopped onion
1/4 cup honey
2 tablespoons lemon juice

1 tablespoon prepared mustard
1 teaspoon seasoned salt
2 garlic cloves, minced

In a large saucepan, combine all ingredients. Bring to a boil. Reduce heat; simmer, uncovered, for 20 minutes or until thickened, stirring occasionally. **Yield:** 3 cups.

Macadamia Nut Pie

(Pictured on page 89)

*When I was young, friends of our family traveled to Hawaii and brought back macadamia nuts.
My mom used them in this recipe. It's a tasty twist on traditional pecan pie.*
—Brenda Hildebrandt, Moosomin, Saskatchewan

1 sheet refrigerated pie pastry
3 eggs
1 cup dark corn syrup
2/3 cup sugar
2 tablespoons butter, melted
2 teaspoons vanilla extract
2 cups chopped macadamia nuts

Unroll pastry and place in a 9-in. pie plate; flute edges and set aside. In a small mixing bowl, beat the eggs, corn syrup, sugar, butter and vanilla until combined. Stir in the nuts. Pour into pastry shell.

Bake at 325° for 50-55 minutes or until center is set and top is golden brown. Cool on a wire rack. Refrigerate leftovers. **Yield:** 8-10 servings.

CHOPPING MACADAMIA NUTS

ONE 3-1/4-ounce jar of macadamia nuts yields about 3/4 cup chopped.

To chop macadamia nuts, put them in a heavy-duty resealable plastic bag; seal and break them with a rolling pin. Or chop them in a food processor fitted with the metal blade. Don't overprocess or the nuts will turn to paste.

Roasted Peanut Salsa

(Pictured at right)

It seems I'm always making this zesty salsa packed with peanuts and fruit. And I've passed on the recipe too many times to count.
—Paula Marchesi
Lenhartsville, Pennsylvania

3 tablespoons lime juice
2 tablespoons minced fresh parsley
1 tablespoon vegetable oil
2-1/2 teaspoons brown sugar
1 to 2 garlic cloves, minced
1/2 to 1 teaspoon crushed red pepper flakes
1/4 teaspoon salt
3/4 cup diced peeled jicama
3/4 cup diced unpeeled apple
1/2 cup chopped cucumber
1/2 cup chopped sweet red pepper
1/2 cup fresh dark sweet cherries, pitted and quartered, optional
3 green onions, sliced
1 cup unsalted dry roasted peanuts
Assorted crackers

In a large bowl, combine the first seven ingredients. Add the jicama, apple, cucumber, red pepper, cherries if desired and onions; toss to coat. Cover and refrigerate for at least 2 hours. Just before serving, stir in peanuts. Serve with crackers. **Yield:** 4 cups.

Almond Chicken Strips

Whether I serve these nutty chicken strips as an appetizer or entree, there are never leftovers.
—Wendy Thurston, Bow Island, Alberta

1/4 cup cornstarch
1 teaspoon sugar
1/2 teaspoon salt
1-1/2 teaspoons sherry *or* chicken broth
2 egg whites, lightly beaten
1-1/2 cups ground almonds
1 pound boneless skinless chicken breasts, cut into 1/2-inch strips
2 tablespoons vegetable oil

In a shallow bowl, combine the cornstarch, sugar, salt and sherry or broth until smooth. Gradually stir in egg whites. Place almonds in another shallow bowl. Dip chicken in egg white mixture, then coat with almonds.

In a large skillet or wok, stir-fry chicken strips in oil for 5-7 minutes or until no longer pink; drain on paper towels. **Yield:** 4 servings.

Almond Cherry Pizza

The traditional pairing of almonds and cherries makes for a delicious dessert pizza in this recipe from our home economists. Keep the ingredients on hand for a no-fuss, impressive dessert.

1 prebaked Italian bread shell
  crust (14 ounces)
1/3 cup almond paste
1 package (8 ounces)
  Mascarpone cheese
1/2 cup vanilla *or* white chips
1 can (12 ounces) cherry filling
1 jar (10 ounces) maraschino
  cherries, drained and halved
1/2 cup sliced almonds

Place the crust on an ungreased 12-in. pizza pan. Crumble almond paste into a small microwave-safe bowl; cover and microwave on high for 5 seconds to soften if necessary. Stir in the cheese until combined; spread over crust to within 1 in. of edges. Sprinkle with chips.

Bake at 400° for 12-15 minutes or until edges are lightly browned. Let stand until cheese mixture is set. Spread with cherry filling; top with maraschino cherries and almonds. **Yield:** 10-12 servings.

Editor's Note: This recipe was tested with Solo brand filling. Look for it in the baking aisle of your grocery store.

Butterscotch Pecan Logs

One of my aunts created this recipe more than 30 years ago. It was always one of our favorite treats at Christmas. Soft, chewy butterscotch candy is coated with crunchy pecans.
—*Loraine Meyer, Bend, Oregon*

1 teaspoon plus 1/4 cup butter,
  divided
1-1/2 cups sugar
1-1/2 cups packed brown sugar
1 can (5 ounces) evaporated milk
1 jar (7 ounces) marshmallow
  creme
1-1/2 cups butterscotch chips
2 packages (14 ounces *each*)
  caramels
5 tablespoons heavy whipping
  cream
4 cups finely chopped pecans

Line a 9-in. square pan with foil; grease the foil with 1 teaspoon butter and set aside. In a heavy saucepan, combine the sugars, milk and remaining butter. Bring to a boil, stirring constantly. Reduce heat to medium-low; cook for 5 minutes. Remove from the heat. Stir in marshmallow creme and chips until chips are melted. Spread into prepared pan. Cool completely.

Using foil, lift candy out of pan; discard foil. Cut candy into 2-in. x 1/2-in. pieces. In a large microwave-safe bowl, combine caramels and cream. Microwave, uncovered, on high for 3-4 minutes or until melted; stir until smooth.

Dip candies into caramel mixture; shake off excess. Immediately roll in pecans. Place on waxed paper until set. Store in an airtight container in the refrigerator. Before serving, cut into slices if desired. **Yield:** 4-1/2 pounds.

Editor's Note: This recipe was tested in a 1,100-watt microwave.

Curried Pecans

(Pictured at right)

These buttery pecans have a mild curry flavor that appeals to all palates.
—Joyce Schultz
Swift Current, Saskatchewan

3 tablespoons butter, melted
1-1/4 to 1-1/2 teaspoons curry
    powder
1/2 teaspoon salt
2 cups pecan halves

In a bowl, combine the butter, curry and salt. Add pecans and toss to coat. Transfer to a foil-lined 11-in. x 7-in. x 2-in. baking pan.

Bake at 350° for 15-20 minutes or until toasted and crisp, stirring three times. Cool on a wire rack. Store in an airtight container. **Yield:** 2 cups.

Chow Mein Sunflower Coleslaw

I like recipes that are easy yet delicious. With only eight ingredients, this cabbage salad can be put together in mere minutes. Then just refrigerate for an hour to let the flavors blend.
—Diane Folkerts, Thompson, Iowa

1 package (16 ounces)
    coleslaw mix
1/2 cup sunflower kernels
1/2 cup sliced almonds
4 to 5 green onions, chopped
1/3 cup vegetable oil
1/4 cup rice wine vinegar
1/4 cup packed brown sugar
1 cup chow mein noodles

In a large bowl, combine the coleslaw mix, sunflower kernels, almonds and onions. In a small bowl, combine the oil, vinegar and brown sugar. Pour over the coleslaw mixture and toss to coat. Cover and refrigerate for 1 hour. Just before serving, sprinkle with chow mein noodles. **Yield:** 14 servings.

Walnut-Caramel Sticky Buns

With filbert and walnut trees on the land of my childhood home, I learned to include nuts in a variety of recipes. No one can resist these caramel rolls with walnuts in both the filling and topping.
—*Alice Swayze, Canby, Oregon*

1 package (1/4 ounce) active
   dry yeast
1 cup plus 2 tablespoons warm
   water (110° to 115°)
1/4 cup sugar
2 tablespoons butter, melted
4-1/2 teaspoons nonfat dry milk
   powder
1 teaspoon salt
3 to 3-1/4 cups all-purpose flour
CARAMEL SAUCE:
1/2 cup butter, cubed
1 cup packed brown sugar
3 tablespoons light corn syrup
2 tablespoons honey
2 tablespoons sour cream
1 cup walnut halves, toasted
FILLING:
2 tablespoons butter, melted
3/4 cup finely chopped walnuts
1/3 cup packed brown sugar
1-1/2 teaspoons ground cinnamon

In a large mixing bowl, dissolve yeast in warm water. Add the sugar, butter, milk powder, salt and 2 cups flour; beat until smooth. Stir in enough remaining flour to form a soft dough. Turn onto a floured surface; knead until smooth and elastic, about 6-8 minutes. Place in a greased bowl, turning once to grease top. Cover and let rise in a warm place until doubled, about 1 hour.

Meanwhile, in a small saucepan, melt butter. Add the brown sugar, corn syrup, honey and sour cream. Cook and stir over medium heat until sugar is dissolved. Pour into a greased 13-in. x 9-in. x 2-in. baking pan. Sprinkle with walnut halves.

Punch dough down. Turn onto a lightly floured surface; roll into a 16-in. x 12-in. rectangle. Brush with melted butter. Combine the chopped walnuts, brown sugar and cinnamon; sprinkle over dough. Roll up jelly-roll style, starting with a long side; pinch seam to seal. Cut into 12 slices. Place cut side down over caramel sauce. Cover and let rise until doubled, about 30 minutes.

Bake at 350° for 25-30 minutes or until golden brown. Cool for 5 minutes. Invert onto a serving platter. **Yield:** 1 dozen.

IN A NUTSHELL

A LITTLE knowledge about nuts will serve you well when buying and storing them and when using them in recipes.

- When buying nuts in the shell, look for whole, clean shells without blemishes, holes or cracks.
- Nuts out of the shell should be plump and unbroken. Don't buy nuts that are discolored or shriveled.
- Before using any nuts in recipes, be sure to taste them first. They should be sweet and crunchy. Do not use nuts with a bitter or oily taste.
- To really bring out the flavor of nuts, consider toasting them before using in recipes. Spread nuts on a baking sheet. Bake at 350° for 5 to 10 minutes or until lightly toasted. Watch carefully so they don't burn.
- Because nuts can turn rancid fairly quickly, the best way to store them is in an airtight container in the freezer. They should stay fresh this way for up to a year.

Cashew Tossed Salad

(Pictured at right, top)

A flavorful onion dressing tastefully tops off a tossed salad featuring cashews and dried cranberries. I'm often asked to make this for meetings at church.
—Raelynne Fink-Mahloch
Kansas City, Missouri

8 cups torn mixed salad greens
1 cup salted cashews
3/4 cup dried cranberries
1/2 cup thinly sliced red onion
DRESSING:
1/4 cup sugar
1/4 cup chopped red onion
3 tablespoons olive oil
2 tablespoons vegetable oil
2 tablespoons white vinegar
1 teaspoon prepared mustard
Dash pepper
1/4 teaspoon poppy seeds

In a large bowl, combine the greens, cashews, cranberries and sliced onion. In a blender, combine the sugar, chopped onion, olive oil, vegetable oil, vinegar, mustard and pepper; cover and process until blended. Stir in the poppy seeds. Drizzle over salad and toss to coat. Serve immediately. **Yield:** 8 servings.

Pistachio-Crusted Fried Fish

(Pictured above, bottom)

This nut-crusted fish from our Test Kitchen home economists is so much better than ordinary breaded fish. Pistachios give it great color.

1/2 cup dry bread crumbs
1/2 cup chopped pistachios
1/2 teaspoon seafood seasoning
1/4 teaspoon salt
1/4 teaspoon garlic powder
1/4 teaspoon pepper
1/2 cup all-purpose flour
1/2 cup milk
1-1/2 pounds whitefish *or* cod fillets
3 tablespoons vegetable oil

In a shallow bowl, combine the first six ingredients. Place flour and milk in separate shallow bowls. Dip fillets in flour, then in milk; coat with pistachio mixture.

In a large nonstick skillet, cook fillets in oil over medium heat for 4-5 minutes on each side or until fish flakes easily with a fork. **Yield:** 6 servings.

Cinnamon-Walnut Coffee Cake

My husband and I work outside the home so we only have time for from-scratch breakfasts on the weekends. Our daughter enjoys slices of this coffee cake around the clock!
—*Jill Hanselman, Lexington, North Carolina*

1-1/2 cups chopped walnuts
1-1/2 cups sugar, *divided*
   3 teaspoons ground cinnamon
   2 cups all-purpose flour
  3/4 teaspoon baking soda
  1/2 teaspoon salt
   1 cup buttermilk
  1/4 cup vegetable oil
   1 egg
   1 teaspoon vanilla extract
GLAZE:
  1/3 cup confectioners' sugar
   2 to 2-1/2 teaspoons milk

In a small bowl, combine the walnuts, 3/4 cup sugar and cinnamon; set aside. Combine the flour, baking soda and salt; set aside. In a large mixing bowl, combine the buttermilk, oil, egg, vanilla and remaining sugar. Add flour mixture; beat just until moistened.

Spread half of the batter into a greased 8-in. square baking dish. Sprinkle with 1-1/2 cups walnut mixture. Spread with remaining batter; top with remaining walnut mixture. Cut through batter with a knife to swirl.

Bake at 350° for 35-40 minutes or until a toothpick inserted near the center comes out clean. Combine glaze ingredients; drizzle over coffee cake. Serve warm if desired or cool on a wire rack. **Yield:** 9 servings.

Sugar 'n' Spice Mixed Nuts

A crunchy, spiced seasoning nicely coats a variety of nuts in this tasty recipe. These nuts disappear whenever I set out a bowl.
—*Glynis Belec, Drayton, Ontario*

   1 egg white
   1 tablespoon butter, melted
   1 cup unsalted dry roasted
     peanuts
   1 cup chopped walnuts
  1/2 cup chopped cashews
  1/2 cup slivered almonds
  1/2 cup pecan halves
  1/2 cup unsalted sunflower
     kernels
  3/4 cup sugar
   2 tablespoons cornstarch

1-1/2 teaspoons ground cinnamon
  1/2 teaspoon ground allspice
  1/2 teaspoon ground nutmeg
  1/4 teaspoon salt

In a bowl, combine the egg white and butter. Add the peanuts, walnuts, cashews, almonds, pecans and sunflower kernels. In a large bowl, combine the sugar, cornstarch, cinnamon, allspice, nutmeg and salt. Add nut mixture and toss to coat.

Transfer to a greased shallow 2-1/2-qt. baking dish. Bake at 275° for 45 minutes or until toasted and crisp, stirring every 15 minutes. Cool on a wire rack. Store in an airtight container. **Yield:** 5 cups.

Caramel-Cashew Cake Bars

(Pictured at right)

These rich bars are a hit with everyone who tries them. The moist, cake-like crust pairs well with the chewy caramel and salty cashews.
—Marlene Collins
Detroit Lakes, Minnesota

3/4 cup all-purpose flour
1/2 cup sugar
1/2 cup packed brown sugar
1/2 teaspoon baking powder
1/4 teaspoon salt
  2 eggs
1/2 cup salted cashews, chopped
CASHEW TOPPING:
1/2 cup salted cashews, chopped
1/4 cup packed brown sugar
  2 tablespoons butter, melted
4-1/2 teaspoons heavy whipping
     cream

In a large mixing bowl, combine the flour, sugars, baking powder and salt. Beat in the eggs just until combined. Fold in the cashews. Spread into a greased 8-in. square baking dish. Bake at 350° for 20-25 minutes or until top springs back when lightly touched.

In a small bowl, combine the topping ingredients. Spread over cake. Broil for 1-2 minutes or until bubbly and lightly browned. Cut into bars while warm. Cool on a wire rack. **Yield:** 16 bars.

'TIS THE *Season*

St. Nick Celebration

ST. NICHOLAS was a fourth century bishop, who would secretly give gifts to children in need. When Europeans settled in the United States, many brought with them the tradition of remembering his generous spirit on December 6.

The night before, kids hang up their stockings or put out their shoes. In the morning, they rush to see the fruits, nuts, candies or small gifts that St. Nick magically left for them.

Why not introduce this little-known holiday to friends by hosting a St. Nick party?

Slow Cooker Pizza Casserole, Herbed Garlic Bread and Colorful Caesar Salad is a mouth-watering meal that will appeal to young and old alike. (All recipes shown at right.)

For a fun, finger-licking dessert, have the kids decorate an array of tasty cupcakes. (See page 107 for inviting ideas.)

FAMILY FARE
(Clockwise from bottom)

Slow Cooker Pizza Casserole (p. 102)

Colorful Caesar Salad (p. 105)

Herbed Garlic Bread (p. 102)

Herbed Garlic Bread

(Pictured on page 101)

No Italian meal is complete without bread. This garlic herb version comes from our home economists. If desired, sprinkle with shredded provolone cheese.

1/2 cup butter, softened
1/4 cup grated Romano cheese
2 tablespoons minced fresh basil
or 2 teaspoons dried basil
1 tablespoon minced fresh parsley
3 garlic cloves, minced
1 loaf (1 pound) French bread, halved lengthwise
4 ounces provolone cheese, shredded, optional

In a small bowl, combine the butter, Romano cheese, basil, parsley and garlic. Spread over cut sides of bread. Sprinkle with provolone cheese if desired.

Place on an ungreased baking sheet. Bake at 425° for 10-12 minutes or until cheese is melted. Slice and serve warm. **Yield:** 8 servings.

Slow Cooker Pizza Casserole

(Pictured on page 100)

A comforting casserole with mass appeal is just what you need when cooking for a crowd. For added convenience, it stays warm in a slow cooker.
—Virginia Krites, Cridersville, Ohio

1 package (16 ounces) rigatoni *or* large tube pasta
1-1/2 pounds ground beef
1 small onion, chopped
4 cups (16 ounces) shredded part-skim mozzarella cheese
2 cans (15 ounces *each*) pizza sauce
1 can (10-3/4 ounces) condensed cream of mushroom soup, undiluted
1 package (8 ounces) sliced pepperoni

Cook pasta according to package directions. Meanwhile, in a skillet, cook beef and onion over medium heat until meat is no longer pink; drain.

Drain pasta; place in a 5-qt. slow cooker. Stir in the beef mixture, cheese, pizza sauce, soup and pepperoni. Cover and cook on low for 2-3 hours or until heated through and the cheese is melted. **Yield:** 12-14 servings.

Christmas Gelatin Cutouts

(Pictured at right)

Cool, fruity and creamy, these gelatin treats from our Test Kitchen are richer than plain gelatin and cut easily into whatever shape you want.

- **2 packages (6 ounces *each*) strawberry gelatin**
- **2 packages (6 ounces *each*) lime gelatin**
- **5 cups boiling water, *divided***
- **2 cups cold milk**
- **2 packages (3.4 ounces *each*) instant vanilla pudding mix**

In a large bowl, dissolve strawberry gelatin in 2-1/2 cups boiling water. In another bowl, dissolve lime gelatin in remaining boiling water; set both aside for 30 minutes.

In a bowl, whisk milk and pudding mixes until smooth, about 1 minute. Quickly pour half of the pudding into each bowl of gelatin; whisk until well blended. Pour into two 13-in. x 9-in. x 2-in. dishes coated with nonstick cooking spray. Chill for 3 hours or until set. Cut with 2-in. Christmas cookie cutters. **Yield:** 4 dozen.

VARIATIONS OF CHRISTMAS GELATIN CUTOUTS

THE RECIPE for Christmas Gelatin Cutouts makes about 4 dozen. If a smaller yield is desired, use only one flavor of gelatin and half of the water, milk and pudding.

You can also use other flavors of red gelatin, such as cherry, cranberry and raspberry. If your family isn't fond of lime, just use all red gelatin.

Mandarin Fruit Dip

With all the heavy foods around the holidays, fruit is a refreshing change of pace.
For more kid appeal, our home economists pair fruit with a sweet and creamy dip.

1 package (8 ounces) cream cheese, softened
1/4 cup confectioners' sugar
1 can (11 ounces) mandarin oranges, drained
1/2 teaspoon vanilla extract
1/2 teaspoon orange extract
1 cup whipped topping
Assorted fresh fruit

In a small mixing bowl, combine cream cheese, confectioners' sugar, oranges and extracts; beat on medium speed until combined. Fold in whipped topping. Transfer to a serving bowl. Refrigerate or serve immediately with fruit. **Yield:** 2 cups.

Bacon-Tomato Dip in a Bread Bowl

This tasty dip disappears whenever I serve it. I like that it is quick and can be made ahead.
—Laura Mahaffey, Annapolis, Maryland

1 package (8 ounces) cream cheese, softened
1/4 cup mayonnaise
1 medium tomato, peeled and chopped
8 bacon strips, cooked and crumbled
1/4 teaspoon dried basil
1/4 teaspoon pepper

1 round loaf (1/2 pound) unsliced sourdough bread
Assorted crackers

In a small mixing bowl, beat cream cheese and mayonnaise until smooth. Stir in the tomato, bacon, basil and pepper. Cover and refrigerate for 1 hour.

Cut a 1-1/2-in. thick slice off the top of bread; set aside. Carefully hollow out loaf, leaving a 1/2-in. shell. Cut removed bread into cubes. Fill bread shell with dip. Serve with crackers and bread cubes. **Yield:** 2 cups.

MAKING A BREAD BOWL

YOU can't go wrong with a dip container that's both attractive and edible! First cut a thick slice off the top of the bread. Cut around the perimeter of the bread, about 1/2 inch from the crust.

Insert your fingers along the cut and loosen the bread from the bottom of loaf. Remove the bread; cut into cubes to serve with the dip. Fill the bread bowl with any savory dip of your choice.

Colorful Caesar Salad

(Pictured at right and on page 100)

*We guarantee you'll enjoy our
Test Kitchen's take on this classic salad.
The dressing can be prepared
up to 3 days in advance.*

12 cups torn romaine
 3 medium tomatoes, cut into
    wedges
 1 medium cucumber, halved and
    sliced
 3 hard-cooked eggs
 6 anchovy fillets
1/4 cup red wine vinegar
 2 tablespoons lemon juice
 2 tablespoons Dijon mustard
 1 tablespoon Worcestershire
    sauce
 4 garlic cloves, minced
 1 teaspoon sugar
1/2 teaspoon pepper
3/4 cup olive oil
1-1/2 cups Caesar salad croutons
3/4 cup shredded Parmesan
    cheese

In a large salad bowl, combine the romaine, tomatoes and cucumber. Slice eggs in half; remove yolks. (Refrigerate whites for another use.) In a blender, combine the anchovies, vinegar, lemon juice, mustard, Worcestershire sauce, garlic, sugar, pepper and egg yolks; cover and process until smooth. While processing, gradually add oil in a steady stream.

   Drizzle desired amount of dressing over salad and toss to coat. Sprinkle with croutons and Parmesan cheese. Serve immediately. Refrigerate any leftover dressing for up to 3 days. **Yield:** 12 servings.

Creamy Hot White Chocolate

(Pictured at right)

We enjoy this hot beverage all year long but especially around the holidays. It's a nice change of pace from traditional hot chocolate.
—*Karen Riordan, Fern Creek, Kentucky*

6 cups half-and-half cream, *divided*
1-1/3 cups vanilla *or* white chips
2 cinnamon sticks (3 inches)
1/4 teaspoon ground cinnamon
Dash ground nutmeg
3 teaspoons vanilla extract

In a large saucepan, combine 1/2 cup cream, vanilla chips, cinnamon sticks, cinnamon and nutmeg. Cook and stir over low heat until chips are melted. Stir in remaining cream; heat through. Discard cinnamon sticks. Stir in vanilla. **Yield:** 8 servings.

Classic Chocolate Frosting

This fast, fudge-like frosting is so fantastic. It even makes cakes from a box mix taste like homemade!
—*Karen Ann Bland, Gove, Kansas*

1-2/3 cups confectioners' sugar
3/4 cup heavy whipping cream
4 squares (1 ounce *each*) unsweetened chocolate, chopped
2 teaspoons vanilla extract
6 tablespoons butter, softened

In a saucepan, combine confectioners' sugar and cream. Bring to a boil, stirring constantly. Remove from the heat; stir in chocolate until melted and smooth. Stir in vanilla. Cool until mixture is thickened, about 25 minutes, stirring occasionally.

In a mixing bowl, cream butter. Gradually beat in chocolate mixture until blended. Cover and refrigerate until ready to use. **Yield:** 1-1/2 cups.

Editor's Note: This recipe makes enough to frost 24 cupcakes or the top of a 13-inch x 9-inch cake. Recipe can be easily doubled.

Cupcake Decoration Station

(Pictured above)

WHEN hosting a party for children, there's no need for a fancy dessert. Just have some plain, baked cupcakes on hand!

As a fun food craft during the party, have kids frost the cupcakes, then decorate with assorted toppings, like colored sugar, sprinkles, chocolate jimmies and small candies.

Or for a little more creativity, have guests put on a happy holiday face by making St. Nick or Reindeer Cupcakes. Here's how:

St. Nick Cupcakes. Start with 2 cups (or one 16-ounce can) vanilla frosting. Place 2/3 cup in a bowl; tint with red food coloring.

Frost part of the cupcake top with white frost-ing for the face and the other part with red frost-ing for the hat. If desired, pipe white frosting to create the fur band of the hat. Press a miniature marshmallow on one side of the hat for pom-pom.

Add chocolate chips for the eyes and a red-hot candy for the nose. Gently press flaked co-conut below the nose for the beard.

Reindeer Cupcakes. Frost cupcakes with Classic Chocolate Frosting or chocolate frosting of your choice. Add chocolate chips for the eyes and a red-hot candy for the nose. Break apart large pretzel twists; add two pieces for antlers.

For a mouth-watering centerpiece, display the decorated cupcakes in a tiered cupcake stand.

GIVING *Thanks*

Looking for a way to liven up your standard
Thanksgiving dinner? Try Citrus-Scented
Brined Turkey along with some deliciously
different side dishes. Then awe dinner guests
with our special selection of incredible
autumn desserts. Your family will also
fall for the splendid second-time-around
recipes that delightfully dress up
ordinary Thanksgiving leftovers.

Thanksgiving With a Twist

IT'S NO SURPRISE that turkey is at the top of the list when it comes to Thanksgiving Day main courses. It's rather easy to make, feeds lots of folks and makes excellent leftovers!

But this year, why not do something a little different by preparing turkey in a delicious, new way?

Before being baked, Citrus-Scented Brined Turkey marinates in a simple salt solution overnight, resulting in a moist and tender entree.

For a flavorful first course, serve guests steaming cupsful of Curried Squash Soup.

Then pass a bowl brimming with Cranberry-Pear Stuffing. (All recipes are shown at right.)

A New Take on Turkey
(Top to bottom)

Citrus-Scented Brined Turkey (p. 112)

Cranberry Pear Stuffing (p. 116)

Curried Squash Soup (p. 113)

Citrus-Scented Brined Turkey

(Pictured on page 111 and on cover)

Our home economists marinate this turkey to keep it tender and moist while roasting.

11 garlic cloves, peeled
6 cups unsweetened apple juice
1 cup kosher salt
3/4 cup packed brown sugar
1/3 cup soy sauce
3 tablespoons minced fresh
  gingerroot
4 bay leaves
6 cups cold water
1 turkey (12 to 14 pounds)
1 medium lemon, cut into
  wedges
1 medium orange, cut into
  wedges
1 medium onion, cut into wedges
4 sprigs fresh thyme
1 tablespoon vegetable oil

Mince five garlic cloves; halve the remaining garlic cloves and set aside. In a large kettle, combine the apple juice, salt, brown sugar, soy sauce, ginger, bay leaves and minced garlic. Bring to a boil; cook and stir until salt and sugar are dissolved. Remove from the heat. Add cold water to cool the brine to room temperature.

Remove giblets from turkey; discard. Place a turkey-size oven roasting bag inside a second roasting bag; add turkey. Carefully pour cooled brine into bag. Squeeze out as much air as possible. Seal bags; turn to coat. Place in a roasting pan. Refrigerate for 18-24 hours, turning several times.

Drain and discard brine. Rinse turkey under cold water; pat dry. Place the lemon, orange, onion, thyme and reserved garlic in both cavities. Rub oil over skin. Skewer turkey openings; tie drumsticks together.

Place turkey, breast side up, on a rack in a roasting pan. Bake, uncovered, at 325° for 4 to 4-1/2 hours or until a meat thermometer inserted in the thigh reads 180° (cover loosely with foil if turkey browns too quickly). Let stand for 15 minutes before removing contents from cavities and carving the turkey. **Yield:** 12-14 servings.

Editor's Note: This recipe was tested with Morton brand kosher salt. It is best not to use a prebasted turkey for this recipe. However, if you do, omit the salt in the recipe.

BENEFITS OF BRINING

LEAN TYPES of meat, like turkey, can quickly dry out if overcooked for even a few extra minutes. One easy way to improve a meat's moisture content, as well as flavor and texture, is by first soaking it in a brine.

At a minimum, a brine consists of water and either kosher, table or sea salt. To add even more flavor, some brines also include juices, seasonings and sugars.

Use a food-safe, non-reactive container (such as an oven roasting bag) and make sure the brine completely covers the meat.

Here are some guidelines for brining times: Whole turkey, up to 24 hours; large whole chicken, 3-4 hours; pork chops, 4 hours; shrimp, 30 minutes; thin fish, 10 minutes.

After brining, rinse the meat and pat dry with paper towels. Bake as directed.

Curried Squash Soup

(Pictured at right and on page 111)

Growing up on a farm, I helped in the kitchen and had three brothers who liked to eat! My love of cooking continues today.
—*Dianne Conway, London, Ontario*

4 pounds butternut squash
1 large onion, diced
1 medium apple, peeled and diced
1 garlic clove, minced
1/4 cup butter
2 teaspoons curry powder
1/2 teaspoon ground ginger
3 cups chicken broth
1/2 cup heavy whipping cream
1/2 teaspoon salt
1/4 teaspoon pepper
1/8 teaspoon cayenne pepper, optional

Cut squash in half; discard seeds. Place squash cut side down in a 15-in. x 10-in. x 1-in. baking pan. Add 1/2 in. of hot water to pan. Bake, uncovered, at 350° for 40 minutes. Drain water from pan; turn squash cut side up. Bake 20-30 minutes longer or until tender. Cool slightly.

Carefully scoop out squash into a blender or food processor; cover and process until smooth. Set aside.

In a large saucepan, saute the onion, apple and garlic in butter until tender. Stir in curry powder and ginger; cook and stir for 1 minute. Stir in broth and pureed squash. Bring to a boil. Reduce heat; simmer, uncovered, for 15 minutes. Reduce heat to low. Add the cream, salt, pepper and cayenne if desired; heat through (do not boil). **Yield:** 8 servings (2 quarts).

THANKSGIVING TIMELINE

A Few Weeks Before:

- Prepare two grocery lists—one for non-perishable items to purchase now and one for perishable items to purchase a few days before Thanksgiving Day.
- Order a fresh turkey or buy and freeze a frozen turkey.

Five Days Before:

- Thaw the frozen turkey in a pan in the refrigerator. (Allow 24 hours of thawing for every 5 pounds.)

Two to Three Days Before:

- Set the table.
- Buy remaining grocery items, including the fresh turkey if you ordered one.
- Purchase flowers for the Fall Floral Centerpiece (see page 117).

The Day Before:

- Marinate and refrigerate the Citrus-Scented Brined Turkey as directed.
- Prepare Curried Squash Soup. Cover and chill.
- For Pineapple Sweet Potato Boats, make the filling as directed. Stuff the potatoes but do not sprinkle with pineapple tidbits and brown sugar. Cover and refrigerate.
- Bake Autumn Streusel Cake. Cool completely then store in a covered container at room temperature.
- Assemble the centerpiece.

Thanksgiving Day:

- Drain the turkey and discard the brine. Rinse the turkey under cold water and pat dry. Prepare the turkey and bake as directed.
- Assemble the Cranberry Pear Stuffing and bake as directed.
- Remove the Pineapple Sweet Potato Boats from the refrigerator 30 minutes before baking. Sprinkle with the pineapple tidbits and brown sugar; bake as directed.
- Reheat the Curried Squash Soup in a saucepan over low heat; do not boil.
- Let the cooked turkey stand 15 minutes. Remove contents from the cavity and carve.
- For dessert, serve the Autumn Streusel Cake.

Pineapple Sweet Potato Boats

(Pictured at right)

Crushed pineapple adds a tasty twist to these twice-baked sweet potatoes. Mini-marshmallows can be used in place of the pineapple if you prefer.
—Phy Bresse, Lumberton, North Carolina

8 medium sweet potatoes
2 cans (8 ounces *each*)
   unsweetened crushed
   pineapple, drained
1/2 cup butter, melted
1 teaspoon salt
1/2 teaspoon *each* ground
   cinnamon, ginger and allspice
1/4 teaspoon ground nutmeg
TOPPING:
2 cans (14 ounces *each*)
   unsweetened pineapple
   tidbits, drained
6 tablespoons brown sugar

SWEET POTATO POINTERS

LOOK for sweet potatoes with smooth skins and without bruises. Store in a cool, dry place for up to 2 weeks, but do not refrigerate. Scrub them well with a vegetable brush before using.

Scrub and pierce sweet potatoes; place on a microwave-safe plate. Microwave, uncovered, on high for 12-14 minutes or until tender, turning once.

When cool enough to handle, cut a thin slice off the top of each potato and discard. Scoop out pulp, leaving a thin shell. In a large mixing bowl, mash the pulp. Add the crushed pineapple, butter, salt, cinnamon, ginger, allspice and nutmeg; mix well. Spoon into sweet potato shells.

Place on a baking sheet. Sprinkle with pineapple tidbits and brown sugar. Bake, uncovered, at 325° for 30-35 minutes or until heated through. **Yield:** 8 servings.

Editor's Note: This recipe was tested in a 1,100-watt microwave.

Cranberry Pear Stuffing

(Pictured on page 111)

Our family came up with this recipe when we decided to add something new to our traditional Thanksgiving menu. Now this tasty dressing has become a standard dish on our holiday table.
—Juanita Haugen, Pleasanton, California

1 cup chopped celery
1/2 cup butter
1 package (16 ounces) seasoned stuffing cubes
1-1/2 cups dried cranberries
1-1/2 cups chopped ripe pears
1 cup chopped pecans
1/4 cup minced fresh parsley
2 to 3 teaspoons poultry seasoning
1/2 teaspoon pepper

2 cups chicken broth
3/4 cup egg substitute

In a small saucepan, saute celery in butter until tender; set aside. In a large bowl, combine the stuffing cubes, cranberries, pears, pecans, parsley, poultry seasoning and pepper. Add the broth, egg substitute and celery mixture; toss until combined.

Spoon into a greased 2-1/2-qt. baking dish. Cover and bake at 325° for 50-60 minutes or until a thermometer inserted near the center reads 160°. **Yield:** 8-10 servings.

Autumn Streusel Cake

Pears, pecans and cranberries flavor this pretty cake from our Test Kitchen.

1/2 cup butter, softened
1/2 cup sugar
3 eggs
1/2 teaspoon vanilla extract
2 cups all-purpose flour
1-1/4 teaspoons baking powder
1/4 teaspoon baking soda
1/3 cup orange juice
FILLING:
1/2 cup packed brown sugar
1/2 cup chopped peeled ripe pear
1/2 cup chopped pecans
1/4 cup dried cranberries
3 tablespoons all-purpose flour
1/2 teaspoon ground cinnamon
1/4 teaspoon ground ginger
1 tablespoon butter, melted

GLAZE:
1/2 cup confectioners' sugar
2-1/2 teaspoons orange juice

In a large mixing bowl, cream butter and sugar. Add eggs, one at a time, beating well after each addition. Beat in vanilla. Combine the flour, baking powder and baking soda; add to creamed mixture alternately with orange juice just until combined (batter will be stiff).

Spoon half of the batter into a greased 10-in. tube pan. Combine the filling ingredients; sprinkle half over batter. Carefully spread remaining batter over the top; sprinkle with remaining filling. Cut through with a knife to swirl.

Bake at 350° for 40-45 minutes or until a toothpick inserted near the center comes out clean. Cool for 15 minutes before removing from pan to a wire rack to cool completely. Combine glaze ingredients until smooth; drizzle over cake. **Yield:** 12-16 servings.

Fall Floral Centerpiece

(Pictured above)

"MUM'S" the word when it comes to fall flower arrangements. After all, when the summer blooms have faded away, you can always depend on chrysanthemums to liven up your tabletop.

Plus, with a range of colors including white, yellow, orange, bronze, red, purple and pink, you're sure to find a variety that ties into your home's color scheme.

For the arrangement shown above, we pur-chased an assortment of daisy, spider and pom-pon mums. Ferns and other greens complete the lovely look.

Instead of using a vase, we reached for the veg-etable bowl in the same pattern as the china used on the dinner table. (See page 110.)

Below we show you how easy it is to arrange a professional-looking floral arrangement with a little tape and creativity!

EASY FLORAL ARRANGING

BY MAKING a grid with tape, you can arrange flowers like a pro and create a stunning centerpiece.

Put a handful of floral marbles or stones in the bottom of your bowl or vase. Place strips of transparent or floral tape parallel to one another across the top of the container. Then place strips perpendicular to the first set to form a grid.

Fill the container with water. To make a mounded shape, trim the center flowers to be longer than the flowers that will be used around the outer edge. Insert flowers within the taped grid. Smaller flowers can be bunched together, while larger flowers can stand alone.

GIVING *Thanks*

Seasonal Side Dishes

THANKSGIVING dinner featuring a succulent roasted turkey is likely the year's most anticipated holiday meal.

Although they don't get quite as much attention as the main course, side dishes play an important role in rounding out this memorable dinner.

In addition to serving your own tried-and-true mashed potatoes, bring new taste twists to the table by dishing out any of this chapter's seasonal vegetables, delicious condiments, reliable rice dishes and more.

Bearnaise Sauce draped over a favorite vegetable and Apple-Sweet Potato Bake are just two of the palate-pleasing accompaniments that will earn you a bushel of compliments. (Both recipes are shown at right.)

Bountiful Harvest
(Pictured above)

Apple-Sweet Potato Bake (p. 120)

Bearnaise Sauce (p. 129)

Apple-Sweet Potato Bake

(Pictured on page 118)

*Apples and sweet potatoes are perfect partners in this
slightly sweet casserole from our home economists. Every bite tastes like fall!*

3 pounds sweet potatoes
4 medium Golden Delicious
  apples, peeled
1/4 cup lemon juice
1/2 cup chopped pecans
1/2 cup butter, cubed
1/2 cup packed brown sugar
1/2 cup honey
2 tablespoons orange juice
1/2 teaspoon ground cinnamon
1/4 teaspoon ground ginger

Wash sweet potatoes and pierce skin in several places; place on a baking sheet. Bake at 400° for 35-45 minutes or until almost tender. When cool enough to handle, peel potatoes and cut into 1/4-in. slices.

Cut the apples into 1/4-in. slices; toss with lemon juice. In a greased 11-in. x 7-in. x 2-in. baking dish, alternately arrange sweet potato and apple slices. Sprinkle with pecans.

In a small saucepan, combine the butter, brown sugar, honey, orange juice, cinnamon and ginger. Bring to a boil, stirring constantly. Remove from the heat; pour over potatoes and apples. Bake, uncovered, at 400° for 25-30 minutes or until tender. **Yield:** 8 servings.

Parmesan Risotto

(Pictured on page 37)

*Risotto is a creamy Italian rice dish. In this version from our Test Kitchen,
the rice is briefly sauteed, then slowly cooked in wine and seasonings.*

8 cups chicken broth
1/2 cup finely chopped onion
2 garlic cloves, minced
1/4 cup olive oil
3 cups arborio rice
1 cup dry white wine *or* water
1/2 cup shredded Parmesan
  cheese
1/4 teaspoon salt
1/4 teaspoon pepper
3 tablespoons minced fresh
  parsley

In a large saucepan, bring broth to a boil. Reduce heat; cover and maintain at a simmer. In a large skillet, saute onion and garlic in oil until tender. Add rice; cook and stir for 3 minutes. Add wine or water; cook and stir until absorbed.

Stir in 1 cup simmering broth. Cook until broth is almost completely absorbed, stirring frequently, then add another cup of simmering broth. Repeat until less than 1 cup broth remains; reserve 1/4 cup broth. (The process should take 20-25 minutes.) Rice should be slightly firm in the center and look creamy.

Remove from the heat. Stir in the Parmesan cheese, salt, pepper and reserved broth. Sprinkle with parsley. Serve immediately. **Yield:** 12 servings.

Cranberry Rice Salad

(Pictured at right)

Our home economists devised this make-ahead recipe with the hectic holidays in mind. Cranberries and green onions add a bit of color.

1 cup uncooked long grain rice
3/4 cup dried cranberries
2 green onions, sliced
2 tablespoons sugar
1/2 teaspoon dried minced onion
1/2 teaspoon poppy seeds
1/8 teaspoon paprika
1 tablespoon white wine vinegar
1 tablespoon cider vinegar
2 tablespoons vegetable oil
3/4 cup sliced almonds, toasted

Cook rice according to package directions; drain and rinse with cold water. In a large bowl, combine the rice, cranberries and green onions.

In a small bowl, combine the sugar, minced onion, poppy seeds and paprika; whisk in the vinegars and oil. Drizzle over rice mixture and toss to coat. Cover and refrigerate for up to 2 hours. Just before serving, stir in the almonds. **Yield:** 5 servings.

Saucy Green Beans

Your family will fall for this deliciously different green bean casserole. Lemon peel provides the right amount of tartness.
—*Mrs. Scott Carpenter, Kings Mountain, North Carolina*

2 packages (10 ounces *each*) frozen French-style green beans
1/2 cup chopped onion
1 tablespoon minced fresh parsley
2 tablespoons butter
1 cup (8 ounces) sour cream
1 teaspoon grated lemon peel
1 teaspoon salt
1/4 teaspoon pepper
1/2 cup shredded cheddar cheese

Cook green beans according to package directions. Meanwhile, in a saucepan, saute onion and parsley in butter until tender. Stir in the sour cream, lemon peel, salt and pepper. Drain beans; add sauce and gently stir until coated.

Transfer to a greased 1-qt. baking dish. Sprinkle with cheese. Broil 6 in. from the heat until cheese is bubbly, about 5 minutes. **Yield:** 6-8 servings.

Tomato Broccoli Parmesan

I came up with this recipe when I was learning to cook healthier meals for my family.
I can quickly prepare it while focusing on the main course.
—Daisy Williams, Harrison, Arkansas

3 cups fresh broccoli florets
1 cup julienned carrots
1 small onion, chopped
4 garlic cloves, minced
2 tablespoons olive oil
1/4 cup chicken broth
1 medium tomato, peeled and chopped
3 tablespoons shredded Parmesan cheese

Place the broccoli in a small saucepan; add 1 in. of water. Bring to a boil. Reduce heat; cover and simmer for 5-8 minutes or until crisp-tender.

Meanwhile, in a large skillet, saute the carrots, onion and garlic in oil until carrots are crisp-tender. Drain broccoli. Add broccoli and broth to the carrot mixture; cook, uncovered, for 3-5 minutes. Remove from the heat. Add tomato; toss to combine. Sprinkle with Parmesan cheese. **Yield:** 4 servings.

Swiss Scalloped Onions

This rich, special side dish makes frequent appearances on my Thanksgiving menu.
Simmering the onions before assembling the casserole mellows their flavor.
—Suzy Sullivan, Royal Palm Beach, Florida

2 quarts water
7 cups sliced onions
1/2 cup butter, *divided*
1/4 cup all-purpose flour
1 teaspoon Worcestershire sauce
3/4 teaspoon salt
1/2 teaspoon paprika
1/2 teaspoon pepper
2 cups milk
2 packages (5 ounces *each*) shredded Swiss cheese
4 cups cubed French bread

In a large saucepan, bring water to a boil; add onions. Return to a boil. Reduce heat; cover and simmer for 10-12 minutes or until tender. Drain well. Place onions in an ungreased 13-in. x 9-in. x 2-in. baking dish.

In a small saucepan, melt 1/4 cup butter. Whisk in the flour, Worcestershire sauce, salt, paprika and pepper until smooth. Gradually stir in milk. Bring to a boil; cook and stir for 2 minutes or until thickened. Remove from the heat; stir in cheese until melted. Pour over onions; toss to coat.

Top with bread cubes. Melt remaining butter; drizzle over the top. Bake, uncovered, at 350° for 30-35 minutes or until golden brown. **Yield:** 10 servings.

Winter Vegetables

(Pictured at right)

The flavor of thyme shines through in this recipe. The colorful array of vegetables is so appealing on the table. It's a great way to showcase often unused broccoli stalks.
—Charlene Augustyn
Grand Rapids, Michigan

3 medium turnips, peeled and
   cut into 2-inch julienne strips
1 large rutabaga, peeled and
   cut into 2-inch julienne strips
4 medium carrots, cut into
   2-inch julienne strips
3 fresh broccoli spears
1 tablespoon butter
1 tablespoon minced fresh
   parsley
1/2 teaspoon salt
1/2 teaspoon dried thyme
Pepper to taste

Place the turnips, rutabaga and carrots in a large saucepan and cover with water. Bring to a boil. Reduce heat; cover and cook for 10 minutes.

Meanwhile, cut florets from broccoli and save for another use. Cut broccoli stalks into 2-in. julienne strips; add to saucepan. Cover and cook 5 minutes longer or until vegetables are crisp-tender; drain well.

In a large skillet, saute vegetables in butter. Stir in the parsley, salt, thyme and pepper. **Yield:** 10-12 servings.

BASIC MASHED POTATOES

THANKSGIVING isn't complete without a bowl brimming with mashed potatoes. Here's a basic recipe that's simply delicious.

Peel and cube 6 medium russet potatoes (about 2 pounds). Place in a saucepan and cover with water. Cover and bring to a boil; cook for 20 to 25 minutes or until very tender. Drain well. Add 1/2 cup warm milk, 1/4 cup butter, 3/4 teaspoon salt and a dash of pepper. Mash until light and fluffy. **Yield:** 6 servings.

Hominy Squash Skillet

This original recipe from my mother captures the flavors of the south.
I make it for family dinners and barbecues as well as Thanksgiving.
—Maureen Chilton, Winona, Missouri

4 cups sliced yellow summer
   squash
1 egg, lightly beaten
1 cup cornmeal
1/2 cup plus 1 tablespoon butter,
   divided
3/4 cup chopped onion
1/3 cup chopped sweet red pepper
1/3 cup chopped green pepper
1 can (15 ounces) white
   hominy, rinsed and drained
1 can (15 ounces) yellow
   hominy, rinsed and drained
3/4 teaspoon salt
1/4 teaspoon pepper

In a large bowl, toss squash with egg. Place the cornmeal in a large resealable plastic bag. Add squash slices, a few at a time, and shake to coat. Let stand for 10 minutes.

In a large skillet, melt 1/4 cup butter. Add half of the squash. Cook over medium heat until browned on both sides, about 5 minutes. Remove to paper towels to drain. Repeat with remaining squash and 1/4 cup butter; set aside and keep warm.

In another skillet, saute the onion and peppers in remaining butter until tender. Add the hominy, salt and pepper; cook and stir until heated through and golden brown. Stir in the reserved squash. Serve immediately. **Yield:** 10 servings.

Maple Candied Sweet Potatoes

A traditional sweet potato bake like this one from our Test Kitchen never
goes out of style. It's perfect when you're cooking for a large group.

4 pounds sweet potatoes
2/3 cup packed brown sugar
1 teaspoon ground cinnamon
1/2 teaspoon ground nutmeg
1/4 cup butter, cubed
1/4 cup maple syrup

Place the sweet potatoes in a Dutch oven and cover with water. Bring to a boil. Reduce heat; cook for 30-45 minutes or until potatoes can be easily pierced with the tip of a sharp knife.

When cool enough to handle, peel potatoes and cut into wedges. Place in an ungreased 15-in. x 10-in. x 1-in.

baking pan. Combine the brown sugar, cinnamon and nutmeg; sprinkle over potatoes. Dot with butter; drizzle with syrup.

Bake, uncovered, at 375° for 25-30 minutes or until bubbly, basting with sauce occasionally. **Yield:** 12-14 servings.

SECOND-TIME AROUND SWEET POTATOES

INSTEAD of just reheating any leftovers of Maple Candied Sweet Potatoes, set aside 1 cup to make Maple Candied Sweet Potato Pie on page 148.

Scalloped Cranberries

(Pictured at right)

This warm cranberry casserole is a nice substitute for traditional cranberry relish. It's been a staple on my holiday table ever since my aunt gave me the recipe many years ago.
—*Ellan Streett, Clear Spring, Maryland*

    4 cups fresh *or* frozen
        cranberries (about 1 pound)
1-1/4 cups sugar
1-1/4 cups water
4-1/2 cups cubed bread (about 5
        slices)
  1/2 cup raisins
  1/3 cup butter, melted
    2 teaspoons grated lemon peel

In a large saucepan, combine the cranberries, sugar and water. Cook over medium heat for 12-15 minutes or until the berries pop. Remove from the heat; stir in the remaining ingredients.

Transfer to a greased 1-1/2-qt. baking dish. Bake, uncovered, at 350° for 25-30 minutes or until heated through. **Yield:** 6 servings.

Veggie Brown Rice

*This simple side dish has the flavor of fried rice but is better for you.
It would pair well with a meaty entree.*
—*Paula Davis, Athens, Alabama*

  1 cup shredded cabbage
  1 cup sliced fresh mushrooms
1/2 cup diced onion
1/4 cup butter
  3 cups cold cooked brown rice
  1 cup frozen peas and carrots
1/4 cup teriyaki sauce
  2 tablespoons soy sauce
1/4 teaspoon pepper

In a large skillet, saute the cabbage, mushrooms and onion in butter for 6-7 minutes or until tender. Add the remaining ingredients. Cook and stir over medium heat until heated through, about 3-4 minutes. **Yield:** 4-6 servings.

Walnut Cranberry Applesauce

I made this homemade applesauce the first time I hosted Thanksgiving dinner for my family. Everyone loved the addition of cranberries and walnuts.
—Alysha Braun, St Catharines, Ontario

1/4 cup dried cranberries
1 tablespoon brandy, optional
3 pounds tart apples, peeled and thinly sliced
1/3 to 1/2 cup packed brown sugar
3 tablespoons butter
1/4 cup coarsely chopped walnuts, toasted

In a small bowl, combine cranberries and brandy if desired; set aside. Place the apples in a large saucepan and cover with water. Bring to a boil. Reduce heat; cover and simmer for 8-10 minutes or until tender. Drain, reserving 2-3 tablespoons cooking liquid.

Place the apples in a food processor; cover and process until smooth. Gradually add reserved cooking liquid until applesauce reaches desired consistency. Return all to the saucepan.

Add brown sugar and cranberries. Bring to a boil. Reduce heat. Stir in butter until melted. Serve warm or refrigerate until serving. Just before serving, stir in the walnuts. **Yield:** 6 servings.

Baked Creamy Spinach

Even folks not fond of spinach find this creamy casserole irresistible. It's a favorite of my family at the holidays.
—Sue Dodd, Friendsville, Tennessee

1 large onion, chopped
1 tablespoon butter
1 package (8 ounces) cream cheese, cubed
1/4 cup milk
1-1/2 cups (6 ounces) shredded Parmesan cheese, *divided*
1/2 teaspoon cayenne pepper
1/4 teaspoon salt
1/8 teaspoon pepper
2 packages (10 ounces *each*) frozen chopped spinach, thawed and squeezed dry

In a large saucepan, saute onion in butter until tender. Add cream cheese and milk; stir until melted. Stir in 1 cup Parmesan cheese, cayenne, salt and pepper. Stir in the spinach.

Transfer to a greased 1-1/2-qt. baking dish. Sprinkle with remaining Parmesan. Bake, uncovered, at 350° for 30-35 minutes or until hot and bubbly. **Yield:** 6-8 servings.

Carrot Potato Casserole

(Pictured at right)

I've been relying on this recipe for more than 30 years. That's a true testament to how delicious it is!
—Louise Piper, Rolfe, Iowa

3 tablespoons butter
3 tablespoons all-purpose flour
1 teaspoon salt
1/4 teaspoon pepper
1-1/2 cups milk
1 cup (4 ounces) shredded cheddar cheese, *divided*
3 cups grated peeled uncooked potatoes
1 cup grated carrots
2 tablespoons grated onion

In a saucepan over medium heat, melt butter. Whisk in the flour, salt and pepper until smooth. Gradually stir in milk. Bring to a boil; cook and stir for 2 minutes. Reduce heat; add 1/2 cup cheese, stirring until melted. Add the potatoes, carrots and onion.

Transfer to a greased 8-in. square baking dish. Cover and bake at 350° for 1 hour. Uncover; sprinkle with the remaining cheese. Bake 15 minutes longer or until potatoes are tender. **Yield:** 6 servings.

Rich Mushroom Bake

I developed this recipe to camouflage mushrooms for my family. Stuffing gives great flavor and Parmesan adds the "mandatory" cheese topping for the kids.
—Phylis Dillon, Gibsonia, Pennsylvania

1 pound sliced fresh mushrooms
6 tablespoons butter, *divided*
2 tablespoons all-purpose flour
1/2 cup milk
1/2 cup beef broth
1/8 teaspoon pepper
1/2 cup crushed seasoned stuffing
1/2 cup grated Parmesan cheese

In a large skillet, saute mushrooms in 2 tablespoons butter; remove and set aside. In the same skillet, melt remaining butter; stir in flour until smooth. Gradually add the milk, broth and pepper. Bring to a boil; cook and stir for 2 minutes or until thickened. Return mushrooms to the pan; stir in stuffing until blended.

Transfer to a greased 1-qt. baking dish; sprinkle with Parmesan cheese. Bake, uncovered, at 350° for 30-35 minutes or until bubbly. **Yield:** 6 servings.

White Sauce

(Pictured at far right, top)

Our Test Kitchen's White Sauce enhances many kinds of veggies. In the photo on the oppopsite page, we topped cooked broccoli florets with the Lemon Chive Sauce variation.

1 tablespoon butter
1 tablespoon all-purpose flour
1/8 teaspoon salt
Dash pepper
3/4 cup milk

In a small saucepan, melt butter. Stir in the flour, salt and pepper until smooth. Gradually add milk. Bring to a boil; cook and stir for 2 minutes or until thickened. **Yield:** 2/3 cup.

Cheese Sauce: Prepare as directed, omitting salt. Add 3/4 cup shredded cheddar, Swiss, American or Gruyere cheese; cook and stir over low heat until cheese is melted. **Yield:** 1 cup.

Herb Garlic Sauce: Prepare as directed, except saute 1/2 teaspoon minced garlic in the melted butter for 1-2 minutes or until tender. Stir in 1/4 teaspoon herb of your choice (caraway seed, celery seed, dried basil, oregano or rubbed sage) with the flour. **Yield:** 3/4 cup.

Lemon Chive Sauce: Prepare as directed. Stir in 1 tablespoon minced chives and 1/2 teaspoon finely shredded lemon peel. **Yield:** 3/4 cup.

Parmesan Sauce: Prepare as directed, omitting salt. Add 1/4 cup grated Parmesan cheese; cook and stir over low heat until cheese is melted. **Yield:** 2/3 cup.

Hollandaise Sauce

This basic sauce from our home economists delightfully dresses up ordinary vegetables. We also offer two variations for tasty twists.

3 egg yolks
1/4 cup water
2 tablespoons lemon juice
1/2 cup cold butter
1/8 teaspoon salt
1/8 teaspoon paprika
Dash pepper

In a small heavy saucepan or double boiler, whisk the egg yolks, water and lemon juice. Cook and stir over low heat or simmering water until mixture bubbles around edges and reaches 160°, about 20 minutes.

Cut cold butter into eight pieces; add to yolk mixture, one piece at a time, stirring after each addition until melted. Stir in the salt, paprika and pepper. Serve immediately. **Yield:** 1 cup.

Sauce Mousseline: Prepare as directed. Gently fold in 1/2 cup whipped cream. **Yield:** 1-1/3 cups.

Ancho Chili Sauce: Prepare as directed, except decrease lemon juice to 1/2 teaspoon. Stir in 1/2 to 1 teaspoon ground ancho chili pepper and 1/4 teaspoon ground cumin. **Yield:** 1 cup.

Bearnaise Sauce

(Pictured at right, bottom, and on page 118)

Bearnaise sauce is closely related to Hollandaise sauce but features wine and tarragon. This version from our Test Kitchen is delicious served over cooked vegetables or beef tenderloin.

   3 egg yolks
1/4 cup water
   3 tablespoons white wine *or* chicken broth
   2 tablespoons tarragon vinegar
   2 teaspoons minced shallot
2-1/2 teaspoons minced fresh tarragon, *divided*
   8 whole peppercorns, crushed
1/2 cup cold butter

In a small heavy saucepan or double boiler, whisk the egg yolks and water. Cook and stir over low heat or simmering water until mixture bubbles around edges and reaches 160°, about 20 minutes.

Meanwhile, in a small saucepan, combine the wine or broth, vinegar, shallot, 1-1/2 teaspoons tarragon and peppercorns. Bring to a boil. Reduce heat; simmer, uncovered, for 10 minutes or until reduced to 2 tablespoons. Strain and set liquid aside.

Cut cold butter into eight pieces; add to egg yolk mixture, one piece at a time, stirring after each addition until melted. Stir reserved liquid and remaining tarragon into prepared sauce. Serve immediately. **Yield:** 1 cup.

SUCCESS WITH SAUCES

WHILE sauces are fairly simple to prepare, keep these tips in mind to ensure perfection every time.
- Unless the recipe states otherwise, cook the sauce over low to medium heat only for the time specified. High heat and lengthy cooking can make a sauce curdle.
- To prevent lumps in a sauce thickened with flour or cornstarch, be sure to stir the mixture constantly while boiling. If lumps do form, break them up by beating briskly with a wire whisk.

Awesome Autumn Desserts

MANY FOLKS would agree that when it comes to Thanksgiving, an assortment of delectable desserts is almost as important as the turkey itself!

But why restrict your mouth-watering repertoire to just the usual pumpkin and apple pies?

Relatives will reap the benefits of your creativity when other tempting treats crop up on your holiday table.

Pumpkin is presented in a whole new light with elegant Pumpkin Napoleons.

With apples, cranberries, pears and peaches, every slice of Four-Fruit Pie has the fabulous flavor of fall.

And cool Cranberry Creme Brulee will become a new-found family favorite throughout the year. (All recipes shown at right.)

Fitting Finales
(Left to right)

Four-Fruit Pie (p. 132)

Pumpkin Napoleons (p. 134)

Cranberry Creme Brulee (p. 133)

Four-Fruit Pie

(Pictured on page 130)

Your holiday guests will be sweet on slices of this fruit-filled pie!
For a special touch, cut out fall shapes in the top pastry.
—Melissa Jane Robinson, Indianapolis, Indiana

1 cup dried cranberries
1-1/2 cups boiling water
2 medium tart apples, peeled and sliced
1 medium fresh peach, peeled and sliced *or* 1 cup frozen unsweetened sliced peaches
1 medium ripe pear, peeled and sliced
1 tablespoon lemon juice
1/2 cup sugar
1/2 cup packed brown sugar
1 teaspoon apple pie spice
1/2 teaspoon vanilla extract
3 tablespoons quick-cooking tapioca
1 package (15 ounces) refrigerated pie pastry
2 tablespoons butter, melted

Place the cranberries in a bowl; cover with boiling water. Let stand for 5 minutes; drain well and set aside. In a large bowl, toss the apples, peach and pear with lemon juice. Stir in the sugars, apple pie spice and vanilla. Add tapioca; let stand for 15 minutes. Stir in the cranberries.

Line a 9-in. deep-dish pie plate with one sheet of pastry; trim even with edge of plate. Add filling. Unroll second sheet of pastry; cut slits in pastry. Place over filling; seal and flute edges. Brush with butter. Bake at 375° for 50-55 minutes or until crust is golden brown and filling is bubbly. Cool on a wire rack. **Yield:** 6-8 servings.

Honey Pecan Tart

As soon as I stumbled across this recipe several years ago, I knew I had to try it.
The lovely tart is scrumptious and makes an impression at the end of a meal.
—Cathie Groesbeck, Charlotte, North Carolina

3/4 cup butter, softened
1-1/2 cups all-purpose flour
1/2 cup confectioners' sugar
FILLING:
3 cups pecan halves, *divided*
4 eggs
3/4 cup honey
1/3 cup light corn syrup
1/4 cup packed brown sugar
1/4 cup butter, melted
1 teaspoon vanilla extract
1/2 teaspoon salt

In a small mixing bowl, beat the butter, flour and confectioners' sugar until crumbly. Press onto the bottom and up the sides of an ungreased 9-in. tart pan with removable bottom.

Chop 2-1/4 cups pecans. In a small mixing bowl, combine the eggs, honey, corn syrup, brown sugar, butter, vanilla and salt. Stir in chopped pecans. Pour into crust. Arrange the remaining pecan halves around edge of tart.

Bake at 350° for 40-45 minutes or until a toothpick inserted near the center comes out clean. Cool on a wire rack. Store in the refrigerator. **Yield:** 10-12 servings.

Cranberry Creme Brulee

(Pictured at right and on page 131)

Our home economists dress up classic creme brulee with an easy-to-make cranberry sauce. The sweet-tart sauce complements the rich, creamy custard.

1 package (12 ounces) fresh *or* frozen cranberries
1 cup granulated sugar
3/4 cup water
1/8 teaspoon salt
CUSTARD:
2-1/2 cups heavy whipping cream, *divided*
1 teaspoon vanilla extract
10 egg yolks
2/3 cup granulated sugar
8 teaspoons superfine sugar

In a large saucepan, combine the cranberries, sugar, water and salt. Cook over medium heat until berries pop, about 15 minutes. Remove from the heat. Spoon 2 tablespoons into each of eight 6-oz. custard cups; chill for 10 minutes. Refrigerate remaining cranberry sauce until serving.

In a small saucepan, heat 1 cup cream over medium heat until bubbles form around sides of pan. Remove from the heat; stir in vanilla. In a large bowl, whisk egg yolks and granulated sugar until smooth. Gradually whisk in heated cream mixture. Gradually stir in remaining cream. Ladle into prepared custard cups.

Place cups in a baking pan. Add 1 in. of boiling water to pan. Bake, uncovered, at 325° for 35-40 minutes or until center is set but jiggles slightly. Remove cups from water bath to a wire rack; cool to room temperature. Cover and refrigerate for 8 hours or overnight.

Just before serving, blot custard with paper towels to remove any moisture. Sprinkle each cup with 1 teaspoon superfine sugar; place on a baking sheet. Broil 3-4 in. from the heat for 1-2 minutes or until sugar turns golden brown. Serve with remaining cranberry sauce. **Yield:** 8 servings.

Pumpkin Napoleons

(Pictured on page 131)

*This is an outstanding dessert for special fall gatherings.
The smooth pumpkin puree pairs well with the crunchy puff pastry.*
—Priscilla Weaver, Hagerstown, Maryland

3/4 cup plus 2 tablespoons sugar
1/3 cup all-purpose flour
1/8 teaspoon salt
1-3/4 cups milk
8 egg yolks, beaten
2/3 cup canned pumpkin
1-1/4 teaspoons vanilla extract
1/4 teaspoon ground cinnamon
1/4 teaspoon ground ginger
1/8 teaspoon ground nutmeg
1 sheet frozen puff pastry, thawed
2 tablespoons confectioners' sugar

In a large saucepan, combine the sugar, flour and salt. Stir in milk until smooth. Cook and stir over medium-high heat until thickened and bubbly. Reduce heat; cook and stir 2 minutes longer. Remove from the heat. Stir a small amount of hot filling into egg yolks; return all to the pan, stirring constantly. Bring to a gentle boil; cook and stir 2 minutes longer.

Remove from the heat. Stir in the pumpkin, vanilla, cinnamon, ginger and nutmeg. Transfer to a bowl. Press plastic wrap onto surface of custard. Refrigerate for 2 hours or until cool.

On a lightly floured surface, roll out pastry into a 12-in. x 10-in. rectangle. With a sharp knife, cut into 15 rectangles, 4 in. x 2 in. Place 1 in. apart on ungreased baking sheets. Bake at 375° for 15-20 minutes or until puffed and golden brown. Remove to wire racks to cool.

To assemble, split pastries in half horizontally. Place 10 bottom layers on a work surface; spread each with a scant 2 tablespoons pumpkin custard. Top with 10 pastries, remaining custard and remaining pastries. Sprinkle with confectioners' sugar. Refrigerate for 1-2 hours before serving. **Yield:** 10 servings.

Ginger Leaf Cutouts

(Pictured at right)

My father enjoyed these cookies with apple cider when he returned home from hunting on Thanksgiving morning. I like to decorate them with colored sugar.
—*Susan Frantz, Pittsburgh, Pennsylvania*

1 cup shortening
1 cup sugar
1 egg
1 cup molasses
2 tablespoons white vinegar
5 cups all-purpose flour
2-1/2 teaspoons ground ginger
1-1/2 teaspoons baking soda
1 teaspoon ground cinnamon
1 teaspoon ground cloves
1/2 teaspoon salt

In a large mixing bowl, cream shortening and sugar. Beat in the egg, molasses and vinegar. Combine the flour, ginger, baking soda, cinnamon, cloves and salt; gradually add to creamed mixture. Divide dough into fourths. Wrap each portion in plastic wrap; refrigerate for 4 hours or until easy to handle.

On a lightly floured surface, roll out one portion of dough at a time to 1/8-in. thickness. Cut with floured 3-in. leaf-shaped cookie cutters. Place 1 in. apart on greased baking sheets. With a sharp knife, score veins in leaves.

Bake at 375° for 6-8 minutes or until edges are firm and lightly browned. Remove to wire racks to cool. Store in an airtight container. **Yield:** 5 dozen.

PLACE CARD COOKIES

YOU CAN use Ginger Leaf Cutouts to make edible place cards for your Thanksgiving dinner table. Bake and cool the cookies as directed.

Fill a pastry bag with your favorite white frosting. Using a No. 1, 2 or 3 round tip, write your guests' names on the cookies. Let the frosting dry; store in a single layer in an airtight container at room temperature. Before guests arrive, set place card cookies on dinner plates.

Golden Delicious Apple Pie

I make this pie using apples from my own orchard. The addition of cider really enhances the appealing flavor.
—Juanita Patterson, Franksville, Wisconsin

7 cups thinly sliced peeled
  Golden Delicious apples
1/4 cup sugar
2 tablespoons cornstarch
1-1/3 cups apple cider *or* apple juice
1 egg, beaten
1 tablespoon lemon juice
1 unbaked deep-dish pastry
  shell (9 inches)
TOPPING:
1/2 cup all-purpose flour
1/4 cup sugar
1/8 teaspoon salt
1/4 cup cold butter
1/4 cup chopped pecans

Place the apples in a large bowl; set aside. In a saucepan, combine the sugar and cornstarch. Stir in apple cider until smooth. Cook and stir over medium-high heat until thickened and bubbly. Reduce heat; cook and stir 2 minutes longer. Remove from the heat. Stir a small amount of hot filling into egg; return all to the pan, stirring constantly. Bring to a gentle boil; cook and stir 2 minutes longer. Remove from the heat. Gently stir in lemon juice.

Pour over apples; toss to coat. Pour into pastry shell. For topping, combine the flour, sugar and salt in a bowl; cut in butter until crumbly. Stir in pecans. Sprinkle over filling.

Bake at 400° for 10 minutes. Reduce heat to 350°; bake 45-50 minutes longer or until apples are tender. Cool on a wire rack. Store in the refrigerator. **Yield:** 6-8 servings.

Banana Bundles with Caramel Sauce

These attractive bundles from our Test Kitchen have the fantastic flavor of Bananas Foster.
It's best to use firm bananas in this recipe.

CARAMEL SAUCE:
1 cup packed brown sugar
1 tablespoon water
3 tablespoons cold butter, *divided*
3/4 cup heavy whipping cream
1/2 teaspoon vanilla extract
Dash salt
BANANA BUNDLES:
1 cup sliced firm bananas
1 tablespoon butter, melted
1 tablespoon brown sugar
1/4 teaspoon ground ginger
Dash ground cinnamon
1 sheet frozen puff pastry,
  thawed
Confectioners' sugar

In a heavy saucepan, combine the brown sugar, water and 1 tablespoon butter. Bring to a boil over medium heat without stirring. Cover and cook for 3 minutes. Stir in cream. Cook and stir over medium-high heat just until mixture comes to a boil, about 1 minute. Remove from the heat. Whisk in vanilla and salt. Cut remaining butter into small pieces; whisk into sauce, a few pieces at a time, until smooth. Set aside and keep warm.

In a bowl, combine the bananas, butter, brown sugar, ginger and cinnamon. On a lightly floured surface, roll out pastry to a 12-in. square. Cut into four squares; lightly brush edges with water. Place 1/4 cup banana mixture in the center of each square. Bring corners of pastry over filling and twist to form a bundle; pinch edges closed.

Place on an ungreased baking sheet. Bake at 400° for 15-18 minutes or until golden brown. Sprinkle with confectioners' sugar; serve warm with sauce. **Yield:** 4 servings.

White Chocolate Pumpkin Cheesecake

(Pictured at right)

Although my family enjoys all of the dishes I serve on Thanksgiving Day, it's this rich and creamy cheesecake they look forward to the most.
—Joyce Schmidt, Lilburn, Georgia

1-1/4 cups cream-filled chocolate
    sandwich cookie crumbs
   2 packages (8 ounces *each*)
    cream cheese, softened
 2/3 cup sugar
   2 teaspoons vanilla extract
   3 eggs, lightly beaten
1-1/4 cups vanilla *or* white chips,
    melted and cooled
 1/2 cup canned pumpkin
 1/4 teaspoon *each* ground ginger,
    cinnamon and nutmeg
White chocolate curls, optional

Press cookie crumbs onto the bottom of a greased 9-in. springform pan; set aside. In a large mixing bowl, beat the cream cheese, sugar and vanilla until smooth. Add eggs; beat on low speed just until combined. Stir in melted chips. In a small bowl, combine pumpkin and spices; gently fold into cream cheese mixture. Pour into prepared pan.

Place on a double thickness of heavy-duty foil (about 16 in. square). Securely wrap foil around pan. Place in a large baking pan; add 1 in. of hot water to larger pan. Bake at 325° for 60-65 minutes or until center is just set. Remove springform pan from water bath. Cool on a wire rack for 10 minutes. Carefully run a knife around edge of pan to loosen; cool 1 hour longer. Refrigerate overnight.

Remove sides of pan. Garnish with white chocolate curls if desired. Refrigerate leftovers. **Yield:** 10-12 servings.

Pumpkin Spice Cookies

*These soft cookies are almost like little pieces of cake. With chopped pecans sprinkled over
a confectioners' sugar frosting, they're a pretty addition to a dessert table.*
—Bev Martin, Shippensburg, Pennsylvania

1 package (8 ounces) cream
  cheese, softened
1-1/2 cups packed brown sugar
1/2 cup sugar
2 eggs
1 cup canned pumpkin
1 teaspoon vanilla extract
3-1/2 cups all-purpose flour
1 to 1-1/2 teaspoons pumpkin
  pie spice
1 teaspoon baking soda
1 teaspoon salt
1/2 teaspoon baking powder
FROSTING:
2 cups confectioners' sugar
1/4 cup butter, melted
1 teaspoon vanilla extract
2 to 3 tablespoons boiling water
2 cups chopped pecans

In a large mixing bowl, beat cream cheese and sugars until
smooth. Add eggs, one at a time, beating well after each
addition. Beat in pumpkin and vanilla. Combine the dry
ingredients; gradually add to pumpkin mixture.

Drop by rounded teaspoonfuls 2 in. apart onto ungreased
baking sheets. Bake at 350° for 10-12 minutes or until
golden brown. Remove to wire racks to cool.

For frosting, in a bowl, combine the confectioners' sugar, butter, vanilla and enough water to achieve desired consistency. Frost cookies; sprinkle with pecans. **Yield:** *7* dozen.

Walnut-Maple Chiffon Cake

The men in the family often request this chiffon cake for their birthdays. The glaze is irresistible.
—Karen Nelson, Sullivan, Wisconsin

2 cups all-purpose flour
1 cup finely chopped walnuts
3/4 cup sugar, *divided*
3/4 cup packed brown sugar
1 teaspoon baking powder
1 teaspoon salt
7 eggs, *separated*
3/4 cup water
1/2 cup vegetable oil
2 teaspoons maple flavoring
1/2 teaspoon cream of tartar

BROWNED BUTTER GLAZE:
3 tablespoons butter
1-1/2 cups confectioners' sugar
1 teaspoon vanilla extract
2 to 3 tablespoons warm water

In a large mixing bowl, combine the flour, walnuts, 1/2 cup
sugar, brown sugar, baking powder and salt. In another bowl,
whisk the egg yolks, water, oil and maple flavoring; add to
dry ingredients and beat until well blended. In a small mixing bowl, beat egg whites, cream of tartar and remaining sug-

ar on medium speed until stiff peaks form; fold into batter.

Gently spoon into an ungreased 10-in. tube pan. Cut through batter with a knife to remove air pockets. Bake on the lowest oven rack at 325° for 60-70 minutes or until top springs back when lightly touched. Immediately invert cake pan onto a wire rack; cool completely. Carefully run a knife around edges of pan and center tube to loosen; remove cake.

For glaze, heat butter in a small saucepan over medium heat until golden brown. Remove from the heat; stir in confectioners' sugar, vanilla and enough water to achieve desired consistency. Drizzle over cake. **Yield:** 12-16 servings.

Cornucopia of Color

(Pictured above)

HARVEST a bushel of compliments with a dazzling Thanksgiving Day dessert buffet!

To create pretty pedestals like the ones shown above, hunt in your cupboards for glass plates, platters, cake stands, vases, bowls and other containers in various shapes and sizes.

Fill the pedestals with any number of autumn elements. We used acorns, miniature ornamental pumpkins and assorted silk leaves. Other ideas include candy corn, fresh cranberries, Indian corn kernels, cinnamon sticks, miniature gourds and pinecones.

Set the serving platters on the pedestals, making sure they're sitting steadily. (You may want to use double stick tape or floral adhesive to hold them in place.)

To finish off the lovely look, we filled a glass vase with stems of dried Japanese lanterns and set out orange candles in crystal candlesticks. (See the photo on page 130.)

Lively Thanksgiving Leftovers

ALTHOUGH it's hard to believe after eating to your heart's content on Thanksgiving, your appetite inevitably comes back the next day…especially if you hit the malls early in the morning!

So if you're in the market for ways to dress up leftover turkey, pumpkin, cranberry sauce, mashed potatoes and more, check out this chapter's super second-time-around specialties.

Shopping around for ways to give new life to cooked turkey? Make grilled Turkey Sandwiches with Red Pepper Hummus!

With canned pumpkin, spices and ice cream, Pumpkin Shakes are sure to become the hottest trend of the season. (Both recipes are shown at right.)

TWICE IS NICE
(Pictured above)

Turkey Sandwiches with Red Pepper Hummus (p. 143)

Pumpkin Shakes (p. 145)

Cranberry Salsa Turkey Wraps

*Once your family tastes these mouth-watering roll-ups, they'll never look at
leftover turkey the same way! The cranberry salsa combines both sweet and spicy flavors.*
—Elke Rose, Waukesha, Wisconsin

2 cups fresh cranberries,
  coarsely chopped
1/4 cup sugar
1/4 cup sliced green onions
1 tablespoon minced fresh
  cilantro
1 tablespoon lime juice
1 jalapeno pepper, seeded and
  chopped
1/4 teaspoon grated fresh
  gingerroot
3/4 cup spreadable cream cheese

6 flour tortillas (8 inches), warmed
3 cups shredded cooked turkey
6 lettuce leaves

In a small bowl, combine the cranberries, sugar, onions, cilantro, lime juice, jalapeno and ginger. Cover and refrigerate for 1 hour.

Just before serving, spread 2 tablespoons of cream cheese over each tortilla. Top with 3-4 tablespoons cranberry salsa, 1/2 cup turkey and a lettuce leaf; roll up. **Yield:** 6 servings.

Editor's Note: When cutting or seeding hot peppers, use rubber or plastic gloves to protect your hands. Avoid touching your face.

Gobbler Cobbler

*I often save some turkey and freeze it so I can make this
hot turkey salad pie on New Year's Day. Pineapple adds a bit of crunch and sweetness.*
—Darlene Brenden, Salem, Oregon

1-1/2 cups all-purpose flour
1/2 teaspoon salt
1/2 cup shortening
1/2 cup shredded cheddar cheese
1/4 cup milk
FILLING:
2 cups cubed cooked turkey
1 cup pineapple tidbits, drained
1 cup chopped walnuts
1/4 cup chopped onion
1/4 cup chopped celery
1 cup (8 ounces) sour cream
2/3 cup mayonnaise
1/4 cup shredded cheddar cheese
1/4 cup sliced ripe olives, optional

In a bowl, combine the flour and salt; cut in shortening until crumbly. Fold in cheese. Gradually add milk, tossing with a fork until dough forms a ball. Roll out pastry to fit a 9-in. pie plate.

Transfer pastry to pie plate. Trim to 1/2 in. beyond edge of plate; flute edges. Line unpricked pastry shell with a double thickness of heavy-duty foil. Bake at 450° for 8 minutes. Remove foil; bake 5 minutes longer. Cool on a wire rack. Reduce heat to 350°.

In a bowl, combine the turkey, pineapple, walnuts, onion and celery. Combine sour cream and mayonnaise; fold into turkey mixture. Spoon into crust. Sprinkle with cheese and olives if desired. Bake, uncovered, for 25-30 minutes or until heated through. **Yield:** 6-8 servings.

Editor's Note: Reduced-fat or fat-free mayonnaise is not recommended for this recipe.

Turkey Sandwiches With Red Pepper Hummus

(Pictured at right and on page 141)

A homemade red pepper hummus from our home economists sets this grilled sandwich apart from any other. Feel free to experiment with different breads, meats and cheeses.

1/3 cup mayonnaise
 1 tablespoon lime juice
 1 can (15 ounces) garbanzo beans *or* chickpeas, rinsed and drained
1/4 cup chopped roasted sweet red peppers, drained
 2 garlic cloves, peeled
1/2 teaspoon chili powder
1/4 teaspoon ground cumin
 2 tablespoons butter, softened
 8 slices rye bread
 4 slices Muenster cheese
 8 thin slices cooked turkey
 1 small red onion, sliced
 2 medium tomatoes, sliced

For hummus, combine the first seven ingredients in a blender or food processor; cover and process until smooth. Transfer to a small bowl; cover and refrigerate for 1 hour.

Spread butter on one side of each slice of bread; spread hummus on the other side. Place four slices buttered side down on a griddle. Layer with cheese, turkey, onion, tomatoes and remaining bread, hummus side down. Toast for 2-3 minutes on each side or until bread is lightly browned and cheese is melted. **Yield:** 4 servings.

Family Traditions

FOR my sister Steph and me, part of our Thanksgiving is spent poring over the store ads for the next day. We make a game plan as to who we would like to shop for and where we would like to shop for the best selection and prices. This kick-off to the Christmas shopping season has been special "sister" time for years.
—*Maria Conway*
Wauwatosa, Wisconsin

Golden Honey Sweet Rolls

*I turn leftover sweet potatoes into these soft, tender sweet rolls packed with honey flavor.
It's a great way to surprise the family the day after Thanksgiving.*
—Arline Hofland, Deer Lodge, Montana

2 tablespoons active dry yeast
1-1/4 cups warm 1% buttermilk
  (110° to 115°)
1 tablespoon honey
3 eggs, lightly beaten
3/4 cup cold mashed sweet potatoes
  (without added milk or butter)
1/2 cup butter, softened
1/3 cup packed brown sugar
2 teaspoons salt
1/2 to 3/4 teaspoon ground mace
5 to 5-1/2 cups all-purpose flour
TOPPING:
2 tablespoons butter, melted
1/2 cup packed brown sugar
1/2 cup chopped pecans
1/2 cup honey, warmed
FILLING:
2 tablespoons butter, softened
3/4 cup sugar
1-1/2 teaspoons ground cinnamon

In a large mixing bowl, dissolve yeast in warm buttermilk. Stir in honey; let stand for 5 minutes. Add the eggs, sweet potatoes, butter, brown sugar, salt, mace and 3 cups flour; beat until smooth. Stir in enough remaining flour to form a firm dough.

Turn onto a floured surface; knead until smooth and elastic, about 6-8 minutes. Place in a greased bowl, turning once to grease top. Cover and let rise in a warm place until doubled, about 1 hour.

Pour melted butter into a greased 13-in. x 9-in. x 2-in. baking pan. Sprinkle with brown sugar and pecans. Drizzle with honey; set aside.

Punch dough down. Turn onto a lightly floured surface; roll into a 16-in. x 10-in. rectangle. Spread with softened butter; sprinkle with sugar and cinnamon. Roll up jelly-roll style, starting from a long side; pinch seam to seal. Cut into 12 slices. Place cut side down in prepared pan. Cover and let rise until doubled, about 40 minutes.

Bake at 350° for 40-50 minutes or until golden brown. Immediately invert onto a serving platter. Serve warm. **Yield:** 1 dozen.

Editor's Note: Warmed buttermilk will appear curdled.

PREPARATION POINTER

WHEN mashing sweet potatoes on Thanksgiving Day, set aside 3/4 cup before adding milk, butter and any other ingredients. Refrigerate in a covered container and use it to make Golden Honey Sweet Rolls within 3 to 5 days.

Fried Mashed Potato Balls

(Pictured at right)

The key to making this recipe from our home economists is to use mashed potatoes, which are firm from chilling. Serve with sour cream or ranch salad dressing on the side.

2 cups cold mashed potatoes
1 egg, lightly beaten
3/4 cup shredded cheddar cheese
1/2 cup chopped green onions
1/4 cup real bacon bits
1/2 cup dry bread crumbs
Oil for frying

Place the mashed potatoes in a bowl; let stand at room temperature for 30 minutes. Stir in the egg, cheese, onions and bacon bits. Shape into 1-in. balls; roll in bread crumbs. Let stand for 15 minutes.

In an electric skillet, heat 1 in. of oil to 375°. Fry potato balls, a few at a time, for 2-1/2 to 3 minutes or until golden brown. Remove with a slotted spoon to paper towels to drain. Serve warm. **Yield:** 6 servings.

Pumpkin Shakes

(Pictured on page 140)

This wonderfully rich dessert has a terrific pumpkin flavor that definitely feels like fall. Sprinkle some nutmeg on top if you like.
—Melissa Jelinek, Menomonee Falls, Wisconsin

1 cup half-and-half cream
4 cups vanilla ice cream
1/4 cup canned pumpkin
1/4 teaspoon pumpkin pie spice
Whipped cream and ground nutmeg

In a blender, combine half of the cream, ice cream, pumpkin and pumpkin pie spice; cover and process until smooth. Pour into chilled glasses. Repeat. Garnish with whipped cream and nutmeg. Serve immediately. **Yield:** 4 servings.

Caramel Pumpkin Dip

Served with vanilla wafers, graham cracker sticks or even apple slices,
this cool, creamy dip from our home economists makes a special autumn snack.

4 ounces cream cheese, softened
1/2 cup confectioners' sugar
1/2 cup canned pumpkin
1/3 cup caramel ice cream topping
1/4 cup sour cream
1/2 teaspoon ground cinnamon
1/4 teaspoon ground nutmeg
Vanilla wafers *or* graham cracker
  sticks

In a small mixing bowl, beat cream cheese and confectioners' sugar until smooth. Gradually add the pumpkin, caramel topping, sour cream, cinnamon and nutmeg, beating until smooth. Serve with vanilla wafers or graham cracker sticks. Refrigerate leftovers. **Yield:** 2-1/2 cups.

Day After Thanksgiving Salad

I originally developed this recipe as a way to use Thanksgiving leftovers.
But it's such a hit, I make it throughout the year.
—Laura Driscoll, Enfield, Connecticut

1 tablespoon butter
3/4 cup chopped walnuts
1 tablespoon sugar
1 package (8 ounces)
  ready-to-serve salad greens
3 cups cubed cooked turkey
  breast
1 small red onion, sliced
1 medium sweet yellow pepper,
  sliced
1 cup grape tomatoes
1 cup chow mein noodles
3/4 cup jellied cranberry sauce
3 tablespoons seedless raspberry
  preserves
2 tablespoons balsamic vinegar
4-1/2 teaspoons vegetable oil
1 tablespoon water

In a small heavy skillet, melt butter. Add walnuts; cook over medium heat until toasted, about 4 minutes. Sprinkle with sugar. Cook and stir for 2-4 minutes or until sugar is melted. Spread on foil to cool.

In a large bowl, combine the salad greens, turkey, onion, yellow pepper, tomatoes, chow mein noodles and sugared walnuts. In a blender, combine the remaining ingredients; cover and process until smooth. Pour over salad and toss to coat. **Yield:** 5 servings.

Cranberry Cheesecake Tartlets

(Pictured at right)

Ordinary cranberry sauce becomes extraordinary when spooned on top of a cheesecake filling inside a nutty crust. The recipe comes from our Test Kitchen.

1 cup slivered almonds, toasted
1/4 cup all-purpose flour
3 tablespoons sugar
1/4 cup cold butter, cubed
2 packages (3 ounces *each*) cream cheese, softened
1/4 cup confectioners' sugar
2 tablespoons lemon juice
1 cup whipped topping
1 cup whole-berry cranberry sauce

In a food processor, combine the almonds, flour and sugar; cover and process until blended. Add butter; cover and process until mixture forms coarse crumbs.

Press onto the bottom and up the sides of four greased 4-in. tart pans with removable bottoms. Bake at 350° for 13-15 minutes or until golden brown. Cool completely on a wire rack.

In a small mixing bowl, beat cream cheese until smooth. Add confectioners' sugar and lemon juice; mix well. Fold in whipped topping. Spoon into crusts. Cover and refrigerate for 4 hours or until set. Just before serving, top with cranberry sauce. **Yield:** 4 servings.

OTHER WAYS TO ENJOY CRANBERRY SAUCE

HERE are some different ways to use up any cranberry sauce left over from your Thanksgiving meal.
- Stir a few tablespoons into hot, cooked oatmeal.
- Melt cranberry sauce in a saucepan. Serve over pound cake, angel food cake or ice cream; drizzle with chocolate sauce if desired.
- Spread some sauce on a flour tortilla. Layer with sliced cooked turkey and lettuce. Roll up to make a mouth-watering wrap.

Maple Candied Sweet Potato Pie

Our home economists turn leftovers of a sweet potato side dish into this tasty dessert! It can also be prepared with canned sweet potatoes.

3/4 cup packed brown sugar
3 tablespoons all-purpose flour
1 cup leftover Maple Candied Sweet Potatoes (recipe on page 124)
3/4 cup evaporated milk
1/2 cup butter, melted
2 eggs
1/4 teaspoon ground nutmeg
Pinch salt
1 unbaked pastry shell (9 inches)
TOPPING:
1 tablespoon butter
2/3 cup chopped pecans
1 tablespoon sugar

In a large mixing bowl, combine brown sugar and flour. Beat in the sweet potatoes, milk, butter, eggs, nutmeg and salt. Pour into pastry shell. Bake at 350° for 55-60 minutes or until a knife inserted near the center comes out clean. Cool on a wire rack.

For topping, in a small heavy skillet, melt butter. Add pecans; cook over medium heat until toasted, about 4 minutes. Sprinkle with sugar. Cook and stir for 2-4 minutes or until sugar is melted. Sprinkle over pie. Refrigerate leftovers. **Yield:** 8 servings.

Turkey Biscuit Bake

As a college student, I appreciate stick-to-your-ribs foods like this that are also easy on the budget. I often double the recipe to ensure leftovers.
—*Stephanie Denning, Mt. Pleasant, Iowa*

1 can (10-3/4 ounces) condensed cream of chicken soup, undiluted
1 cup diced cooked turkey *or* chicken
1 can (4 ounces) mushroom stems and pieces, drained
1/2 cup frozen peas
1/4 cup milk
Dash *each* ground cumin, dried basil and thyme
1 tube (12 ounces) refrigerated biscuits

In a bowl, combine the soup, turkey, mushrooms, peas, milk, cumin, basil and thyme. Pour into a greased 8-in. square baking dish. Arrange biscuits over the top. Bake, uncovered, at 350° for 20-25 minutes or until biscuits are golden brown. **Yield:** 5 servings.

Stuffed Acorn Squash

(Pictured at right)

Our Test Kitchen offers up this unique way to present leftover stuffing. Serve this squash as a hearty side dish or as a meatless entree.

  3 small acorn squash
  1 egg, beaten
1/4 teaspoon salt
1/8 teaspoon pepper
  1 teaspoon chicken bouillon granules
  2 tablespoons boiling water
  2 cups cooked stuffing
1/4 cup grated Parmesan cheese, optional
  1 teaspoon paprika

Cut squash in half; discard seeds. Place cut side down in a 15-in. x 10-in. x 1-in. baking pan; add 1/2 in. of hot water.

Bake, uncovered, at 400° for 30 minutes or until tender.

When cool enough to handle, scoop out pulp, leaving a 1/4-in. shell (pulp will measure about 3 cups). Drain water from pan; place squash cut side up in pan and set aside.

In a large bowl, combine the pulp, egg, salt and pepper. Dissolve bouillon in boiling water; add to squash mixture. Add stuffing; spoon into squash shells. Top with Parmesan cheese if desired. Sprinkle with paprika. Bake, uncovered, at 400° for 20-25 minutes or until heated through. **Yield:** 6 servings.

Turkey Dinner Pasta Shells

This special pasta dish created in our Test Kitchen uses a variety of Thanksgiving leftovers, like stuffing, gravy and turkey. Prepare it ahead of time, chill and bake when ready.

      2 cups shredded cooked turkey
1-1/2 cups cooked stuffing
  1/2 cup mayonnaise
     18 jumbo pasta shells, cooked and drained
      2 cups turkey gravy
Paprika

In a bowl, combine the turkey, stuffing and mayonnaise. Spoon into pasta shells. Place in a greased 13-in. x 9-in. x 2-in. baking dish. Pour gravy over shells. Sprinkle with paprika. Cover and bake at 350° for 30-35 minutes or until heated through. **Yield:** 6 servings.

EASTER Gatherings

Hop to it this Easter and offer to host a
mid-morning brunch. It's easy with our
early day recipe ideas. Or maybe you prefer
to celebrate the arrival of the season with
a more formal sit-down dinner featuring
mouth-watering roasted chicken. Either way,
you can round out these special springtime
menus with sweet and savory oven-fresh breads.

Rise-and-Shine Easter Brunch

SPRING has sprung. So set aside the heavy fare you've served all winter and bring out a sunnier selection suited for warmer weather.

Hop to it this Easter and invite your family over for an inviting mid-morning brunch.

Even cooks who are green in the kitchen can prepare the "eggs-cellent" foods featured here with confidence.

Asparagus Strudel is an elegant entree that starts with convenient frozen phyllo dough.

Cool, creamy Mock Devonshire Cream pairs well with both tender Citrus Scones and assorted fresh fruit. (All recipes are shown at right.)

Round out your delicious brunch buffet with a selection of this chapter's enticing egg dishes, French toast and crepes.

EARLY DAY DINING
(Clockwise from bottom)

Asparagus Strudel (p. 154)

Mock Devonshire Cream (p. 154)

Citrus Scones (p. 156)

Mock Devonshire Cream

(Pictured on page 153)

I always serve this tasty, no-fuss cream with fresh fruit to usher in a new season.
Prepare it the day before for added convenience.
—Lillian Julow, Gainesville, Florida

1 package (3 ounces) cream
    cheese, softened
1 cup (8 ounces) sour cream
3 tablespoons confectioners'
    sugar
1 cup heavy whipping cream

In a small mixing bowl, beat cream cheese until fluffy. Beat in sour cream and confectioners' sugar until smooth. Add whipping cream. Beat on medium speed until combined; beat on high speed until stiff peaks form. Refrigerate until serving. **Yield:** 3-1/4 cups.

Asparagus Strudel

(Pictured on page 152)

Celebrate the arrival of spring by serving this delightful strudel for
Easter brunch. Watch the savory slices disappear from the table!
—Dona Erhart, Stockbridge, Michigan

2 cups water
3/4 pound fresh asparagus,
    trimmed and cut into 1-inch
    pieces
2 medium leeks (white portion
    only), thinly sliced
1-1/4 cups butter, *divided*
2 cups (8 ounces) shredded
    Gruyere *or* Swiss cheese
3 eggs, lightly beaten
2 tablespoons lemon juice
2 tablespoons minced fresh
    parsley
1 tablespoon minced fresh mint
1 tablespoon minced fresh dill
1/3 cup sliced almonds, toasted
Dash cayenne pepper
32 sheets phyllo dough (14 inches
    x 9 inches)

In a large skillet, bring water to a boil. Add the asparagus; cover and boil for 3 minutes. Drain and immediately place the asparagus in ice water. Drain and pat dry. In the same skillet, saute the leeks in 1/4 cup butter for 5 minutes or until tender.

In a large bowl, combine the asparagus, leeks, cheese, eggs, lemon juice, parsley, mint, dill, almonds and cayenne.

Melt remaining butter. Place one sheet of phyllo dough on a work surface (keep remaining dough covered with plastic wrap and a damp towel to avoid drying out). Brush with butter. Repeat layers seven times. Spoon a fourth of the vegetable mixture along the short end of dough to within 1 in. of edges. Fold long sides 1 in. over filling. Roll up jelly-roll style, starting with a short side. Place seam side down on a greased baking sheet.

Repeat, making three more strudels. Brush tops with remaining butter. Bake at 350° for 40-45 minutes or until golden brown. Cool for 10 minutes before slicing. **Yield:** 8 servings.

Blueberry-Stuffed French Toast

(Pictured at right)

I came across this recipe in a local newspaper several years ago. The fruity French toast is truly company fare.
—Myrna Koldenhoven, Sanborn, Iowa

1-1/2 cups fresh *or* frozen blueberries
   3 tablespoons sugar, *divided*
   8 slices Italian bread (1-1/4 inches thick)
   4 eggs
1/2 cup orange juice
   1 teaspoon grated orange peel
Dash salt
BLUEBERRY ORANGE SAUCE:
   3 tablespoons sugar
   1 tablespoon cornstarch
1/8 teaspoon salt
1/4 cup orange juice
1/4 cup water
1-1/2 cups orange segments
   1 cup fresh *or* frozen blueberries
1/3 cup sliced almonds

In a small bowl, combine blueberries and 2 tablespoons sugar. Cut a pocket in the side of each slice of bread. Fill each pocket with about 3 tablespoons berry mixture.

In a shallow bowl, whisk the eggs, orange juice, orange peel, salt and remaining sugar. Carefully dip both sides of bread in egg mixture (do not squeeze out filling). Place in a greased 15-in. x 10-in. x 1-in. baking pan. Bake at 400° for 15 minutes, gently turning once.

Meanwhile, in a small saucepan, combine the sugar, cornstarch and salt. Gently whisk in orange juice and water until smooth. Bring to a boil; cook and stir for 1-2 minutes or until thickened. Reduce heat; stir in oranges and blueberries. Cook for 5 minutes or until heated through. Serve over French toast; sprinkle with almonds. **Yield:** 8 servings.

Family Traditions

EACH YEAR, Easter dinner at my house concludes with an assortment of my homemade pies—coconut cream, banana cream, lemon meringue and butterscotch. The pie crust recipe was passed on to me from my mother, and it has received uncountable compliments over the years.
—Janis Engle, San Jose, California

Citrus Scones

(Pictured on page 153)

My family enjoys these tender scones fresh from the oven with cream cheese.
The recipe makes enough to include the scones on a brunch buffet.
—Debra Savory, Simcoe, Ontario

4 cups all-purpose flour
1 cup sugar
2-1/2 teaspoons baking powder
1 teaspoon salt
1/2 teaspoon baking soda
1 cup cold butter, cubed
1/2 cup buttermilk
1/3 cup orange juice
1 egg
2 tablespoons lemon juice
1 tablespoon grated orange peel
2 teaspoons grated lemon peel
1 teaspoon lemon extract

In a large bowl, combine the flour, sugar, baking powder, salt and baking soda. Cut in butter until mixture is crumbly. Combine the remaining ingredients; stir into crumb mixture just until moistened.

Turn dough onto a floured surface; knead gently 5-6 times. Gently pat into two 8-in. circles; transfer to two greased 9-in. round baking pans. Cut each circle into eight wedges but do not separate. Bake at 350° for 20-25 minutes or until lightly browned. Remove from pans to wire racks. **Yield:** 16 scones.

Sausage and Cheese Souffle

I created this souffle based on a recipe from my great aunt.
I even make it for Sunday dinner with applesauce, bread and a tossed salad.
—Linda Paxton, Halethorpe, Maryland

1/2 pound bulk pork sausage
1/4 cup butter
1/4 cup all-purpose flour
1/4 teaspoon salt
1-1/4 cups milk
1 cup (4 ounces) shredded
   cheddar cheese
4 eggs, *separated*

In a small skillet, cook sausage over medium heat until no longer pink; drain and set aside. In a large saucepan, melt butter over medium heat. Stir in flour and salt; gradually stir in milk. Bring to a boil; cook and stir for 2 minutes or until thickened. Reduce heat; stir in cheese until melted.

Remove from the heat. Stir a small amount of hot mixture into the egg yolks; return all to the pan, stirring constantly. Stir in the sausage. In a small mixing bowl, beat egg whites on high speed until stiff peaks form. Fold into sausage-cheese mixture.

Transfer to an ungreased 2-qt. baking dish. Place in a large baking pan. Add 1 in. of hot water to larger pan. Bake, uncovered, at 325° for 45-50 minutes or until a knife inserted near the center comes out clean. **Yield:** 4-6 servings.

Ham and Apricot Crepes

(Pictured at right)

A sweet apricot sauce nicely complements these savory ham crepes.
—Candy Evavold
Sammamish, Washington

1-1/2 cups milk
  2 eggs, lightly beaten
  1 tablespoon butter, melted
  1 cup all-purpose flour
 20 thin slices deli ham
SAUCE:
  1 can (15-1/4 ounces) apricot
    halves
2/3 cup sugar
  2 tablespoons cornstarch
1/8 teaspoon salt
  2 cans (5-1/2 ounces *each*)
    apricot nectar
  2 tablespoons butter
  2 teaspoons lemon juice

In a large mixing bowl, combine the milk, eggs and butter. Add flour and mix well. Cover and chill for 1 hour.

Heat a lightly greased 8-in. nonstick skillet; pour 2 tablespoons batter into the center of skillet. Lift and tilt pan to evenly coat bottom. Cook until top appears dry; turn and cook 15-20 seconds longer. Remove to a wire rack. Repeat with remaining batter, greasing skillet as needed. When cool, stack crepes with waxed paper or paper towels in between.

Place a slice of ham on each crepe; roll up. Place in two greased 13-in. x 9-in. x 2-in. baking dishes. Bake, uncovered, at 350° for 20 minutes.

Meanwhile, drain apricots, reserving syrup. Cut apricots into 1/4-in. slices; set aside. In a large saucepan, combine the sugar, cornstarch and salt. Add apricot nectar and reserved syrup; stir until smooth. Bring to a boil; cook and stir for 1-2 minutes or until thickened. Remove from the heat; stir in the butter, lemon juice and apricot slices. Serve with crepes. **Yield:** 10 servings.

CREPE-MAKING POINTERS

- Let the batter sit at least 1 hour before using to reduce any air bubbles.
- Lightly coat the pan with nonstick cooking spray, butter or oil; heat over medium-high.
- Add a small amount of batter to the hot pan. Tilt the pan to evenly coat the bottom.
- When the edges are dry and pull away from pan, gently turn; cook the other side.
- To prevent crepes from sticking before filling, let them cool on a wire rack or waxed paper. Then stack crepes with waxed paper or paper towel in between.

Potato Sausage Frittata

With sausage, bacon, eggs and potatoes, this frittata is a meal in one.
I usually double the recipe and rarely have leftovers.
—*Patricia Lee, Eatonton, Georgia*

1/2 **pound bulk pork sausage**
6 **bacon strips, diced**
1-1/2 **cups finely chopped red**
   potatoes
1 **medium onion, finely chopped**
8 **eggs**
2 **teaspoons dried parsley flakes**
3/4 **teaspoon salt**
1/8 **teaspoon pepper**

In a large ovenproof skillet, cook sausage over medium heat until no longer pink. Remove and set aside. In the same skillet, cook bacon over medium heat until crisp. Using a slotted spoon, remove to paper towels; drain, reserving 2 tablespoons drippings.

In the drippings, saute potatoes and onion until tender. In a large bowl, whisk the eggs, parsley, salt and pepper. Return sausage and bacon to the skillet; top with egg mixture.

Cover and cook over low heat for 8-10 minutes or until eggs are almost set. Uncover; broil 6 in. from the heat for 2 minutes or until eggs are set. Cut into wedges. **Yield:** 4 servings.

Curried Eggs in Shrimp Sauce

I like to dress up ordinary hard-cooked eggs with a special shrimp sauce.
You can assemble this casserole the day before and bake it the next morning.
—*M. Beatrice Mann, Vernon, Vermont*

3 **tablespoons butter,** *divided*
2 **tablespoons all-purpose flour**
1 **can (10-3/4 ounces)**
   condensed cream of shrimp
   soup, undiluted
1 **cup milk**
1/2 **cup shredded cheddar cheese**
1/2 **pound frozen cooked small**
   shrimp, thawed and chopped
12 **hard-cooked eggs**
1/2 **cup mayonnaise**
1/4 **teaspoon curry powder**
1/4 **teaspoon ground mustard**
1/4 **teaspoon paprika**
1/8 **teaspoon salt**
1 **cup soft bread crumbs**

In a large saucepan, melt 2 tablespoons butter; whisk in flour until smooth. Gradually add soup and milk. Bring to a boil; cook and stir over medium heat for 2 minutes or until thickened. Remove from the heat; stir in cheese until melted. Stir in shrimp.

Pour 2 cups of sauce into a greased 13-in. x 9-in. x 2-in. baking dish; set remaining sauce aside. Cut the eggs in half lengthwise; arrange whites over sauce. In a bowl, mash the yolks. Stir in the mayonnaise, curry powder, mustard, paprika and salt. Spoon into egg whites. Top with the reserved sauce.

Melt the remaining butter; toss with bread crumbs. Sprinkle over the top. Bake, uncovered, at 350° for 15-20 minutes or until heated through. **Yield:** 12 servings.

Bunny
Napkin Fold

(Pictured at right)

FOR a "hare-raising" reaction at your Easter brunch, fashion these festive napkin folds in the shape of bunnies!

All you need are well-starched square napkins in the color of your choice. (In keeping with our green theme, we used green polka dot napkins.) Then just follow the folding instructions below.

For a brunch buffet, you may want to create a "warren" of rabbits by placing the folded napkins on a nest of shredded scrapbook papers. We selected a variety of papers, then shredded them with a paper cutter. But a 1/4-inch straight-edge paper shredder could also be used.

BUNNY NAPKIN FOLD

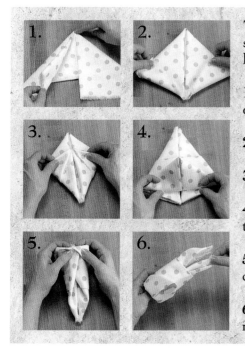

TO MAKE these festive napkin folds, start with well-starched square napkins. Fold the bottom third of the napkin up and the top third down, making a rectangle.

1. Find the center along the top fold and fold the top corners down, making sure the bottom ends are even.

2. Fold up the outside bottom corners.

3. Fold left and right sides so that they meet in the center.

4. Turn the napkin over and flip the top to bottom. Fold bottom point up.

5. Fold the left and right corners to the back and tuck one corner into the other to hold.

6. Hold the tucked corners securely and pull out the bunny ears on the other end.

Easter Gatherings

Elegant Easter Dinner

EASTER is a terrific time to plan a marvelous menu around the fresh flavors of spring.

If you're hosting a dinner for six, roasted chicken is an easy, elegant entree that's sized just right.

Citrus-Rosemary Roasted Chicken features juicy grapefruit and fresh rosemary. The appealing aroma will have guests heading to the dinner table in a hurry.

Two special sides—Poppy Seed Crescents and Orange Rice Pilaf—round out the lovely meal in a mouth-watering way.

Land lots of compliments by shaping a chocolate and hazelnut mixture into tempting Truffle Eggs. (All recipes shown at right.)

TRUE BLUE MENU
(Top to bottom)

Poppy Seed Crescents (p. 166)

Citrus-Rosemary Roasted Chicken (p. 164)

Orange Rice Pilaf (p. 162)

Truffle Eggs (p. 163)

EASTER DINNER TIMETABLE

A Few Weeks Before:

- Prepare two grocery lists—one for non-perishable items to purchase now and one for perishable items to purchase a few days before Easter.
- Bake Poppy Seed Crescents; cool. Freeze in a single layer in heavy-duty resealable plastic bags.

Two to Three Days Before:

- Buy remaining grocery items.
- For the Bird Nest Centerpiece, prepare hard-cooked eggs. The next day, make Marbled Easter Eggs (page 167).
- Make Truffle Eggs; refrigerate.

The Day Before:

- Set the table.
- Make Festive Apricot Tart. Cover; chill.

- Toast the slivered almonds for Orange Rice Pilaf. Store in a covered container at room temperature.

Easter:

- Assemble the Bird Nest Centerpiece.
- Thaw Poppy Seed Crescent Rolls at room temperature.
- Place Truffle Eggs in small twig nests on each place setting if desired.
- Bake the Citrus-Rosemary Roasted Chicken.
- Make Orange Rice Pilaf.
- Let the roasted chicken stand for 10 to 15 minutes before slicing.
- Prepare Cauliflower with Buttered Crumbs.
- For dessert, serve Festive Apricot Tart and additional Truffle Eggs if desired.

Orange Rice Pilaf

(Pictured on page 160)

Rice is favored in my family so I make this pleasant, citrus side dish often.
—Linda Schneekloth, Apple Valley, Minnesota

1/2 cup chopped celery
1/4 cup chopped green onions
1/4 cup butter
  1 cup uncooked long grain rice
  1 cup orange juice
  1 cup water
  1 teaspoon salt
  1 medium orange, peeled, seeded and cut into small pieces
1/4 cup slivered almonds, toasted

In a large saucepan, saute celery and onions in butter until tender. Add rice; cook and stir for 5 minutes or until lightly browned.

Add the orange juice, water and salt. Bring to a boil. Reduce heat; cover and simmer for 20 minutes or until liquid is absorbed and rice is tender.

Remove from the heat. Gently stir in orange pieces; sprinkle with almonds. **Yield:** 6 servings.

Truffle Eggs

(Pictured at right and on page 161)

These rich chocolate candies from our Test Kitchen feature a fabulous hazelnut flavor. They're an eye-catching addition to your Easter table.

1/4 **cup heavy whipping cream**
1 **tablespoon butter**
1/2 **teaspoon light corn syrup**
4 **squares (1 ounce** *each***) semisweet chocolate**
2 **tablespoons chocolate hazelnut spread**
1 **pound white candy coating**
5 to 6 **drops blue food coloring**
1/2 to 1 **teaspoon instant coffee granules**

In a saucepan, bring the cream, butter and corn syrup to a boil. Add chocolate and remove from the heat (do not stir). Let stand for 5 minutes. Whisk in hazelnut spread until combined. Transfer to a bowl. Cover and refrigerate for 45-60 minutes or until thickened, stirring every 15 minutes.

Shape 1 heaping teaspoonful of the chocolate mixture into an egg. Place on a parchment paper-lined baking sheet. Repeat with the remaining mixture. Refrigerate until firm, about 5-10 minutes.

Meanwhile, in a small saucepan, melt candy coating over medium-low heat. Stir in food coloring. Dip eggs into candy coating; allow excess to drip off. Return to baking sheet and immediately sprinkle with coffee granules. Let stand until set. Store in an airtight container in the refrigerator. **Yield: 3 dozen.**

SERVING TRUFFLE EGGS

DYED a robin's egg blue, Truffle Eggs bring a bit of spring to the table. To tie into our Bird Nest Centerpiece on page 167, we purchased small twig nests from a craft store, set one on each dinner plate and set a Truffle Egg inside.

Another presentation idea is to make a "nest" of toasted flaked coconut on a large serving tray and then top with a dozen or so Truffle Eggs.

Citrus-Rosemary Roasted Chicken

(Pictured on page 161)

Grapefruit and rosemary blend together beautifully to create this moist and delicious chicken.
It's an excellent entree to make when hosting a smaller group.
—Kathy Rundle, Fond du Lac, Wisconsin

2 tablespoons grated onion
1 tablespoon minced fresh rosemary
2 teaspoons minced fresh marjoram
3 garlic cloves, minced
1 teaspoon grated grapefruit peel
1/2 teaspoon salt, *divided*
1/2 teaspoon pepper, *divided*
1 roasting chicken (6 to 7 pounds)
1 medium onion, cut into wedges
1 small pink grapefruit, cut into wedges
3 fresh rosemary sprigs
3 fresh marjoram sprigs
2 tablespoons olive oil

In a small bowl, combine the first five ingredients. Add 1/4 teaspoon salt and 1/4 teaspoon pepper; set aside.

Place chicken on a rack in a shallow roasting pan. Sprinkle remaining salt and pepper inside cavity; fill with onion and grapefruit wedges. With fingers, carefully loosen the skin from both sides of chicken breast. Place rosemary and marjoram sprigs under the skin. Brush chicken with oil; rub with reserved herb mixture.

Bake, uncovered, at 325° for 2-1/2 to 3 hours or until a meat thermometer reads 180°. Let stand for 10-15 minutes. Discard herb sprigs and contents of cavity before slicing. **Yield:** 6 servings.

Festive Apricot Tart

I like to bring dishes to potlucks that are a little different from others.
Everyone reaches for this attractive apricot tart.
—Kathy Friesen, Grande Praire, Alberta

1/2 cup butter, softened
3 tablespoons confectioners' sugar
1 cup all-purpose flour
FILLING:
3/4 cup cold milk
1 package (3.4 ounces) instant lemon pudding mix
1 package (8 ounces) cream cheese, softened

1/4 cup confectioners' sugar
3 tablespoons lemon juice, *divided*
1/2 cup heavy whipping cream, whipped
2 cans (15 ounces *each*) apricot halves, well drained
1/3 cup apricot jam

In a small mixing bowl, cream butter and confectioners' sugar. Add flour; beat until well mixed. Press dough onto the bottom and 1/2 in. up the sides of a 9-in. springform pan. Prick well with a fork; chill for 30 minutes.

Place pan on a baking sheet. Bake at 425° for 12-15 minutes or until light golden brown. Cool on a wire rack.

For filling, in a bowl, whisk milk and pudding mix for 2 minutes. Let stand for 2 minutes or until soft-set. In a small mixing bowl, beat cream cheese, confectioners' sugar and 2 tablespoons lemon juice until smooth. Stir in pudding until blended. Fold in whipped cream. Spread over crust.

Arrange apricots over filling. Combine jam and remaining lemon juice; brush over apricots. Cover and chill for at least 3 hours or overnight. **Yield:** 8 servings.

Cauliflower With Buttered Crumbs

(Pictured at right)

Our home economists offer this home-style way to add flavor and interest to steamed cauliflower. Serve this simple side dish with a variety of entrees.

- 1 **large head cauliflower, broken into florets**
- 1/3 **cup butter**
- 1 **tablespoon lemon juice**
- 1/4 **cup dry bread crumbs**
- 1/4 **cup grated Parmesan cheese**
- 2 **tablespoons minced fresh parsley**
- 1/8 **teaspoon salt**
- 1/8 **teaspoon pepper**

Place 1 in. of water in a large saucepan; add cauliflower. Bring to a boil. Reduce heat; cover and simmer for 10-12 minutes or until crisp-tender.

Meanwhile, in a small heavy saucepan, cook butter over medium heat for 5 minutes or until golden brown, stirring frequently. Remove from the heat; stir in lemon juice. In a small bowl, combine the bread crumbs, Parmesan cheese, parsley, salt and pepper; stir in 3 tablespoons browned butter.

Drain cauliflower and place in a serving dish. Drizzle with the remaining browned butter; sprinkle with bread crumb mixture. **Yield:** 6 servings.

Poppy Seed Crescents

(Pictured on page 161)

I've been relying on this recipe for more than 40 years.
With a slightly sweet flavor, these rolls can be served for both brunch and dinner.
—Loraine Meyer, Bend, Oregon

1 package (1/4 ounce) active
    dry yeast
1/2 cup warm water (110° to 115°)
1 can (5 ounces) evaporated milk
1/4 cup sugar
1/4 cup butter, softened
1 egg
1 teaspoon salt
3 to 3-1/2 cups all-purpose flour
FILLING:
2 tablespoons sugar
2 tablespoons poppy seeds
2 tablespoons water
1/2 teaspoon grated lemon peel
1/4 teaspoon ground cinnamon
EGG WASH:
1 egg yolk
1 tablespoon water

In a large mixing bowl, dissolve yeast in warm water. Add the milk, sugar, butter, egg, salt and 2 cups flour; beat until smooth. Stir in enough remaining flour to form a soft dough.

Turn onto a floured surface; knead until smooth and elastic, about 6-8 minutes. Place in a greased bowl, turning once to grease top. Cover and let rise in a warm place until doubled, about 1 hour.

In a small saucepan, combine the filling ingredients. Bring to a boil, stirring constantly. Remove from the heat and set aside.

Punch down dough. Turn onto a lightly floured surface. Divide dough in half; roll each portion into a 12-in. circle. Spread with filling to within 1/2 in. of edges. Cut each circle into 12 wedges. Roll up wedges from the wide end and place point side down 2 in. apart on greased baking sheets. Curve ends to form a crescent. Cover and let rise until doubled, about 30 minutes.

In a small bowl, beat egg yolk and water; brush over rolls. Bake at 350° for 15-20 minutes or until golden brown. Remove from pans to wire racks. **Yield:** 2 dozen.

REHEATING ROLLS

THE Poppy Seed Crescents can be baked and frozen. To reheat, wrap thawed crescent rolls in foil. Bake at 350° for 15 to 20 minutes.

Bird Nest Centerpiece

(Pictured at right)

To bring a bit of spring to your Easter table, we hatched this clever centerpiece idea. First, make Marbled Easter Eggs (see directions below), then perch them in purchased twig nests. Set several nests down the length of your table.

White hard-cooked eggs
Liquid food coloring in color of
** your choice**
White vinegar
Vegetable oil

Place about 1-1/2 cups of water in a deep-sided bowl. Add food coloring one drop at a time, testing color with a hard-cooked egg until desired color is reached. Add 1 tablespoon each of white vinegar and vegetable oil to colored water.

Swirl the water with a fork to break up the oil. Immediately lower an egg into the bowl using a wire egg holder, spoon or fork, swirling it in a circle as it enters the water. Raise and lower egg until desired color is achieved. Remove egg and let dry on paper towels.

MARBLED EASTER EGGS

1. With a wire egg holder, spoon or fork, dip the egg into the food coloring with vinegar and oil mixture, swirling it in a circle.

2. When desired color is achieved, remove egg and let dry on paper towels.

Special Springtime Breads

SWEET and savory breads have herald the arrival of Easter—as well as the departure of religious fasting—for centuries.

Why not beckon family and friends to the table this Easter with a bounty of fresh-baked goodies?

Instead of the usual currants or raisins, Candied-Fruit Hot Cross Buns feature delicious mixed candied fruit.

Old-world flavor abounds in slightly sweet Cream Cheese Nut Bread.

For a pretty presentation, prepare Swedish Pastry Rings. The recipe makes two loaves so you can keep one and share the other with a friend or neighbor. (All recipes are shown at right.)

Fresh from the Oven
(Clockwise from bottom)

Swedish Pastry Rings (p. 170)

Cream Cheese Nut Bread (p. 172)

Candied-Fruit Hot Cross Buns (p. 171)

Swedish Pastry Rings

(Pictured on page 168)

Although my family is of Polish and German descent, we sure enjoy this sweet bit of Sweden!
Mom was always sure to make this for Easter breakfast.
— Myra Pratt, Fairview, Pennsylvania

2-1/4 cups all-purpose flour
2 tablespoons plus 1 teaspoon sugar, *divided*
1 teaspoon salt
1/2 cup cold butter
1 package (1/4 ounce) active dry yeast
1/4 cup warm water (110° to 115°)
1/4 cup warm evaporated milk (110° to 115°)
1 egg
1/4 cup dried currants *or* raisins
FILLING:
1/4 cup butter, softened
1/2 cup packed brown sugar
1/2 cup chopped pecans
BROWNED BUTTER GLAZE:
2 tablespoons butter
1 cup confectioners' sugar
1/2 teaspoon vanilla extract
3 to 4 teaspoons evaporated milk

In a large bowl, combine flour, 2 tablespoons sugar and salt. Cut in butter until mixture resembles fine crumbs. In a large mixing bowl, dissolve yeast and remaining sugar in warm water. Add milk, egg and crumb mixture; beat until well blended. Stir in currants. Cover and refrigerate overnight.

Line two baking sheets with foil and grease the foil; set aside. For filling, in a small mixing bowl, cream butter and brown sugar; stir in pecans. Punch down dough. Turn onto a lightly floured surface; divide in half. Roll each portion into a 14-in. x 7-in. rectangle; spread filling to within 1/2 in. of edges. Roll up jelly-roll style, starting with a long side; pinch seams to seal.

Place loaves seam side down on prepared pans; pinch ends together to form a ring. With scissors, cut from outside edge two-thirds of the way toward center of ring at 1-in. intervals. Separate strips slightly; twist to allow filling to show. Cover and let rise in a warm place until doubled, about 45 minutes.

Bake at 350° for 18-22 minutes or until golden brown. Remove from pans to wire racks to cool.

For glaze, in a small saucepan, cook butter over medium heat until lightly browned, stirring constantly. Remove from the heat. Stir in confectioners' sugar, vanilla and enough milk to achieve desired consistency. Drizzle over pastry rings. **Yield:** 2 pastry rings (12-16 servings each).

Candied-Fruit Hot Cross Buns

(Pictured at right and on page 169)

My family looks forward to my mom's hot cross buns every year. She's a wonderful lady and cook who makes our holidays memorable.
—*Gloria Wiebe, Winkler, Manitoba*

2 packages (1/4 ounce *each*) active dry yeast
2 cups warm milk (110° to 115°)
6 tablespoons butter, softened
2 eggs, lightly beaten
3/4 cup sugar
1 teaspoon salt
6 to 6-1/2 cups all-purpose flour
1 cup chopped mixed candied fruit
2 teaspoons ground cinnamon
1 egg yolk
2 tablespoons water

ICING:
1-1/4 cups confectioners' sugar
2 tablespoons milk
1 tablespoon butter, melted
1/4 teaspoon vanilla extract

In a large mixing bowl, dissolve yeast in warm milk. Stir in the butter, eggs, sugar and salt. Combine 3 cups flour, candied fruit and cinnamon; add to the yeast mixture and mix well. Stir in enough remaining flour to form a soft dough.

Turn onto a floured surface; knead until smooth and elastic, about 6-8 minutes. Place in a greased bowl, turning once to grease top. Cover and let rise in a warm place until doubled, about 1 hour.

Punch dough down; shape into 2-in. balls. Place 2 in. apart on greased baking sheets. Using a sharp knife, cut a cross on top of each bun. Cover and let rise until doubled, about 30 minutes.

Beat egg yolk and water; brush over buns. Bake at 350° for 12-15 minutes or until golden brown. Remove from pans to cool on wire racks. Combine icing ingredients; pipe an "X" on top of each bun. **Yield:** 3 dozen.

HOT CROSS BUNS IN BRIEF

PEOPLE have been making hot cross buns since the days of ancient Greece. At that time, the round shape represented the sun and the cross stood for either the four seasons or four moon phases.

In the 14th century, monks baked the buns for the poor on Good Friday using leftover dough from sacramental bread.

Banana Brickle Muffins

(Pictured at far right)

Toffee bits add great flavor to these delicious banana muffins.
Serve them at breakfast, lunch, dinner or as a special snack.
—Andra Cogan, Grosse Pointe Park, Michigan

2 cups all-purpose flour
1/2 cup packed brown sugar
1 tablespoon baking powder
1 cup mashed ripe bananas
1/2 cup milk
1/3 cup vegetable oil
1 egg
1 package (10 ounces) English toffee bits *or* almond brickle chips (7-1/2 ounces), *divided*

In a large bowl, combine the flour, brown sugar and baking powder. In a small bowl, combine the bananas, milk, oil and egg. Stir into dry ingredients just until moistened. Fold in 1 cup toffee bits.

Fill greased muffin cups three-fourths full. Sprinkle with remaining toffee bits. Bake at 350° for 18-20 minutes or until a toothpick comes out clean. Cool for 5 minutes before removing from pan to a wire rack. Serve warm. **Yield:** 1 dozen.

Cream Cheese Nut Bread

(Pictured on page 168)

I went to a luncheon with some girlfriends a few years ago, and the
hostess served this bread. We all marveled at the wonderful flavor and texture.
—Patricia Sawtell, Kinston, New York

2 packages (3 ounces *each*) cream cheese, softened
1/4 cup sugar
2 egg whites
1 tablespoon all-purpose flour
1 tablespoon grated orange peel
BATTER:
2-1/2 cups all-purpose flour
1/3 cup sugar
1 teaspoon baking soda
1/2 teaspoon salt
1 egg
2/3 cup milk
2/3 cup honey
1/2 cup vegetable oil
1 cup chopped walnuts, toasted

In a small mixing bowl, beat cream cheese and sugar; beat in the egg whites. Stir in flour and orange peel; set aside.

In a large bowl, combine the flour, sugar, baking soda and salt. In a small bowl, beat the egg, milk, honey and oil; stir into dry ingredients just until moistened. Fold in walnuts.

Spoon a fourth of the batter into two greased 8-in. x 4-in. x 2-in. loaf pans. Spread reserved cream cheese mixture to within 1/2 in. of edges. Spoon remaining batter over filling and carefully spread to cover (pans will not be very full).

Bake at 325° for 50-55 minutes or until a toothpick comes out clean. Cool for 10 minutes before removing from pans to wire racks to cool completely. Store in the refrigerator. **Yield:** 2 loaves.

Maple Twists

(Pictured at right)

Mashed potatoes are the secret ingredient that makes these flavorful treats nice and moist. My mother made them when I was young, and now my grandchildren request them.
— *Eunice Knipp, Elmore, Ohio*

1 package (1/4 ounce) active dry yeast
1/4 cup warm water (110° to 115°)
1 cup warm milk (110° to 115°)
1 cup warm mashed potatoes (without added milk and butter)
1/2 cup shortening
1/2 cup sugar
1 egg
1 teaspoon salt
3-3/4 to 4-1/4 cups all-purpose flour
ICING:
4 cups confectioners' sugar
4 tablespoons milk
1-1/2 teaspoons maple flavoring

In a large mixing bowl, dissolve yeast in warm water. Add the milk, potatoes, shortening, sugar, egg and salt; mix well. Add 1 cup flour; beat until smooth. Stir in enough remaining flour to make a soft dough.

Turn onto a floured surface; knead until smooth and elastic, about 6-8 minutes. Place in a greased bowl, turning once to grease top. Cover and let rise in a warm place until doubled, about 1 hour.

Punch dough down. Turn onto a lightly floured surface. Roll into a 12-in. x 10-in. rectangle. Cut into 24 strips (5 in. x 1 in.). Twist strips; place on greased baking sheets. Cover and let rise until doubled, about 30 minutes.

Bake at 375° for 15-20 minutes or until golden brown. Remove from pans to wire racks. Combine the icing ingredients until smooth; drizzle over warm rolls. **Yield:** 2 dozen.

Lemony Nut Rolls

*My grandmother had these light, lemon rolls waiting for the men when they came in from
working the fields on our farm. They're still a favorite with our family today.*
—Barbara Rejzer, Waterford, Pennsylvania

1 package (1/4 ounce) active
  dry yeast
1/4 cup warm water (110° to 115°)
1/2 cup warm mashed potatoes
  (without added milk and
  butter)
1/2 cup warm milk (110° to 115°)
1/3 cup sugar
1/3 cup shortening
1 egg
1 tablespoon lemon juice
1-1/2 teaspoons grated lemon peel
1 teaspoon salt
3 to 3-1/2 cups all-purpose flour
FILLING:
2 tablespoons butter, melted
3/4 cup sugar
1/2 cup chopped pecans
2 teaspoons grated lemon peel
FROSTING:
1/2 cup confectioners' sugar
1 tablespoon heavy whipping
  cream
1 teaspoon grated lemon peel
1/2 teaspoon lemon juice

In a large mixing bowl, dissolve yeast in warm water. Add
the potatoes, milk, sugar, shortening, egg, lemon juice and
peel, salt and 2 cups flour; beat until smooth. Stir in enough
remaining flour to form a firm dough.

Turn onto a floured surface; knead until smooth and elastic, about 6-8 minutes. Place in a greased bowl, turning once
to grease top. Cover and let rise in a warm place until doubled, about 1 hour.

Punch dough down. Turn onto a lightly floured surface.
Roll into a 16-in. x 12-in. rectangle. Brush with butter to
within 1/2 in. of edges. Combine the sugar, pecans and
lemon peel; sprinkle over dough. Roll up jelly-roll style,
starting with a long side; pinch seam to seal. Cut into 16
rolls. Place cut side up in two greased 9-in. round baking
pans. Cover and let rise in a warm place until doubled, about
30 minutes.

Bake at 375° for 25-30 minutes or until golden brown.
Cool for 10 minutes on a wire rack. Combine frosting ingredients; spread over warm rolls. **Yield:** 16 rolls.

Easter Bunny Breads

(Pictured at right)

These cute bunny breads are a must at our house during the Easter season. Kids of all ages love the chocolate egg surprise found inside.
—Molly Hurd, Newcastle, Washington

2 packages (1/4 ounce *each*)
    active dry yeast
1 cup warm water (110° to 115°)
1 cup warm milk (110° to 115°)
2 tablespoons sugar
2 tablespoons vegetable oil
1 egg
1 teaspoon salt
5-1/2 to 6-1/2 cups all-purpose flour
16 small milk chocolate eggs
ICING:
    1 tablespoon confectioners' sugar
1/4 teaspoon water
    1 drop red food coloring

In a large mixing bowl, dissolve yeast in warm water. Add milk, sugar, oil, egg, salt and 4 cups flour. Beat on medium speed for 3 minutes; beat until smooth. Stir in enough remaining flour to form a soft dough (dough will be sticky).

Turn onto a floured surface; knead until smooth and elastic, about 6-8 minutes. Place in a greased bowl, turning once to grease top. Cover and let rise in a warm place until doubled, about 1 hour.

Punch dough down. For each bunny, shape a 3-in. ball for the body; press a chocolate egg into each ball. Shape dough around egg so it is completely covered. For each head, shape a 2-in. ball; press a chocolate egg into each. Shape dough around egg so it is completely covered. Add a 1-in. ball for the tail and two 2-in. x 3/4-in. pieces for the ears.

Place bunnies 2 in. apart on greased baking sheets. Bake at 400° for 12-15 minutes or until golden brown. Carefully remove from pans to wire racks to cool.

For icing, in a small bowl, combine confectioners' sugar and water; tint pink with red food coloring. With a small new paintbrush, paint a nose and whiskers on each bunny. **Yield:** 8 servings.

Polish Sauerkraut Bread

Hearty, chewy slices of this light rye bread are terrific by themselves or with a favorite meal.
—Cecilia Kowalski, Fontana, Wisconsin

6 cups all-purpose flour
1 cup rye flour
1 tablespoon sugar
3 teaspoons salt
1 package (1/4 ounce) active
   dry yeast
2 cups water
2 tablespoons butter
3/4 cup sauerkraut, rinsed and
   well drained
Cornmeal

In a large mixing bowl, combine 3 cups all-purpose flour, rye flour, sugar, salt and yeast. In a saucepan, heat water and butter to 120°-130°. Add to dry ingredients; beat until smooth. Stir in sauerkraut and enough remaining all-purpose flour to form a soft dough.

Turn onto a floured surface; knead until smooth and elastic, about 6-8 minutes. Place in a greased bowl, turning once to grease top. Cover and let rise in a warm place until doubled, about 1 hour.

Punch dough down. Turn onto a lightly floured surface; divide in half. Shape into two loaves, about 9 in. long. Grease two baking sheets or 9-in. x 5-in. x 3-in. loaf pans and sprinkle with cornmeal. Place loaves in prepared pans. Cover and let rise in a warm place until doubled, about 45 minutes.

Lightly brush tops of loaves with water. With a very sharp knife, make four to five diagonal slashes across the top of each loaf. Bake at 400° for 20 minutes. Reduce heat to 350°; bake 10-15 minutes longer or until lightly browned. Remove from pans to wire racks to cool. **Yield:** 2 loaves.

SCORING THE TOP OF BREAD

SLASHING or scoring the top of a bread loaf allows steam to vent and helps prevent cracking. It also gives ordinary-looking bread a pretty appearance. For more interest, make slashes in a crisscross pattern.

Garlic Cheese Bubble Bread

My daughter makes this easy bread when she serves spaghetti and lasagna. It's really delicious.
—Evelyn Backhaus, Pollock, South Dakota

1 loaf (1 pound) frozen bread
   dough, thawed
3 pieces string cheese
1/4 cup butter, softened
2 tablespoons grated Parmesan
   cheese
1/2 teaspoon garlic salt

Divide dough into 10 portions. Cut string cheese into 1-in. pieces. Wrap each portion of dough around a piece of cheese; shape into balls. Place in a greased 9-in. x 5-in. x 3-in. loaf pan. In a bowl, combine the butter, Parmesan cheese and garlic salt until blended; spread over top of dough. Cover and let rise in a warm place until doubled, about 1 hour.

Bake at 375° for 20-25 minutes or until golden brown. Cool for 10 minutes before removing from pan to a wire rack. Serve warm. **Yield:** 1 loaf.

Strawberry Streusel Muffins

(Pictured at right)

My friends and I enjoy trying new recipes that are good nutritionally. These tasty muffins rely on yogurt and sour cream instead of oil. Everyone loves them!
—Caroline Galicic, Kent, Washington

2 cups all-purpose flour
3/4 cup sugar
1 teaspoon cream of tartar
1/2 teaspoon baking soda
1/2 teaspoon salt
2 eggs
3/4 cup strawberry yogurt
1/4 cup sour cream
1 cup chopped fresh strawberries
STREUSEL TOPPING:
1/4 cup packed brown sugar
5 tablespoons all-purpose flour
1/2 teaspoon ground cinnamon
2 tablespoons cold butter

In a bowl, combine the flour, sugar, cream of tartar, baking soda and salt. In another bowl, combine eggs, yogurt and sour cream; stir into dry ingredients just until moistened. Fold in strawberries. Fill greased or paper-lined muffin cups two-thirds full.

For topping, combine the brown sugar, flour and cinnamon in a bowl; cut in butter until mixture resembles coarse crumbs. Sprinkle over batter. Bake at 350° for 30-35 minutes or until a toothpick comes out clean. Cool for 5 minutes before removing from pan to a wire rack. **Yield:** 1 dozen.

SPECIAL
Celebrations

Occasions throughout the year call for special gatherings with family and friends. On Valentine's Day, treat your sweetie to a romantic dinner for two. Southern comfort is in the spotlight at a Kentucky Derby bash, while on Memorial Day, a patriotic picnic is perfect. Have a teen turning Sweet 16? Plan a fun-filled Mexican fiesta! Celebrate summer with recipes showcasing colorful, juicy berries. Then as the season winds down, host a farm-inspired hoedown— and on Halloween, throw a mad scientist "spooktacular!"

Valentine's Day Dinner

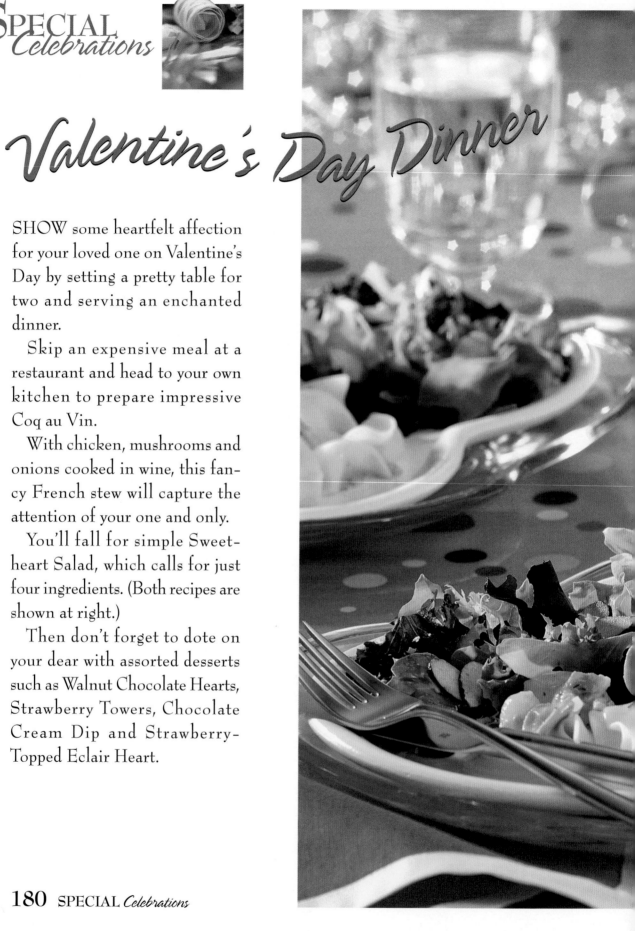

SHOW some heartfelt affection for your loved one on Valentine's Day by setting a pretty table for two and serving an enchanted dinner.

Skip an expensive meal at a restaurant and head to your own kitchen to prepare impressive Coq au Vin.

With chicken, mushrooms and onions cooked in wine, this fancy French stew will capture the attention of your one and only.

You'll fall for simple Sweetheart Salad, which calls for just four ingredients. (Both recipes are shown at right.)

Then don't forget to dote on your dear with assorted desserts such as Walnut Chocolate Hearts, Strawberry Towers, Chocolate Cream Dip and Strawberry-Topped Eclair Heart.

ROMANTIC MEAL
(Pictured above)

Coq au Vin (p. 182)

Sweetheart Salad (p. 182)

Coq au Vin

(Pictured on page 181)

Coq au Vin is a chicken dish typically made with red wine.
This wonderful white wine version was created in our Test Kitchen.

4 cups water
1 cup pearl onions
4 bacon strips, cut into 1-inch
   pieces
2 bone-in chicken breast halves
   (8 ounces *each*)
1/4 teaspoon salt
1/8 teaspoon pepper
3/4 cup sliced fresh mushrooms
2 garlic cloves, minced
4-1/2 teaspoons all-purpose flour
3/4 cup chicken broth
3/4 cup white wine *or* additional
   chicken broth
1 bay leaf
1/2 teaspoon dried thyme
Hot cooked noodles

In a large saucepan, bring water to a boil. Add onions; boil for 3 minutes. Drain and rinse in cold water; peel and set aside.

In a large skillet, cook bacon over medium heat until crisp. Using a slotted spoon, remove to paper towels. Sprinkle chicken with salt and pepper. Brown chicken in the drippings; remove and keep warm. Add onions to drippings; saute until crisp-tender. Add mushrooms and garlic; saute 3-4 minutes longer or until almost tender.

Combine flour and broth; stir into onion mixture. Add wine or additional broth, bay leaf and thyme; bring to a boil. Return chicken and bacon to the pan. Reduce heat; cover and simmer for 25-30 minutes or until a meat thermometer reads 170°.

Remove chicken and keep warm. Cook sauce over medium heat until slightly thickened. Discard bay leaf. Serve chicken and sauce with noodles. **Yield:** 2 servings.

Sweetheart Salad

(Pictured on page 180)

Our home economists share the recipe for this speedy salad featuring convenient
salad mix, dried cranberries, bottled salad dressing and purchased honey-roasted almonds.

3 cups spring mix salad greens
1/4 cup dried cranberries
1/4 cup balsamic vinaigrette
2 tablespoons honey-roasted
   sliced almonds

Divide salad greens and cranberries between two salad plates. Drizzle with vinaigrette and sprinkle with almonds. Serve immediately. **Yield:** 2 servings.

Strawberry Towers

(Pictured at right)

A few years ago, I hosted a Valentine's Day party with a heart theme. This stunning grand finale received rave reviews.
—Nancy Donato, Uniontown, Ohio

1 **sheet frozen puff pastry, thawed**
1 **tablespoon cinnamon-sugar**
1/4 **cup semisweet chocolate chips**
1/4 **teaspoon shortening**
3/4 **cup heavy whipping cream**
1 **tablespoon sugar**
1/4 **teaspoon clear vanilla extract**
1 **cup sliced fresh strawberries**

On a lightly floured surface, roll pastry sheet into a 14-in. x 10-in. rectangle. Using three different sizes of heart-shaped cookie cutters (3-1/2 in., 3 in. and 1 in.), cut out 12 hearts, four of each size (discard scraps).

Place 2 in. apart on a greased baking sheet. Sprinkle with cinnamon-sugar. Bake at 400° for 8-10 minutes or until golden brown; remove smallest hearts to a wire rack. Bake medium and large hearts 2 minutes longer; remove to a wire rack.

In a small microwave-safe bowl, melt chocolate chips and shortening; stir until smooth. Transfer mixture to a small resealable plastic bag; cut a small hole in a corner of bag. In a small mixing bowl, beat cream until it begins to thicken. Add sugar and vanilla; beat until stiff peaks form.

To assemble, place large pastry hearts on dessert plates; top with a third of the whipped cream and half of the strawberries. Drizzle with chocolate. Top with medium hearts, another third of the whipped cream and remaining strawberries. Drizzle with chocolate. Dollop with remaining whipped cream. Pipe chocolate around edge of small hearts; insert into whipped cream at top of tower. **Yield:** 4 servings.

SIMPLE CINNAMON-SUGAR

YOU can buy bottles of prepared cinnamon-sugar in the spice aisle of your grocery store. Or make your own by combining 1/2 cup sugar and 1 tablespoon ground cinnamon. Store in an airtight container to use in a variety of recipes or to sprinkle over buttered toast at breakfast.

Basil Shrimp

My husband loves shrimp and agrees nothing beats this incredibly easy,
enjoyable dish. You can double the recipe when entertaining.
—Natalie Corona, Maple Grove, Minnesota

1 tablespoon minced fresh basil
1 tablespoon olive oil
1 tablespoon butter, melted
1 tablespoon Dijon mustard
2 teaspoons lemon juice
1 garlic clove, minced
Dash salt and white pepper
8 uncooked large shrimp,
   peeled and deveined

In a small bowl, combine the basil, oil, butter, mustard, lemon juice, garlic, salt and pepper. Pour 3 tablespoons into a small resealable plastic bag; add shrimp. Seal bag and turn to coat; let stand at room temperature for 15-20 minutes. Set remaining marinade aside.

Drain and discard marinade. Thread shrimp onto two metal or soaked wooden skewers. Grill, covered, over medium heat for 2-3 minutes on each side or until shrimp turn pink, basting occasionally with reserved marinade. **Yield:** 2 servings.

Spinach-Stuffed Salmon

These moist salmon fillets are filled with spinach, pesto,
sun-dried tomatoes and pine nuts. They're both pretty and delicious!
—Betty Stewart, Leola, Pennsylvania

2 thick-cut salmon fillets
   (5 ounces *each*)
Dash salt and pepper
2 cups packed fresh baby
   spinach
1 tablespoon prepared pesto
1 tablespoon sun-dried tomatoes
   (not packed in oil), chopped
1 tablespoon pine nuts

Cut a horizontal pocket in each salmon fillet by slicing to within 1/2 in. of opposite side. Sprinkle with salt and pepper. In a small bowl, combine the spinach, pesto, tomatoes and pine nuts. Spoon into each pocket.

Place salmon on a broiler pan coated with nonstick cooking spray. Broil 4-6 in. from the heat for 12-15 minutes or until spinach mixture is heated through and fish flakes easily with a fork. **Yield:** 2 servings.

Walnut Chocolate Hearts

(Pictured at right)

I've been making these cute cookies with my mom since I was a little girl. They're certainly one of my favorites and very fast to make.
—Maria Hull, Bartlett, Illinois

1 cup butter, cubed
2/3 cup packed brown sugar
1 teaspoon vanilla extract
1 egg, beaten
2-1/4 cups all-purpose flour
1/4 cup baking cocoa
1/2 teaspoon salt
3/4 cup finely chopped walnuts
TOPPING:
1-1/2 cups semisweet chocolate chips
2 tablespoons shortening
1/2 cup ground walnuts

In a saucepan, combine butter and brown sugar. Cook and stir over medium-low heat until butter is melted. Remove from the heat; stir in vanilla. Cool for 15 minutes. Stir in egg. Combine the flour, cocoa and salt; add to butter mixture. Fold in walnuts. Cover and chill for 30 minutes or until easy to handle.

On a lightly floured surface, roll dough to 1/4-in. thickness. Cut with a floured 3-in. heart-shaped cookie cutter. Place 1 in. apart on ungreased baking sheets. Bake at 350° for 9-10 minutes or until edges are firm. Remove to wire racks to cool.

In a small saucepan, melt chocolate chips and shortening over low heat; stir until smooth. Dip half of each heart into chocolate mixture; dip edges of dipped side into ground walnuts. **Yield:** about 4 dozen.

VALENTINE KABOBS

IF YOU can't aim Cupid's arrow at the one you love, stick it to them with these fruit and cheese kabobs!

Clean and hull some whole strawberries; set aside. Cut Monterey Jack cheese with a small heart-shaped cookie cutter. Thread the berries and cheese hearts onto small skewers. Serve the kabobs as an appetizer or dessert.

Chocolate Cream Dip

My daughter-in-law shared this recipe with me after sampling it at a party.
I like to serve this dip with Granny Smith apples because of the tasty sweet-tart combination.
—Lois Zigarac, Rochester Hills, Michigan

4 ounces cream cheese, softened
1-1/2 cups whipped topping
1/2 cup caramel ice cream topping
1/4 cup chocolate ice cream topping
Sliced apples and graham cracker
   sticks

In a small mixing bowl, beat cream cheese until smooth. Beat in the whipped topping and ice cream toppings until blended. Transfer to a serving bowl. Serve with apples and graham cracker sticks. **Yield:** 2 cups.

Strawberry-Topped Eclair Heart

This original creation looks like it came straight from a
gourmet bakery. It's impressive to serve and flavorful as well.
—Shelly Platten, Amherst, Wisconsin

3 tablespoons sugar
1 tablespoon cornstarch
1 cup milk
1 egg yolk, lightly beaten
2 teaspoons vanilla extract
5 tablespoons butter, *divided*
1/2 cup water
1/2 cup all-purpose flour
2 eggs
1 cup whipped topping
1 cup sliced fresh strawberries
3 tablespoons semisweet
   chocolate chips, melted

For filling, combine sugar and cornstarch in a saucepan. Stir in milk until smooth. Cook and stir over medium-high heat until thickened and bubbly. Reduce heat; cook and stir 2 minutes longer. Remove from the heat. Stir hot filling into egg yolk; return all to the pan, stirring constantly. Bring to a gentle boil; cook and stir for 2 minutes.

Remove from the heat. Gently stir in vanilla and 1 tablespoon butter. Transfer to a bowl. Cover and refrigerate for 1 hour or until chilled.

Meanwhile, in a large saucepan, bring water and remaining butter to a boil. Add flour all at once and stir until a smooth ball forms. Remove from the heat; let stand for 5 minutes. Add eggs, one at a time, beating well after each addition. Continue beating until mixture is smooth and shiny.

Trace an 8-in. heart on parchment paper; place on a baking sheet. Spread batter evenly over heart. Bake at 400° for 20-25 minutes or until golden brown. Remove to a wire rack to cool completely.

Fold whipped topping into chilled filling; spread over pastry. Arrange strawberries over filling. Refrigerate until serving. Just before serving, drizzle melted chocolate over berries. **Yield:** 4 servings.

Romantic Candles

(Pictured above)

IGNITE a little romance at your Valentine's Day dinner with a few pretty candles.

In the photo above, we showcase three ways to dress up ordinary pink pillars.

One bright idea starts with inexpensive, purchased bangle bracelets. Open them with a wire cutters, slip on colorful beads, then carefully wrap around the candles.

To symbolize that you and your loved one are tied together for eternity, intertwine the candles with a long silver necklace.

Finally, you can simply slip a charm bracelet over a single pillar candle. If needed, use silver elastic cord to tie ends of the bracelet together.

Gentlemen, this is also a fun way to present a gift of jewelry. (Ladies, you may want to light the fire under your significant other by leaving this page open on the table!)

Kentucky Derby Gala

AND THEY'RE OFF! Those three simple words signal the start of the most famous two-minute horse race in history.

The first Kentucky Derby race took place in 1875 and has been held on the first Saturday in May ever since, making it one of America's oldest sporting events.

If you can't get to Churchill Downs to see the Derby in person, host a winning TV-viewing party at home!

Guests will be jockeying for a position at the buffet table to sample born-and-bred Kentucky dishes such as Mint Juleps, Benedictine Spread and Derby Pie.

Finish the meal in fine fashion with other classics like Southern Fried Chicken and Cheese 'n' Grits Casserole. (All recipes are shown at right.)

Southern Comfort Food

(Clockwise from top right)

Cheese 'n' Grits Casserole (p. 197)

Benedictine Spread (p. 192)

Southern Fried Chicken (p. 190)

Mint Juleps (p. 195)

Derby Pie (p. 191)

SPECIAL KENTUCKY DERBY TABLE SETTING

THE "run for the roses" conjures up images of well-to-do gentlemen in suits and Southern belles in flowing dresses and wide-brimmed hats. Pair this chapter's casual food with an elegant table for a lovely look. Here's how:

- As the "mane" attraction on your buffet table, look for an inexpensive horse sculpture. We purchased the one pictured on page 189 at a local gardening and gift store. Or have a field day and set out a collection of horse figurines.
- Remember the red roses! Place stems in one or several silver vases or scatter rose petals on the table.

- Top tables with linen cloths and coordinating napkins.
- This is the perfect occasion for displaying sterling silver platters and bowls. Present silverware in the Cloth Silverware Holder shown on page 197.
- Put aside the paper plates and bring out your everyday dishes or china.
- Consider holding the event outside. If your budget allows, rent a tent and chairs.
- Greet guests with Mint Juleps (see recipe on page 195) served in traditional cups. You can find both silver plated and plastic mint julep cups on-line and at party stores.

Southern Fried Chicken

(Pictured on page 189)

In the South, fried chicken is served with creamy, seasoned gravy.
Our Test Kitchen home economists share their recipe here.

1 cup all-purpose flour
1 teaspoon onion powder
1 teaspoon paprika
3/4 teaspoon salt
1/2 teaspoon rubbed sage
1/2 teaspoon pepper
1/4 teaspoon dried thyme
1 egg
1/2 cup milk
1 broiler/fryer chicken (3 to 3-1/2 pounds), cut up
Oil for frying
CREAMY GRAVY:
1/3 cup all-purpose flour
1/4 teaspoon salt
1/4 teaspoon dried thyme
1/4 to 1/2 teaspoon pepper
2-1/2 cups milk
1/2 cup heavy whipping cream

In a large resealable plastic bag, combine the first seven ingredients. In a shallow bowl, beat egg and milk. Dip chicken pieces into egg mixture, then add to flour mixture, a few pieces at a time, and shake to coat.

In a large skillet, heat 1/4 in. of oil; fry chicken until browned on all sides. Cover and simmer for 35-40 minutes or until juices run clear and chicken is tender, turning occasionally. Uncover and cook 5 minutes longer. Drain on paper towels and keep warm.

Drain skillet, reserving 3 tablespoons drippings. For gravy, in a small bowl, combine the flour, salt, thyme and pepper. Gradually whisk in milk and cream until smooth; add to skillet. Bring to a boil over medium heat; cook and stir for 2 minutes or until thickened. Serve with chicken. **Yield:** 6 servings.

Derby Pie

(Pictured at right and on page 188)

This is our Test Kitchen's version of the regional classic. The chocolate pecan pie is infused with Kentucky bourbon.

- 3 eggs
- 2 egg yolks
- 3/4 cup packed brown sugar
- 2/3 cup light corn syrup
- 1/3 cup butter, melted
- 2 tablespoons Kentucky bourbon, optional
- 1 teaspoon vanilla extract
- Dash salt
- 1 cup coarsely chopped pecans
- 1 unbaked pastry shell (9 inches)
- 1 egg white, lightly beaten
- 3/4 cup semisweet chocolate chips
- 1 cup heavy whipping cream
- 2 tablespoons confectioners' sugar

In a large bowl, whisk the eggs, yolks, brown sugar, corn syrup, butter, bourbon if desired, vanilla and salt. Stir in pecans.

Brush pastry shell with egg white. Sprinkle with chocolate chips. Pour filling over chips. Bake at 350° for 40-45 minutes or until set. Cool on a wire rack.

In a small chilled mixing bowl, beat cream until it begins to thicken. Add confectioners' sugar; beat until stiff peaks form. Dollop on pie just before serving. Refrigerate leftovers. **Yield:** 6-8 servings.

Corn Pillows

We live quite far north and nothing warms us up on cold days like
warm breads and rolls. This wonderful recipe comes from a dear friend.
—Martha Nunn, Vanderhoof, British Columbia

1 tablespoon active dry yeast
1/4 cup warm water (110° to 115°)
1-3/4 cups milk
1/2 cup cornmeal
1/3 cup vegetable oil
1/3 cup sugar
2 teaspoons salt
1 can (18-1/2 ounces) cream-style corn
2 eggs, beaten
6 to 7 cups all-purpose flour
Oil for deep-fat frying
Confectioners' sugar

In a large mixing bowl, dissolve yeast in warm water. In a large saucepan, heat the milk, cornmeal, oil, sugar and salt to 110°-115°, add to yeast mixture. Add corn, eggs and 6 cups flour; beat until smooth. Stir in enough remaining flour to form a soft dough.

Turn onto a lightly floured surface; knead until smooth and elastic, about 6-8 minutes. Place in a greased bowl, turning once to grease top. Cover and let rise until doubled, about 1 hour.

Punch dough down. Turn onto a lightly floured surface; divide in half. Roll each portion into a 15-in. x 12-in. rectangle. Cut into 3-in. x 1-1/2-in. strips.

In a deep-fat fryer, heat oil to 375°. Drop dough strips in batches into oil; fry for 45-75 seconds or until golden brown. Drain on paper towels. Dust with confectioners' sugar. **Yield:** about 6-1/2 dozen.

Benedictine Spread

(Pictured on page 189)

This variation of a traditional, Kentucky cucumber spread comes from our
Test Kitchen. Serve it as an appetizer dip or sandwich filling.

1 package (8 ounces) cream cheese, softened
1 tablespoon mayonnaise
1/4 teaspoon salt
1/8 teaspoon white pepper
1/8 teaspoon dill weed
1 drop green food coloring, optional
3/4 cup finely chopped peeled cucumber, patted dry
1/4 cup finely chopped onion
Pita bread wedges *or* snack rye bread

In a small mixing bowl, combine the cream cheese, mayonnaise, salt, white pepper, dill and food coloring if desired; beat until smooth. Stir in cucumber and onion. Cover and refrigerate until serving. Serve with pita or snack rye bread. **Yield:** 1-3/4 cups.

Hot Brown Sandwiches

(Pictured at right)

Our home economists suggest that you prepare these open-faced turkey sandwiches with leftover turkey. Or pick up sliced, cooked turkey from the deli counter.

1/4 cup butter
1/4 cup all-purpose flour
 1 cup milk
 1 cup chicken broth
1/2 teaspoon Worcestershire
   sauce
3/4 cup shredded cheddar cheese
1/4 teaspoon salt
1/8 teaspoon white pepper
 8 slices Italian bread (1/2 inch
   thick), toasted
1-1/2 pounds sliced cooked turkey
 8 cooked bacon strips, halved
 2 medium tomatoes, sliced
 1 cup (4 ounces) shredded
   Parmesan cheese

In a large saucepan, melt butter over low heat. Stir in flour until smooth; gradually add milk, broth and Worcestershire sauce. Bring to a boil; cook and stir for 2 minutes or until thickened. Stir in the cheese, salt and white pepper until cheese is melted. Remove from the heat.

Place slices of toast on a baking sheet. Top each with turkey, cheese sauce, bacon, tomatoes and Parmesan cheese. Broil 3-4 in. from the heat for 3-4 minutes or until cheese is melted. **Yield:** 8 servings.

HISTORIC HOT BROWNS

A HOT BROWN is an open-faced turkey sandwich, which was created at the Brown Hotel in Louisville by chef Fred K. Schmidt in 1926.

Victory Corn Salad

This crisp vegetable salad from our Test Kitchen adds color and unique freshness to your table.

    3 cans (11 ounces *each*) white *or*
       shoepeg corn, drained
    3 plum tomatoes, seeded and
       chopped
3/4 cup chopped celery
1/2 cup chopped sweet red pepper
1/3 cup thinly sliced green onions
    2 tablespoons minced fresh
       parsley
    3 tablespoons cider vinegar
    3 tablespoons vegetable oil
    1 teaspoon sugar
1/2 teaspoon salt
1/4 teaspoon pepper

In a large bowl, combine the corn, tomatoes, celery, red pepper, onions and parsley. In a small bowl, whisk the vinegar, oil, sugar, salt and pepper. Pour over vegetables and toss to coat. Cover and refrigerate for at least 1 hour or until chilled. **Yield:** 8 servings.

Peach Rice Pudding

This old-fashioned rice pudding is layered with sliced peaches, then topped with a sweet raspberry sauce. It makes for a pretty presentation in parfait glasses.
—Lorraine Wisvader, Millbrook, Illinois

    6 cups milk
    1 cup uncooked long grain rice
1/2 teaspoon salt
1/4 cup sugar
    2 tablespoons butter
1/2 teaspoon vanilla extract
RUBY PORT WINE SAUCE:
    1 cup sugar
    1 cup fresh *or* frozen raspberries
    1 cup red currant jelly
    4 teaspoons cornstarch
1/4 cup port wine *or* red grape juice
    4 cups sliced peeled fresh *or*
       frozen peaches, thawed

In a large saucepan, bring milk, rice and salt just to a boil. Reduce heat; cover and simmer for 25-30 minutes or until rice is tender and most of the liquid is absorbed, stirring occasionally. Remove from the heat. Stir in the sugar, butter and vanilla; cool.

In a small saucepan, combine the sugar, raspberries and jelly. Bring to a boil, stirring constantly. Cook and stir over medium heat for 5 minutes. Press mixture through a fine strainer or sieve; discard seeds. Return raspberry sauce to pan. Combine cornstarch and wine or grape juice until smooth; stir into sauce. Bring to a boil; cook and stir for 1-2 minutes or until thickened. Remove from the heat; cool.

In individual dessert dishes or in a 2-1/2-qt. trifle bowl, layer the rice pudding and peaches. Serve with sauce. **Yield:** 12 servings.

Mint Juleps

(Pictured at right and on page 188)

Our home economists know it wouldn't be Kentucky Derby Day without Mint Juleps! They even offer a nonalcoholic version that tastes just as great.

MINT SYRUP:
- **2 cups sugar**
- **2 cups water**
- **2 cups coarsely chopped loosely packed fresh mint**

BEVERAGE:
- **2/3 to 1-1/4 cups bourbon**
- **Cracked ice**
- **10 mint sprigs**

For syrup, combine the sugar, water and mint in a saucepan. Bring to a boil over medium heat; cook until sugar is dissolved, stirring occasionally. Remove from the heat; cool to room temperature.

Line a mesh strainer with a double layer of cheesecloth or a coffee filter. Strain syrup; discard mint. Cover and refrigerate syrup for at least 2 hours or until chilled.

For each serving, combine 1/4 cup mint syrup and 1-2 tablespoons bourbon. Pour into a glass over cracked ice. Garnish with a mint sprig. **Yield:** 10 servings.

Mock Mint Julep: Prepare mint syrup as directed; after straining, add 1/2 cup lemon juice. Cover and refrigerate for at least 2 hours or until chilled. For each serving, combine 1/2 cup club soda and 1/4 cup mint syrup. Pour into a glass over cracked ice. Garnish with a mint sprig.

Family Traditions

HERE in Louisville, the Kentucky Derby is preceded by 3 weeks of festivities. Practically everyone hosts or attends a Derby party. A popular hot dish to serve is Burgoo, a savory stew made of different cooked meats and vegetables. Folks begin preparing Burgoo days in advance.
—*Sherry Hulsman, Louisville, Kentucky*

Derby Day Brie

Derby Day guests will be impressed when you present this attractive cheese spread.
The mellow flavor of the cheese pairs well with the caramel-flavored topping.
—Annette Grahl, Midway, Kentucky

1 round (13.2 ounces) Brie *or* Camembert cheese, rind removed
3/4 cup finely chopped pecans, toasted
1/4 cup Kahlua
3 tablespoons brown sugar
Apple *or* pear slices
2 tablespoons unsweetened pineapple juice

Place cheese on a microwave-safe serving dish. In a small bowl, combine the pecans, Kahlua and brown sugar; spoon over top of cheese. Microwave on high for 1 minute or until cheese is softened. Toss apple or pear slices with pineapple juice. Serve with cheese. **Yield:** 12-14 servings.

Editor's Note: This recipe was tested in a 1,100-watt microwave.

Ham Biscuits

Our home economists make ordinary biscuits even heartier by stirring in
ground ham. These handheld goodies are great fresh from the oven.

1 cup cubed fully cooked ham
1 cup all-purpose flour
1 teaspoon baking powder
1/4 teaspoon baking soda
1/4 teaspoon *each* onion powder, garlic powder and ground mustard
3 tablespoons shortening
1 teaspoon minced chives
6 tablespoons buttermilk
1 tablespoon butter, melted

In a food processor, process ham until ground; set aside. In a large bowl, combine the flour, baking powder, baking soda, onion powder, garlic powder and mustard. Cut in shortening until mixture is crumbly. Fold in ham and chives. Add buttermilk; stir just until the dough clings together.

Turn onto a lightly floured surface; knead gently 10-12 times. Roll dough to 1/2-in. thickness. Cut with a floured 2-1/2-in. biscuit cutter. Place 1 in. apart on a greased baking sheet. Bake at 450° for 13-15 minutes or until golden brown. Brush with butter. Serve warm. **Yield:** 10 biscuits.

BISCUIT BASICS

FOR BISCUITS that are tender and moist instead of tough and dry, be careful not to overmix or overknead the dough. When reworking the trimmings, handle the dough as little as possible and use as little additional flour as needed.

Cloth Silverware Holder

(Pictured at right)

ADD a bit of pizzazz to your Kentucky Derby buffet by displaying cutlery in a unique way.

Place a large, starched cloth napkin wrong side up on a flat surface. (Our napkin measured 22 inches.) Fold up the bottom third of napkin, forming a rectangle.

Carefully turn the napkin over. Fold bottom folded edge halfway up.

On each short end, tuck about 1-1/2 inches of the napkin under to form a long pocket. Insert silverware into the pocket.

Cheese 'n' Grits Casserole

(Pictured on page 189)

Grits are a staple in Southern cooking. Serve this as a brunch item with bacon or as a side dish for dinner.
—Jennifer Wallis, Goldsboro, North Carolina

4 cups water
1 cup uncooked old-fashioned grits
1/2 teaspoon salt
1/2 cup milk
1/4 cup butter, melted
2 eggs, beaten
1 cup (4 ounces) shredded cheddar cheese
1 tablespoon Worcestershire sauce
1/8 teaspoon cayenne pepper
1/8 teaspoon paprika

In a large saucepan, bring water to a boil. Stir in grits and salt. Reduce heat; cover and simmer for 5-7 minutes or until thickened. Cool slightly. Gradually whisk in the milk, butter and eggs. Stir in the cheese, Worcestershire sauce and cayenne.

Transfer to a greased 2-qt. baking dish. Sprinkle with the paprika. Bake, uncovered, at 350° for 30-35 minutes or until bubbly. Let stand 10 minutes before serving. **Yield:** 8 servings.

Memorable Memorial Day

PROUDLY display your patriotism—and salute the arrival of summer—with a spirited celebration on Memorial Day.

This stars-and-stripes supper features make-ahead qualities that busy cooks will eagerly want to tap into.

Be sure to flag the recipe for Grilled Lemon-Basil Chicken. It conveniently marinates overnight, then quickly cooks on the grill.

By assembling Chilled Tomato Salad early in the day, you can visit with guests instead of spending precious time in the kitchen.

Family and friends will be in their glory when you serve generous slices of Star-Studded Blueberry Pie. (All recipes are shown at right.)

True Blue Menu
(Pictured above)

Chilled Tomato Salad (p. 202)

Grilled Lemon-Basil Chicken (p. 200)

Star-Studded Blueberry Pie (p. 201)

Grilled Lemon-Basil Chicken

(Pictured on page 198)

Garden-fresh basil is put to good use in this super summer recipe.
The chicken turns out moist and tender every time.
—Mary Jo Hopkins, Hobart, Indiana

1 cup minced fresh basil
1 cup vegetable oil
1/2 cup lemon juice
1/4 cup white wine vinegar
2 teaspoons grated lemon peel
3 to 4 garlic cloves, minced
1 teaspoon salt
1/2 teaspoon pepper
8 boneless skinless chicken
   breast halves (6 ounces *each*)

In a small bowl, combine the first eight ingredients. Pour 1-1/2 cups into a large resealable plastic bag; add chicken. Seal bag and turn to coat; refrigerate for 4 hours or overnight, turning occasionally. Cover and refrigerate remaining marinade for basting.

Drain and discard marinade. Grill chicken, covered, over medium heat for 6-8 minutes on each side or until juices run clear, basting occasionally with reserved marinade. **Yield:** 8 servings.

CUTTING FRESH BASIL

FRESH BASIL is a wonderful addition to recipes and can be a pretty garnish, too.

But chopping one leaf at a time can be tedious. To quickly chop a lot of basil, try this:

Before cutting the basil, sprinkle a few drops of olive or vegetable oil on the leaves and gently rub to evenly coat the leaves. This will help prevent the leaves from darkening.

Stack several basil leaves and roll them into a tight tube. Slice the leaves widthwise into narrow pieces to create long thin strips. If you'd like smaller pieces, simply chop the strips.

Star-Studded Blueberry Pie

(Pictured at right and on page 199)

Family and friends say this pleasing pie is better than a popular one served at a local restaurant. If desired, use gooseberries for half of the blueberries.
—Nancy Barker, Silverton, Oregon

    4 cups fresh *or* frozen blueberries
    1 cup sugar
    1/4 cup quick-cooking tapioca
    1 tablespoon lemon juice
    1/4 teaspoon salt
Pastry for double-crust pie (9 inches)
    2 tablespoons butter

In a bowl, combine the blueberries, sugar, tapioca, lemon juice and salt; toss gently. Let stand for 15 minutes.

Line a 9-in. pie plate with bottom pastry; add filling. Dot with butter; flute edges.

Cover edges loosely with foil. Bake at 400° for 25 minutes. Remove foil; bake 20-25 minutes longer or until set. Cool on a wire rack.

From remaining pastry, cut out 15 large stars with a 2-in. cookie cutter and 15 small stars with a 1/2-in. cookie cutter. Place on an ungreased baking sheet. Bake at 350° for 5-10 minutes or until golden brown. Remove to wire racks to cool. Randomly place stars over cooled pie. **Yield:** 8 servings.

Roasted Corn and Black Bean Salsa

Sometimes I'll turn this into individual appetizers by putting a spoonful of salsa in a tortilla chip scoop, then topping with a small dollop of sour cream.
—Douglas Wasdyke, Effort, Pennsylvania

    2 cups frozen corn, thawed and
        undrained
    1/4 cup chopped sweet red pepper
    1/4 cup chopped green pepper
    1/4 cup vegetable oil
    2 garlic cloves, chopped
    1 teaspoon ground cumin
    1 teaspoon chili powder
Dash salt
    1 can (15 ounces) black beans,
        rinsed and drained

    1 tablespoon minced fresh cilantro
Tortilla chips

In a small bowl, combine the corn and peppers. In another bowl, whisk the oil, garlic, cumin, chili powder and salt. Drizzle over vegetables and toss to coat. Place in a single layer in an ungreased 15-in. x 10-in. x 1-in. baking pan.

Bake, uncovered, at 425° for 10-15 minutes or until peppers are tender. Cool slightly. Transfer to a serving bowl; stir in the black beans and cilantro. Serve with tortilla chips. **Yield:** 3 cups.

Chilled Tomato Salad

(Pictured on page 198)

I use homegrown veggies to make this special summer salad. It's popular at picnics.
—Cathleen Bushman, Geneva, Illinois

3 large tomatoes, peeled and
  sliced
2 medium cucumbers, sliced
2 medium sweet red peppers,
  sliced into rings
2 medium green peppers, sliced
  into rings
DRESSING:
1/4 cup vegetable oil
1/4 cup minced fresh parsley
2 tablespoons white vinegar

2 teaspoons prepared mustard
1 teaspoon sugar
1 garlic clove, minced
1/4 teaspoon pepper

In a large serving bowl, combine the tomatoes, cucumbers and peppers. In a jar with a tight-fitting lid, combine the dressing ingredients; shake well. Pour over vegetables and toss gently. Cover and refrigerate for at least 3 hours. Serve with a slotted spoon. **Yield:** 8 servings.

Mediterranean Pasta Salad

A zesty mayonnaise dressing is a deliciously different twist in this chilled salad.
You can substitute fresh peas for the frozen ones if desired.
—Jodi Stewart, Beyer, Pennsylvania

2 cups uncooked medium pasta
  shells
1 jar (6-1/2 ounces) marinated
  artichoke hearts, drained
1 cup frozen peas, thawed
1 medium red onion, chopped
1 medium sweet red pepper,
  chopped
1 small zucchini, chopped
1 can (2-1/4 ounces) chopped
  ripe olives, drained
1/2 cup grated Parmesan cheese
1/2 cup mayonnaise
1/2 cup creamy Italian salad
  dressing
1 teaspoon minced fresh parsley
1/2 teaspoon dill weed
1/2 teaspoon pepper

Cook pasta according to package directions; drain and rinse in cold water. In a large bowl, combine the pasta, artichokes, peas, onion, red pepper, zucchini and olives.

In a small bowl, combine the Parmesan cheese, mayonnaise, salad dressing, parsley, dill and pepper. Pour over pasta mixture and toss to coat. Cover and refrigerate until serving. **Yield:** 10 servings.

Club Roll-Ups

(Pictured at right)

Packed with meat, cheese and olives, these roll-ups are always a hit at parties.
—Linda Searl, Pampa, Texas

1 package (3 ounces) cream cheese, softened
1/2 cup ranch salad dressing
2 tablespoons ranch salad dressing mix
8 bacon strips, cooked and crumbled
1/2 cup finely chopped onion
1 can (2-1/4 ounces) sliced ripe olives, drained
1 jar (2 ounces) diced pimientos, drained
1/4 cup diced canned jalapeno peppers
8 flour tortillas (10 inches)

8 thin slices deli ham
8 thin slices deli turkey
8 thin slices deli roast beef
2 cups (8 ounces) shredded cheddar cheese

In a small mixing bowl, beat cream cheese, ranch dressing and dressing mix until well blended. In another bowl, combine bacon, onion, olives, pimientos and jalapenos.

Spread cream cheese mixture over tortillas; layer with ham, turkey and roast beef. Sprinkle with bacon mixture and cheddar cheese; roll up. **Yield:** 8 servings.

Chipotle Rhubarb Sauce

Folks are surprised to hear that rhubarb is this barbecue sauce's secret. Chipotle peppers add a little kick.
—Deborah Clayton, Squamish, British Columbia

2 cups chopped fresh *or* frozen rhubarb
1 cup ketchup
1/2 cup water
1 small onion, chopped
1/4 cup packed brown sugar
2 tablespoons cider vinegar
2 tablespoons Dijon mustard
2 tablespoons chipotle peppers in adobo sauce

2 teaspoons Worcestershire sauce
2 garlic cloves, peeled
1/2 teaspoon salt

In a large saucepan, combine all ingredients. Bring to a boil. Reduce heat; simmer, uncovered, for 18-22 minutes or until rhubarb is tender. Cool slightly.

In a blender or food processor, process the sauce until smooth. Serve warm. **Yield:** 3 cups.

Fruit-Topped Dessert Squares

*I love to try new dessert recipes...and so does my family! We really enjoy these
chocolate chip cookie bars dressed up with strawberries and a fluffy white-chocolate mixture.*
— *Theresa Hoffmann, Hatley, Wisconsin*

1 cup butter, softened
1 cup packed brown sugar
1/2 cup sugar
2 eggs
1 teaspoon vanilla extract
2-1/4 cups all-purpose flour
1 teaspoon baking soda
1/2 teaspoon salt
2 cups (12 ounces) semisweet
   chocolate chips
TOPPING:
2 squares (1 ounce *each*) white
   baking chocolate, chopped
2 tablespoons milk
1 package (8 ounces) cream
   cheese, softened
1/4 cup confectioners' sugar
1 cup whipped topping
2 cups halved fresh strawberries
1 can (11 ounces) mandarin
   oranges, well drained

1/4 cup semisweet chocolate chips
1 tablespoon butter

In a large mixing bowl, cream butter and sugars. Add eggs, one at a time, beating well after each addition. Beat in vanilla. Combine the flour, baking soda and salt; gradually add to creamed mixture. Stir in chocolate chips.

Spread into a greased 15-in. x 10-in. x 1-in. baking pan. Bake at 350° for 20-22 minutes or until golden brown. Cool on a wire rack.

In a microwave-safe bowl, combine white chocolate and milk. Microwave, uncovered, on high for 30-60 seconds or until chocolate is melted. Stir until smooth; set aside. In a small mixing bowl, beat cream cheese and confectioners' sugar until smooth. Gradually beat in white chocolate mixture. Fold in whipped topping. Spread over crust.

Arrange strawberries and oranges over the top. In a microwave-safe bowl, melt chocolate chips and butter; stir until smooth. Drizzle over fruit. Refrigerate for 30 minutes or until chilled. Cut into bars. **Yield:** 3 dozen.

Citrus Flank Steak

A sunny marinade fabulously flavors flank steak. Round out the meal with wild rice and a salad.
— *Linda Gronewaller, Hutchinson, Kansas*

1 beef flank steak (1-1/2 pounds)
1/2 cup grapefruit juice
1/4 cup packed brown sugar
3 tablespoons lemon juice
2 tablespoons lime juice
2 tablespoons Worcestershire
   sauce
2 teaspoons grated lemon peel

Score surface of steak with 1/4-in.-deep diagonal cuts, making diamond shapes. In a large resealable plastic bag, combine the remaining ingredients; add steak. Seal bag and turn to coat; refrigerate for 6-8 hours, turning occasionally.

Drain and discard marinade. Grill steak, covered, over medium heat for 6-7 minutes on each side or until meat reaches desired doneness (for medium-rare, a meat thermometer should read 145°; medium, 160°; well-done, 170°). Let stand for 5 minutes. Thinly slice across the grain. **Yield:** 6 servings.

Beer Cheese

(Pictured at right)

*I like to serve this zesty cheese spread
with crackers and veggie dippers.
It's great to take along to picnics.*
— Pat Wartman
Bethlehem, Pennsylvania

1/3 cup beer *or* nonalcoholic beer
4 ounces cream cheese, cubed
3 ounces crumbled blue cheese
1/4 cup Dijon mustard
2 tablespoons grated onion
1/2 to 1 teaspoon hot pepper sauce
1 garlic clove, minced
3 cups (12 ounces) shredded
    cheddar cheese
Assorted crackers

In a small saucepan, bring beer to a boil. Remove from the heat and cool to room temperature.

In a food processor, combine the beer, cream cheese, blue cheese, mustard, onion, hot pepper sauce and garlic. Add cheddar cheese; cover and process until well blended. Transfer to a bowl. Cover and refrigerate overnight.

Let cheese stand at room temperature for 30 minutes before serving. Serve with crackers. **Yield:** 3 cups.

GI CAP NAPKIN FOLD

AS A HAT'S OFF to all soldiers, turn napkins into GI caps! (See the photo above.) Start with well-starched tan, khaki, army green or grey fabric napkins.

1. Fold the napkin in half. With the fold at the top, bring in the sides so that they meet in the center.

2. Lift up the top layer on each side and pull out, making a triangle at the top.

3. On each side, fold the outer half of each triangle underneath.

4. Fold up the top layer of the bottom edge so that it aligns with the bottom edge of the triangles.

5. Fold up the same edge again to cover about half of the triangles. Turn the napkin over and repeat Steps 4 and 5.

6. Stand the napkin up, pulling the folded sides of the napkin apart and denting the top.

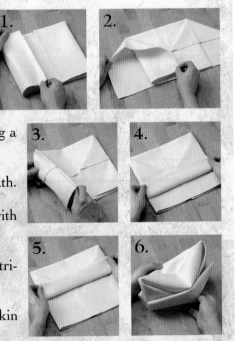

Bursting with Berries!

WHETHER you pick your own, grow them in a garden or buy them at the grocery store, a bounty of fresh berries is the highlight of summer.

But the season often seems to come and go too quickly. So why not plan a party centered around these mouth-watering morsels today?

Sweet and savory slices of deliciously different Raspberry Pork Roast will bring rave reviews to the table.

Surprise relatives and friends with a fun, fruity side dish such as Blueberry Tossed Salad.

Genoise with Fruit 'n' Cream Filling features assorted fresh berries, tender cake layers and an irresistible sweet filling. (All recipes are shown at right.)

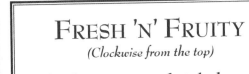

Blueberry Tossed Salad

(Pictured on page 207)

My friends look forward to having this salad at picnics throughout summer. It's deliciously different.
—*Joan Solberg, Ashland, Wisconsin*

8 cups torn mixed salad greens
2 cups fresh blueberries
1 cup (4 ounces) shredded
  Monterey Jack cheese
1/2 cup sliced almonds, toasted
1/2 cup sunflower kernels
DRESSING:
  1/2 cup vegetable oil
  1/3 cup sugar
  1/4 cup chopped onion
    3 tablespoons red wine vinegar
1-1/2 teaspoons ground mustard
1-1/2 teaspoons poppy seeds

In a large bowl, combine the greens, blueberries, cheese, almonds and sunflower kernels. In a blender, combine the oil, sugar, onion, vinegar and mustard; cover and process until blended. Stir in poppy seeds. Drizzle over salad and toss to coat. **Yield:** 10 servings.

Lemon Torte with Fresh Berries

I appreciate recipes like this that can be made ahead and that are guaranteed to be great. A cool slice is so refreshing on warm days.
—*Edith Lyon, Martinsburg, West Virginia*

1 package (3 ounces) lemon
  gelatin
1/2 cup boiling water
1/3 cup lemonade concentrate
1 can (12 ounces) evaporated
  milk
3 cups angel food cake cubes
3 cups fresh raspberries *or*
  sliced strawberries
1 tablespoon sugar

In a large mixing bowl, dissolve gelatin in boiling water. Stir in lemonade concentrate and milk. Cover and refrigerate for 1-2 hours.

Place the cake cubes in a 9-in. springform pan coated with nonstick cooking spray. Beat gelatin mixture on medium speed for 5 minutes or until fluffy; pour over cake cubes. Cover and chill for 4 hours or until firm. In a small bowl, combine the berries and sugar; chill for 2 hours.

Just before serving, carefully run a knife around edge of pan to loosen; remove sides of pan. Spoon berry mixture over torte. Refrigerate leftovers. **Yield:** 12 servings.

Genoise with Fruit 'n' Cream Filling

(Pictured at right and on page 207)

Sweet syrup soaks into the tender layers of this sponge cake from our Test Kitchen. Complete the presentation with sweetened whipped cream and assorted fresh berries.

6 eggs, lightly beaten
1 cup sugar
1 teaspoon grated lemon peel
1 teaspoon lemon extract
1 cup all-purpose flour
1/2 cup butter, melted and cooled
SUGAR SYRUP:
   3 tablespoons boiling water
   2 tablespoons sugar
1/4 cup cold water
1-1/2 teaspoons lemon extract
FILLING:
   1 cup heavy whipping cream
1/2 cup confectioners' sugar
   1 teaspoon vanilla extract,
     optional
   3 cups mixed fresh berries

CAKE CAPERS

Genoise (pronounced zhayn-WAHZ) is a rich, delicate sponge cake that contains lots of eggs and sugar but little or no fat. It was created in Genoa, Italy and adapted by the French.

Line two greased 9-in. round baking pans with waxed paper and grease the paper; set aside. In a large heatproof mixing bowl, combine eggs and sugar; place over a large saucepan filled with 1-2 in. of simmering water. Heat over low heat, stirring occasionally, until mixture reaches 110°, about 8-10 minutes.

Remove from the heat; add lemon peel and extract. Beat on high speed until mixture is lemon-colored and more than doubles in volume. Fold in flour, 1/4 cup at a time. Gently fold in butter. Spread into prepared pans.

Bake at 350° for 25-30 minutes or until a toothpick inserted near the center comes out clean. Cool for 10 minutes before removing from the pans to wire racks to cool completely.

In a bowl, combine boiling water and sugar; stir until sugar is dissolved. Stir in cold water and extract. Using a fork, evenly poke 1/2-in.-deep holes in each cake. Spoon sugar syrup over cake surface. In a small mixing bowl, beat cream until it begins to thicken. Add sugar and vanilla if desired; beat until soft peaks form.

Place one cake on a serving platter; spread with half of the whipped cream and top with half of the berries. Repeat layers. Store in the refrigerator. **Yield:** 10-12 servings.

Raspberry Roast Pork

(Pictured on page 206)

Our home economists pair a sage- and pepper-seasoned pork roast with raspberry sauce for an easy, yet elegant entree.

4-1/2 cups fresh *or* frozen
    raspberries
3 tablespoons sugar
1/2 cup unsweetened apple juice
1/4 cup red wine vinegar
2 garlic cloves, minced
3/4 teaspoon rubbed sage, *divided*
1 tablespoon cornstarch
1 tablespoon water
1/2 teaspoon salt
1/2 teaspoon pepper
1 boneless whole pork loin
    roast (3-1/2 to 4 pounds)

Place raspberries in a bowl; sprinkle with sugar and mash. Let stand for 15 minutes; mash again. Strain, reserving juice; discard pulp and seeds.

In a small saucepan, combine the raspberry juice, apple juice, vinegar, garlic and 1/4 teaspoon sage. Simmer, uncovered, for 5 minutes. In a small bowl, combine cornstarch and water until smooth; stir into raspberry juice mixture until smooth. Bring to a boil; cook and stir for 1 minute or until thickened.

Combine the salt, pepper and remaining sage; rub over roast. Place fat side up on a rack in a shallow roasting pan. Spread with 1/2 cup raspberry sauce. Bake, uncovered, at 350° for 1-3/4 to 2 hours or until a meat thermometer reads 160°. Let stand for 10-15 minutes before slicing. Meanwhile, reheat the remaining raspberry sauce; serve with pork. **Yield:** 8-10 servings.

BERRY BASICS

FOR maximum freshness and flavor, follow these tips for buying and storing berries.
- Purchase berries that are brightly colored and plump. Blueberries should have a silver frosted appearance. While raspberries and blackberries should not have their hulls attached, strawberries should.
- At home, remove any berries that are soft, shriveled or moldy. Place in a single layer on a paper towel-lined plate, cover loosely and refrigerate. Don't wash berries until ready to use.
- Berries are very perishable. Blackberries, raspberries and strawberries stay fresh for up to 2 days. Blueberries should be used within 5 days.
- Whole berries can also be frozen for up to 1 year. Wash, blot dry and arrange in a single layer on a jelly-roll pan. Freeze until firm, then transfer to a heavy-duty resealable plastic bag. You can also freeze sliced or halved strawberries. Place in a heavy-duty resealable plastic bag and sprinkle with sugar if desired; seal bag.
- One pint of blackberries yields 1-1/2 to 2 cups; one pint of blueberries or raspberries equals 2 cups; one pint of strawberries yields 1-1/2 to 2 cups, sliced.

Berry Bruschetta

(Pictured at right)

Our Test Kitchen is the source of this fantastic fruit bruschetta. It's a tasty twist from the traditional tomato variety and can be served as an appetizer or a dessert.

1 French bread baguette
  (1 pound)
2 tablespoons olive oil
1-1/2 cups chopped fresh
  strawberries
3/4 cup chopped peeled fresh
  peaches
1-1/2 teaspoons minced fresh mint
1/2 cup Mascarpone cheese

Cut baguette into 32 slices, about 1/2 in. thick; place on ungreased baking sheets. Brush with oil. Broil 6-8 in. from the heat for 1-2 minutes or until lightly toasted.

In a small bowl, combine the strawberries, peaches and mint. Spread each slice of bread with cheese; top with fruit mixture. Broil for 1-2 minutes or until cheese is slightly melted. Serve immediately. **Yield:** 32 appetizers.

Strawberry Ice

I came across this delightful dessert while looking for a simple recipe to get my daughter some experience in the kitchen. She loves this treat and asks to make it often.
— KeriAnne Zimmerman, Glen Burnie, Maryland

1-1/2 cups water
1/2 cup honey
2 tablespoons lemon juice
3 cups fresh strawberries,
  hulled

In a blender, combine all ingredients; cover and process until smooth. Pour into an 8-in. square dish; cover and freeze for 2-1/2 hours or until almost frozen.

Spoon mixture into a blender; cover and process until smooth. Return to the dish; cover and freeze until firm, about 2 hours. About 15 minutes before serving, place dessert in the refrigerator to soften. **Yield:** 1 quart.

Rhubarb Blueberry Crisp

Although butter and sugar were scarce during World War II, my mom would save her rations to make this tasty treat using wild blueberries and homegrown rhubarb.
—Lydia Garcia, Gouldsboro, Maine

3 cups chopped fresh *or* frozen rhubarb
2 cups fresh *or* frozen blueberries
1/2 cup sugar
2 tablespoons all-purpose flour
TOPPING:
1/2 cup packed brown sugar
1/3 cup all-purpose flour
1/4 cup cold butter
1/2 cup slivered almonds, toasted

In a large bowl, toss rhubarb and blueberries with sugar and flour. Transfer to a greased 2-qt. baking dish. In a small bowl, combine brown sugar and flour; cut in butter until mixture resembles coarse crumbs. Stir in almonds. Sprinkle over fruit. Bake at 350° for 1 hour or until bubbly. Serve warm. **Yield:** 4-6 servings.

Editor's Note: If using frozen rhubarb, measure rhubarb while still frozen, then thaw completely. Drain in a colander, but do not press liquid out. If using frozen blueberries, do not thaw.

Chicken with Mango-Raspberry Salsa

The slight spice from the jalapeno pairs well with the sweet mango and raspberry salsa in this grilled entree. The recipe comes from our Test Kitchen.

3/4 cup chopped peeled mango
1/3 cup chopped sweet onion
1/4 cup minced fresh cilantro
3 tablespoons lime juice
1 tablespoon chopped seeded jalapeno pepper
1/2 teaspoon sugar
1 garlic clove, minced
1/2 teaspoon salt
1/2 teaspoon garlic powder
1/2 teaspoon pepper
6 boneless skinless chicken breast halves
3/4 cup fresh raspberries

For salsa, in a small bowl, combine the first seven ingredients. Cover and refrigerate for 1 hour.

Combine the salt, garlic powder and pepper; sprinkle over both sides of chicken. Grill chicken, covered, over medium heat for 6-8 minutes on each side or until juices run clear. Just before serving, gently fold raspberries into salsa. Serve with chicken. **Yield:** 6 servings.

Editor's Note: When cutting or seeding hot peppers, use rubber or plastic gloves to protect your hands. Avoid touching your face.

Sangria Gelatin Ring

(Pictured at right)

This gelatin is enjoyed by everyone because you just can't go wrong with fresh berries.
—*Nicole Nemeth, Komoka, Ontario*

    2 **packages (3 ounces** *each***)**
       lemon gelatin
1-1/2 **cups boiling white wine** *or*
       white grape juice
    2 **cups club soda, chilled**
    1 **cup sliced fresh strawberries**
    1 **cup fresh** *or* **frozen blueberries**
    1 **cup fresh** *or* **frozen**
       raspberries
 1/2 **cup green grapes, halved**

In a large bowl, dissolve the gelatin in boiling wine or grape juice; cool for 10 minutes. Stir in the club soda; refrigerate until set but not firm, about 45 minutes.

Fold in the berries and grapes. Pour into a 6-cup ring mold coated with nonstick cooking spray. Refrigerate for 4 hours or until set. Invert and unmold onto a serving platter. **Yield:** 10 servings.

Three-Berry Jam

I sold jars of this pretty berry jam at craft fairs. It's a wonderful way to preserve the summer gems.
—*Bernadette Colvin, Tomball, Texas*

    4 **cups fresh blueberries**
    3 **cups fresh strawberries**
    2 **cups fresh raspberries**
1/4 **cup lemon juice**
    2 **packages (1-3/4 ounces** *each***)**
       powdered fruit pectin
    7 **cups sugar**

In a large saucepan, combine berries and lemon juice; crush slightly. Stir in pectin. Bring to a full rolling boil over high heat, stirring constantly. Stir in sugar; return to a full rolling boil. Boil for 1 minute, stirring constantly.

Remove from the heat; skim off foam. Ladle hot mixture into nine hot pint jars and one hot half-pint jar, leaving 1/4-in. headspace. Adjust caps. Process for 15 minutes in a boiling-water bath. Remove jars to wire racks to cool completely. **Yield:** 9 pints and 1 half-pint.

Raspberry Muffins

(Pictured at far right, bottom)

These muffins are my family's favorite and can be made with blueberries as well.
Serve them for breakfast with jam or for dessert with ice cream.
—*Margaret Pache, Mesa, Arizona*

6 tablespoons butter, softened
1 cup sugar
2 eggs
2-1/2 cups all-purpose flour
2 teaspoons baking powder
1/4 teaspoon baking soda
1 teaspoon grated lemon peel
1 cup lemon yogurt
1/4 cup milk
2 cups fresh *or* frozen raspberries
TOPPING:
1 cup quick-cooking oats
1/4 cup sugar
1/4 cup butter, melted
3 tablespoons seedless
   raspberry preserves

In a large mixing bowl, cream the butter and sugar. Add eggs; beat well. Combine the flour, baking powder, baking soda and lemon peel; add to the creamed mixture alternately with yogurt and milk. Gently fold in raspberries. Fill greased or paper-lined muffin cups three-fourths full.

Combine the topping ingredients; spoon over batter. Bake at 375° for 25-30 minutes or until a toothpick comes out clean. Cool for 5 minutes before removing from pans to wire racks. Serve warm. **Yield:** 1-1/2 dozen.

Editor's Note: If using frozen raspberries, do not thaw before adding to batter.

Berry Puff Pancake

Breakfast is my husband's favorite meal of the day.
I use our homegrown blueberries in this sweet morning treat.
—*Cecilia Morgan, Milwaukie, Oregon*

1 tablespoon butter
3 eggs
3/4 cup milk
3/4 cup all-purpose flour
1/2 teaspoon salt
BERRY TOPPING:
1 cup fresh raspberries
1 cup fresh blueberries
1 cup sliced fresh strawberries
1/3 cup orange marmalade
2 tablespoons confectioners'
   sugar

Place the butter in a 9-in. pie plate; place in a 400° oven for 4-5 minutes or until melted. Meanwhile, in a small bowl, whisk the eggs and milk. In another small bowl, combine the flour and salt; whisk in egg mixture until smooth. Pour into prepared pie plate. Bake for 15-20 minutes or until sides are crisp and golden brown.

In a large bowl, gently combine the berries and marmalade. Sprinkle pancake with confectioners' sugar; fill with berry mixture. Serve immediately. **Yield:** 6 servings.

Grandma's Berry Tart

(Pictured at right, top)

With seven children and 12 grandchildren, our household is always busy. But everyone makes time for a slice of this fruity treat from my grandma.
—Lorraine Nuzzo
Staten Island, New York

1-1/4 cups all-purpose flour
  1/4 teaspoon salt
  1/4 cup cold butter
  1/4 cup shortening
  5 to 6 tablespoons cold water
FILLING:
  1 cup *each* fresh blueberries,
    raspberries, blackberries and
    sliced strawberries
  1/2 cup sugar
  2 tablespoons cornstarch
  2 teaspoons grated lemon peel
  1 teaspoon vanilla extract
  1/2 teaspoon ground ginger
  1/4 teaspoon ground allspice
Milk
Additional sugar
TOPPING:
  1/4 cup sugar
  3 tablespoons all-purpose flour
  2 tablespoons cold butter

In a small bowl, combine flour and salt; cut in butter and shortening until crumbly. Gradually add water, tossing with a fork until dough forms a ball. On a lightly floured surface, roll out dough into a 13-in. circle. Transfer to a 9-in. deep-dish pie plate.

Place the berries in a large bowl. Combine the sugar, cornstarch, lemon peel, vanilla, ginger and allspice; add to berries and toss gently to coat. Pour into crust. Fold edges of pastry over filling. Brush folded pastry with milk; sprinkle with sugar.

For topping, combine the sugar and flour in a small bowl; cut in butter until crumbly. Sprinkle over filling. Bake at 400° for 50-55 minutes or until pastry is golden brown. Cool on a wire rack. **Yield:** 6-8 servings.

PASTRY SCRAP SNACKS

DON'T toss out any of the pastry scraps when making Grandma's Berry Tart. Form the scraps into a ball; roll out very thin. Brush with melted butter, then sprinkle with cinnamon and sugar; roll up. Cut into 1-inch slices and place cut side down on a greased baking sheet. Bake the no-fuss delights alongside the tart until they're golden brown.

Raspberry Mousse

This creamy, smooth mousse from our Test Kitchen is a refreshing finale to any summer meal.

2 cups fresh raspberries
1/2 cup sugar
1 tablespoon lemon juice
1-1/2 teaspoons unflavored gelatin
1/4 cup cold water
1 cup heavy whipping cream

Place the raspberries in a food processor; cover and puree. Strain and discard seeds. Place puree in a bowl. Stir in sugar and lemon juice; set aside.

In a small saucepan, sprinkle gelatin over cold water; let stand for 1 minute. Stir over low heat until gelatin is completely dissolved. Stir into raspberry mixture. Refrigerate until slightly thickened, about 1 hour.

Transfer to a mixing bowl. Beat on high speed until foamy. Gradually add cream; beat until thickened, about 2 minutes. Spoon into dessert dishes. Cover and refrigerate for 1-2 hours or until set. **Yield:** 8 servings.

Blueberry Cheese Torte

*Blueberries are plentiful here in the Northwest.
I keep my freezer stocked so I can make this torte any time of year.
—John Eilman, Sequim, Washington*

1-1/2 cups finely chopped
    macadamia nuts
3/4 cup all-purpose flour
1/2 cup packed brown sugar
6 tablespoons butter, melted
3 packages (8 ounces *each*)
    cream cheese, softened
1 can (14 ounces) sweetened
    condensed milk
3 eggs, lightly beaten
1/4 cup lemon juice
3 cups fresh *or* frozen blueberries
1-1/2 teaspoons cornstarch
1 tablespoon cold water

In a bowl, combine the nuts, flour and brown sugar; stir in butter. Set aside 1/3 cup for the filling. Press remaining nut mixture onto the bottom and 2 in. up the sides of a greased 9-in. springform pan. Place pan on a baking sheet. Bake at 350° for 10 minutes. Cool on a wire rack.

In a large mixing bowl, beat cream cheese and milk until smooth. Add eggs; beat on low speed just until combined. Add lemon juice; beat just until blended. Stir in reserved nut mixture. Pour into crust.

Return pan to baking sheet. Bake at 350° for 40-45 minutes or until center is almost set. Cool on a wire rack for 10 minutes. Carefully run a knife around edge of pan to loosen; cool 1 hour longer. Refrigerate overnight.

In a large saucepan, cook blueberries over medium heat until heated through. Combine cornstarch and water until smooth; stir into blueberries. Bring to a boil; cook and stir for 2 minutes or until thickened. Cool; cover and refrigerate until serving. Remove sides of springform pan. Spoon blueberry topping over cheesecake. Refrigerate leftovers. **Yield:** 12 servings.

Chilled Mixed Berry Soup

(Pictured at right)

As a lovely addition to a luncheon menu, our home economists recommend this cool, fruity soup featuring three kinds of berries.

1 cup sliced fresh strawberries
1/2 cup fresh raspberries
1/2 cup fresh blackberries
1 cup unsweetened apple juice
1/2 cup water
1/4 cup sugar
2 tablespoons lemon juice
Dash ground nutmeg
2 cartons (6 ounces *each*) raspberry yogurt

In a heavy saucepan, combine the berries, apple juice, water, sugar, lemon juice and nutmeg. Cook, uncovered, over low heat for 20 minutes or until berries are softened. Strain, reserving juice. Press berry mixture through a fine meshed sieve; discard seeds. Add pulp to reserved juice; cover and refrigerate until chilled.

Place berry mixture in a food processor or blender; add yogurt. Cover and process until smooth. Pour into bowls. **Yield:** 4 servings.

A "SOUPER" SERVING SUGGESTION

SKIP ordinary soup mugs or bowls and serve Chilled Mixed Berry Soup in special stemmed glasses. And for a lovely color contrast, top each serving with a blackberry and fresh mint leaves.

Sweet 16 Celebration

SWEET 16 parties are all the rage these days. But you don't have to break the bank to celebrate in style.

A fun-filled Mexican fiesta with friends is all you need to make cherished memories for your soon-to-be grown-up girl.

Welcome guests to a taco bar buffet with refreshing Mock Strawberry Margaritas.

Then have the teens fix their own nachos and hard- and soft-shell tacos with Mexican Beef and Spicy Seasoned Chicken.

Round out the casual get-together with fixings like shredded lettuce, sliced ripe olives, shredded cheese, sour cream, Traditional Salsa and Spicy Refried Beans. (All recipes are shown at right.)

TEEN SCENE

(Clockwise from top left)

Mock Strawberry Margaritas (p. 221)

Traditional Salsa (p. 220)

Spicy Refried Beans (p. 224)

Mexican Beef (p. 222)

Spicy Seasoned Chicken (p. 220)

Spicy Seasoned Chicken

(Pictured on page 218)

*Seasoned with a zesty combination of garlic and chili powders and cumin, this specialty from
our Test Kitchen can be used as a fabulous filling for tacos, burritos and more.*

1 pound boneless skinless
  chicken breasts, cut into
  strips
1 teaspoon ground cumin
1 teaspoon garlic powder
1 teaspoon chili powder
1/2 teaspoon salt
1 tablespoon vegetable oil

Tortilla chips, taco shells *or* flour tortillas
Shredded cheddar cheese, sliced ripe olives, shredded
  lettuce, sour cream and salsa, optional

In a large skillet, saute the chicken, cumin, garlic powder,
chili powder and salt in oil until chicken is no longer pink.
Serve with tortilla chips, taco shells or flour tortillas. Garnish
with optional toppings. **Yield:** 4 servings.

Traditional Salsa

(Pictured on page 219)

*Why buy bottled salsa when you can make a more flavorful variety at home without a lot of effort?
You may want to double the recipe because it's sure to be a hit!*
—Katie Rose, Pewaukee, Wisconsin

5 plum tomatoes, seeded and
  chopped
1/2 cup chopped onion
1 jalapeno pepper, seeded and
  chopped
1 tablespoon lime juice
1 garlic clove, minced

1/4 teaspoon salt
1/4 cup minced fresh cilantro
Tortilla chips

In a small bowl, combine the first seven ingredients. Cover
and refrigerate until serving. Serve with tortilla chips. **Yield:**
2-1/2 cups.

SURPRISE PARTY INVITATION

KEEP your favorite teen guessing about her very own Sweet 16 event
by making it a surprise party. When you pen the invitations, remember to tell guests not to spill the beans about the bash. For an extra
reminder, tuck a few dried beans into the envelope. Don't forget to
end your invite with a happy "adios!"

Not-Fried Ice Cream Cake

(Pictured at right)

Our home economists created this ice cream cake to mimic the fabulous flavor of a popular dessert in many Mexican restaurants. It's a no-fuss treat that feeds a crowd. Plus, it's conveniently made ahead.

  1 **cup cornflake crumbs**
1/3 **cup sugar**
1/3 **cup butter, melted**
3/4 **teaspoon ground cinnamon**
1/2 **gallon butter pecan ice cream, softened**
  4 **tablespoons honey,** *divided*

In a small bowl, combine the cornflake crumbs, sugar, butter and cinnamon; set aside 1/2 cup. Press remaining crumb mixture into a greased 9-in. springform pan. Spoon half of the ice cream over crust. Sprinkle with reserved crumb mixture; drizzle with 2 tablespoons honey. Cover and freeze for 2 hours.

Top with remaining ice cream. Cover and freeze for 8 hours or overnight.

Remove from the freezer 5 minutes before serving. Remove sides of pan; drizzle with remaining honey. **Yield:** 12-16 servings.

Mock Strawberry Margaritas

(Pictured on page 218)

These refreshing strawberry smoothies from our home economists pair well with spicy Mexican fare. They're a fun addition to any table.

  6 **lime wedges**
  3 **tablespoons plus 1/3 cup sugar,** *divided*
1-1/4 **cups water**
  1 **can (6 ounces) frozen limeade concentrate, partially thawed**
  1 **package (16 ounces) frozen unsweetened strawberries**
25 **ice cubes**

Using lime wedges, moisten the rim of six glasses. Set limes aside for garnish. Sprinkle 3 tablespoons sugar on a plate; hold each glass upside down and dip rim into sugar. Set aside. Discard remaining sugar on plate.

In a blender, combine the water, limeade concentrate, strawberries, ice cubes and remaining sugar; cover and blend until smooth. Pour into prepared glasses. Garnish with reserved limes. Serve immediately. **Yield:** 6 servings.

Green Rice

*Instead of reaching for a box of Mexican rice, round out the
Southwestern menu with this cilantro-spinach dish from our Test Kitchen.*

1 medium green pepper
1 jalapeno pepper
2 cups water, *divided*
1 package (10 ounces) fresh
  baby spinach
2 cups fresh cilantro leaves
2 green onions, chopped
1-1/2 cups uncooked long grain rice
3 tablespoons vegetable oil
1 teaspoon salt

Broil green pepper and jalapeno 4 in. from the heat until skins blister, about 4 minutes. With tongs, rotate peppers a quarter turn. Broil and rotate until all sides are blistered and blackened. Immediately place peppers in a bowl; cover and let stand for 15 minutes. Peel off and discard charred skin. Remove stems and seeds; chop peppers.

Place 1 cup of water in a food processor. Add the peppers, spinach, cilantro and onions; cover and process until smooth.

In a large skillet, saute rice in oil until golden brown. Stir in spinach puree, salt and remaining water. Bring to a boil. Reduce heat; cover and simmer 15 minutes. Remove from heat. Let stand 10 minutes before serving. **Yield:** 5 servings.

Mexican Beef

(Pictured on page 219)

Purchased taco seasoning mixes can't compare to our home economists' flavorful blend.

1 pound ground beef
2 teaspoons chili powder
1-1/2 teaspoons ground cumin
1/4 teaspoon ground coriander
1/2 teaspoon salt
1/2 teaspoon dried oregano
1/2 teaspoon cornstarch
1/3 cup water
Tortilla chips, taco shells *or* flour
  tortillas
Shredded cheddar cheese, sliced
  ripe olives, shredded lettuce,
  sour cream and salsa, optional

In a large skillet, cook beef over medium heat until no longer pink; drain. Stir in the chili powder, cumin, coriander, salt and oregano.

Combine cornstarch and water until smooth. Stir into beef mixture. Bring to a boil; cook and stir for 2 minutes or until thickened. Serve with tortilla chips, taco shells or flour tortillas. Garnish with optional toppings. **Yield:** 4 servings.

Chorizo Cheese Dip

(Pictured at right)

Guests will wipe the bowl clean when you set out this spicy cheese dip from our Test Kitchen. Serve it with tortilla chips or even vegetable dippers.

1/2 pound uncooked chorizo
    sausage, casings removed
1 small green pepper, chopped
1 small sweet red pepper,
    chopped
1 small onion, chopped
3 garlic cloves, minced
1 tablespoon vegetable oil
1/2 teaspoon cayenne pepper
2 cartons (12 ounces *each*)
    white Mexican dipping cheese
Tortilla chips

In a large skillet, cook chorizo over medium heat until no longer pink; drain. Remove and keep warm. In the same skillet, saute the peppers, onion and garlic in oil until tender. Stir in cayenne and chorizo; heat through.

Heat cheese according to package directions; stir into meat mixture. Serve warm with tortilla chips. Refrigerate leftovers. **Yield:** 4 cups.

Baked Jalapenos

(Pictured above)

This baked version of jalapeno poppers was developed by our home economists. The crunchy topping nicely complements the creamy filling.

1 package (3 ounces) cream
    cheese, softened
1/4 teaspoon ground cumin
2/3 cup shredded Monterey Jack
    cheese
1 teaspoon minced fresh
    cilantro
8 jalapeno peppers, halved
    lengthwise and seeded
1 egg, beaten
3/4 cup cornflake crumbs

In a small mixing bowl, beat cream cheese and cumin until smooth. Beat in Monterey Jack cheese and cilantro. Spoon into jalapeno halves.

Place egg and cornflake crumbs in separate shallow bowls. Dip filling side of jalapenos in egg, then coat with crumbs. Place on a greased baking sheet with crumb side up. Bake at 350° for 25-30 minutes or until top is golden brown. Serve immediately. **Yield:** 16 appetizers.

Mexican Macaroni and Cheese

For a classic casserole with a little more grown-up taste, give our
Test Kitchen's zesty macaroni and cheese a try.

3 cups uncooked elbow macaroni
3 tablespoons butter
3 tablespoons all-purpose flour
2 cups milk
1 tablespoon lime juice
2 cups (8 ounces) shredded
    cheddar cheese, *divided*
1-1/2 cups (6 ounces) shredded
    pepper Jack cheese, *divided*
2 tablespoons chopped jalapeno
    pepper
1 to 2 teaspoons chili powder
1/2 teaspoon salt
1/4 teaspoon paprika

Cook macaroni according to package directions. Meanwhile, in a large saucepan, melt butter. Stir in flour until smooth. Gradually stir in milk. Bring to a boil; cook and stir for 2 minutes or until thickened. Reduce heat; stir in lime juice. Stir in 1-1/2 cups cheddar cheese and 1 cup pepper Jack cheese until melted.

Remove from the heat. Stir in the jalapeno, chili powder and salt. Drain macaroni; add to cheese sauce and toss to coat.

Transfer to a greased 8-in. square baking dish. Top with remaining cheeses; sprinkle with paprika. Bake, uncovered, at 350° for 15-20 minutes or until cheese is melted. **Yield:** 6 servings.

Spicy Refried Beans

(Pictured on page 219)

Our home economists jazz up a can of refried beans with jalapeno pepper,
seasonings and cheese. Serve with tortilla chips on the side for scooping.

1 small onion, chopped
1 jalapeno pepper, seeded and
    chopped
1 garlic clove, minced
2 teaspoons vegetable oil
1 can (16 ounces) refried beans
2 tablespoons water
1 teaspoon hot pepper sauce
1/4 teaspoon ground cumin
1/4 teaspoon chili powder
1/8 teaspoon cayenne pepper
1/2 cup shredded Monterey Jack
    cheese

In a large skillet, saute the onion, jalapeno and garlic in oil for 2-3 minutes or until tender. Stir in the beans, water, hot pepper sauce, cumin, chili powder and cayenne. Cook and stir over medium-low heat until heated through. Transfer to a serving bowl; sprinkle with cheese. **Yield:** 2 cups.

JALAPENO PEPPER POINTER

WHEN cutting or seeding hot peppers, use rubber or plastic gloves to protect your hands. Avoid touching your face.

Picture-Perfect Party Favors

(Pictured above)

THE fun times at the Sweet 16 party will go by in a flash. So be sure to capture the special moments forever.

During the party, use your digital camera to snap a photo of the birthday girl with each guest. Then print off the pictures on your home computer.

Place the pictures in cute and quirky photo stands that the guests can take home with them as unforgettable party favors.

You can find these individual photo stands at a variety of discount and department stores. Buy all of the same style or mix and match them for colorful table-toppers.

Hoedown on the Farm

ROUND UP your family and friends for a homespun, end-of-summer celebration featuring a delicious, down-home menu.

To spur on your guests' appetites, set out finger-licking Lemon-Ginger Barbecue Ribs.

Rope in a bushel of compliments by passing around a platter piled high with Skillet Jalapeno Corn Bread and a kettle brimming with Three-Bean Bake.

Of course, nothing says "summer" quite like hot, buttered ears of Cilantro-Lime Sweet Corn!

Then cool off with a thirst-quenching beverage such as Sweet Citrus Iced Tea. (All recipes are shown at right.)

COUNTRY CUISINE
(Pictured above)

Lemon-Ginger Barbecue Ribs (p. 229)

Cilantro-Lime Sweet Corn (p. 228)

Skillet Jalapeno Corn Bread (p. 230)

Three-Bean Bake (p. 232)

Sweet Citrus Iced Tea (p. 228)

Sweet Citrus Iced Tea

(Pictured at far right and on page 227)

My family has been making iced tea this way ever since I was a child. When I recently prepared some for the Elders at church, the men liked it so much that all the wives asked for the recipe.
— Diane Kirkpatrick, Terre Hill, Pennsylvania

14-1/2 cups water, *divided*
  10 individual tea bags
 1-1/2 cups sugar
  2/3 cup lemon juice
  1/4 cup orange juice concentrate
Ice cubes

In a large saucepan, bring 4 cups of water just to a boil. Remove from the heat. Add tea bags; let stand for 10 minutes. Discard tea bags. Pour tea into a large container. Stir in the sugar, lemon juice, orange juice concentrate and remaining water. Refrigerate until chilled. Serve over ice. **Yield:** 1 gallon.

Cilantro-Lime Sweet Corn

(Pictured on page 227)

Our home economists give southwestern flavor to corn on the cob with cilantro and lime juice.

  8 medium ears sweet corn in husks
 1/3 cup plus 1/4 cup butter, softened, *divided*
  2 to 3 tablespoons minced fresh cilantro
1-1/2 teaspoons grated lime peel
  1 teaspoon salt
  1 teaspoon plus 2 tablespoons lime juice, *divided*
  1/2 teaspoon garlic powder

Soak the corn in cold water for 1 hour. Meanwhile, in a small bowl, combine 1/3 cup butter, cilantro, lime peel, salt, 1 teaspoon lime juice and garlic powder; set aside.

Carefully peel back husks from corn to within 1 in. of bottom; remove silk. Spread each ear of corn with butter mixture. Rewrap corn husks and secure with kitchen string. Coat grill rack with nonstick cooking spray before starting the grill. Grill corn, covered, over medium heat for 25-30 minutes or until tender, turning occasionally.

In a small microwave-safe bowl, melt the remaining butter; stir in remaining lime juice. Cut string and peel back husks. Brush corn with butter mixture. **Yield:** 8 servings.

KERNELS OF CORN FACTS

FRESH CORN is at its peak May through September. Look for ears of corn with bright green, tightly closed husks and golden brown silk. The kernels should be plump, milky and in closely spaced rows all the way to the tip.

As soon as corn is picked, the sugar gradually begins to convert to starch, reducing its natural sweetness. So corn is best cooked and served the same day it's picked and purchased.

Lemon-Ginger Barbecued Ribs

(Pictured at right and on page 227)

Although my husband does most of the cooking for us, the kitchen is all mine on weekends! I was inspired to make this recipe for a family member who's allergic to tomatoes.
—Meg Cash, Lady Lake, Florida

  8 **pounds pork baby back ribs, cut into serving-size pieces**
1/2 **cup water**
1/2 **cup lemon juice**
1/2 **cup light corn syrup**
  4 **garlic cloves, peeled**
  2 **tablespoons ground ginger**
  1 **tablespoon onion powder**
  1 **tablespoon dried basil**
  1 **tablespoon dried thyme**
  1 **tablespoon pepper**
1-1/2 **teaspoons salt**
1-1/2 **teaspoons paprika**
  3/4 **cup vegetable oil**

Place the ribs in two shallow roasting pans; add water. Cover and bake at 325° for 2 hours.

For sauce, in a blender or food processor, combine the lemon juice, corn syrup, garlic and seasonings; cover and process until blended. While processing, gradually add oil in a steady stream.

Drain ribs. Coat grill rack with nonstick cooking spray before starting the grill. Spoon some of the sauce over ribs. Grill, uncovered, over medium-low heat for 8-10 minutes or until browned, turning occasionally and brushing with sauce. Serve remaining sauce with ribs. **Yield:** 8 servings.

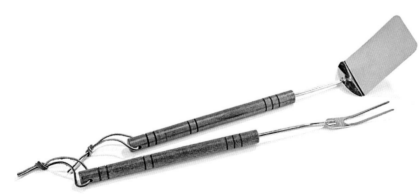

Skillet Jalapeno Corn Bread

(Pictured on page 227)

*Our home economists bake this moist corn bread in an ovenproof skillet to
tie into the Western barbecue theme. A jalapeno pepper adds a bit of zip.*

6 bacon strips, diced
1 cup all-purpose flour
1 cup yellow cornmeal
1/4 cup sugar
3 teaspoons baking powder
1/2 teaspoon salt
2 eggs
1 cup buttermilk
1/2 cup vegetable oil
3/4 cup shredded cheddar cheese
2 tablespoons chopped seeded
    jalapeno pepper

In a 10-in. ovenproof skillet, cook bacon over medium heat until crisp. Remove with a slotted spoon to paper towels. Drain, reserving 1 tablespoon drippings in skillet; set aside.

In a bowl, combine the flour, cornmeal, sugar, baking powder and salt. In another bowl, combine the eggs, buttermilk and oil; stir into dry ingredients just until moistened. Fold in the cheese, jalapeno and bacon.

Pour into the skillet. Bake at 425° for 20-25 minutes or until golden brown. Cut into wedges; serve warm. **Yield:** 8-10 servings.

Editor's Note: When cutting or seeding hot peppers, use rubber or plastic gloves to protect your hands. Avoid touching your face.

BAKING BETTER CORN BREAD

HERE are some hints for making the best corn bread:

- Before using cornmeal, make sure it's fresh. It should have a slightly sweet smell. Rancid cornmeal will smell stale and musty.
- To avoid overmixing, stir the batter by hand just until moistened. Lumps in the batter are normal and desired.
- Don't let the mixed batter stand before baking. Have the oven preheated and the skillet or pan ready to go.
- Corn bread tastes best fresh from the oven. If that's not possible, serve it the same day it's made.
- If you like a more crusty corn bread, use a dark pan or skillet instead of one with a light finish.

Potato Salad with Bacon

(Pictured at right)

My young nephew refuses to eat any potato salad but mine! Italian salad dressing, sour cream and bacon give it a one-of-a-kind flavor.
—Collette Reynolds
Raleigh, North Carolina

3 pounds red potatoes (about 12 medium)
4 hard-cooked eggs
3/4 cup sour cream
2/3 cup mayonnaise
1 teaspoon salt
1 teaspoon prepared mustard
1/2 teaspoon garlic powder
1/4 teaspoon pepper
11 bacon strips, cooked and crumbled
1/2 cup chopped celery
1/4 cup chopped green onions
1/4 cup Italian salad dressing

Cut potatoes into 1/2-in. cubes; place in a large kettle and cover with water. Bring to a boil. Reduce heat; cover and simmer for 10-15 minutes or until tender. Drain and cool to room temperature.

Cut eggs in half; chop egg whites and set aside. In a bowl, mash egg yolks. Stir in the sour cream, mayonnaise, salt, mustard, garlic powder and pepper; set aside.

In a large bowl, combine the potatoes, bacon, egg whites, celery, onions and Italian dressing. Fold in mayonnaise mixture. Cover and refrigerate for at least 2 hours before serving. **Yield:** 16 servings.

Creamy Coleslaw

My mother made this classic coleslaw for my wedding. The big bowl was emptied in no time!
—Shannon Walker, Thermopolis, Wyoming

10 cups shredded cabbage
2 celery ribs with leaves, chopped
1/2 cup chopped green onions
1/2 cup mayonnaise
1/4 cup sugar
1/4 cup lemon juice *or* cider vinegar

1/4 cup sour cream
1/2 teaspoon seasoned pepper
1/4 teaspoon salt

In a large bowl, combine the cabbage, celery and onions. In a small bowl, combine the remaining ingredients until smooth. Pour over cabbage mixture and toss to coat. Serve immediately or refrigerate for several hours. **Yield:** 12 servings.

Three-Bean Bake

(Pictured on page 227)

I've come across many recipes for baked beans through the years, but none have the right amount of "kick."
I created this recipe from several different ideas I've gathered over time. It's my husband's favorite.
—*Romi Plath, Sweetser, Indiana*

6 bacon strips, cut into 1-inch
   pieces
1/2 cup chopped onion
3 garlic cloves, minced
1 can (28 ounces) baked beans
1 can (16 ounces) kidney beans,
   rinsed and drained
1 can (15 ounces) butter beans,
   rinsed and drained
1/3 cup packed brown sugar
1/4 cup ketchup
2 tablespoons Dijon mustard
1/2 teaspoon chili powder
1/2 teaspoon pepper

In a large skillet, partially cook the bacon. Remove with a slotted spoon to paper towels. Drain, reserving 1 tablespoon drippings. In the drippings, saute onion and garlic until tender. In a large bowl, combine the beans, onion mixture and bacon. Stir in the brown sugar, ketchup, mustard, chili powder and pepper.

Transfer mixture to a greased 2-qt. baking dish. Bake, uncovered, at 350° for 50-60 minutes or until bubbly. **Yield:** 8 servings.

Chips Galore Cookies

I created this recipe one day when I decided to revise a family favorite.
My kids loved the variation, and I've been making these cookies this way ever since.
—*Bennet Barlean, Nooksack, Washington*

1 cup butter-flavored shortening
1 cup sugar
1/2 cup packed brown sugar
2 eggs
2 teaspoons vanilla extract
2-1/2 cups all-purpose flour
1 teaspoon baking soda
1/2 teaspoon salt
1 cup chopped pecans
1 cup milk chocolate chips
3/4 cup peanut butter chips
3/4 cup English toffee bits *or*
   almond brickle chips

3/4 cup flaked coconut
2/3 cup vanilla *or* white chips

In a large mixing bowl, cream shortening and sugars. Add eggs, one at a time, beating well after each addition. Beat in vanilla. Combine the flour, baking soda and salt; gradually add to the creamed mixture. Stir in the remaining ingredients.

Drop by 1/4 cupfuls 2 in. apart onto ungreased baking sheets. Bake at 350° for 12-14 minutes or until golden brown. Remove to wire racks. **Yield:** 2 dozen.

Pear-Apple Pie Bars

(Pictured at right)

With two kinds of fruit, these bars from our Test Kitchen have mass appeal. The lovely lattice top makes it special for get-togethers.

4 cups all-purpose flour
1 teaspoon salt
1 teaspoon baking powder
1 cup shortening
4 egg yolks
2 tablespoons lemon juice
9 tablespoons cold water
FILLING:
1-1/2 cups sugar
3 tablespoons all-purpose flour
1 teaspoon ground cinnamon
Dash ground nutmeg
4 cups finely chopped peeled apples
3 cups finely chopped peeled ripe pears
1 egg white, beaten

In a large bowl, combine the flour, salt and baking powder. Cut in shortening until mixture resembles coarse crumbs. In a small bowl, whisk egg yolks, lemon juice and water; gradually add to flour mixture, tossing with a fork until dough forms a ball. Divide in half, making one portion slightly larger. Chill for 30 minutes.

Roll out larger portion of dough between two large sheets of waxed paper into a 17-in. x 12-in. rectangle. Transfer to an ungreased 15-in. x 10-in. x 1-in. baking pan. Press pastry onto the bottom and up the sides of pan; trim pastry even with top edges.

In a large bowl, combine the sugar, flour, cinnamon and nutmeg. Add apples and pears; toss to coat. Spoon over crust. Roll out remaining pastry; make a lattice crust. Trim and seal edges. Brush lattice top with egg white. Bake at 375° for 40-45 minutes or until golden brown. Cool on a wire rack. **Yield:** 2 dozen.

APPEALING PEARS

LOOK for pears that are firm, fragrant and free of blemishes.

To ripen pears, place them in a brown paper bag at room temperature for several days. Ripe pears will give in slightly to pressure.

Use a vegetable peeler or paring knife to remove the skin.

Barbecued Beef Brisket

This tasty brisket conveniently bakes for hours, allowing you lots of time to prepare the rest of the meal. Leftovers make delicious sandwiches.
—*Martha Lewis, Glen Allen, Virginia*

1 teaspoon garlic powder
1/2 teaspoon onion salt
1/2 teaspoon celery salt
1 fresh beef brisket (4 pounds)
3 to 4 teaspoons Liquid Smoke, optional
3 cups water, *divided*
1 cup ketchup
1/2 cup chopped onion
6 tablespoons Worcestershire sauce, *divided*
1/4 cup packed brown sugar
1/4 cup cider vinegar
1 teaspoon celery seed
1 teaspoon pepper
1/2 teaspoon salt

Combine the garlic powder, onion salt and celery salt; rub over brisket. Place in a large resealable plastic bag; sprinkle with Liquid Smoke if desired. Seal bag and turn to coat; refrigerate overnight.

For sauce, in a large saucepan, combine 2 cups water, ketchup, onion, 4 tablespoons Worcestershire sauce, brown sugar, vinegar, celery seed, pepper and salt. Bring to a boil. Reduce heat; cover and simmer for 15 minutes, stirring occasionally. Cool; cover and refrigerate.

Place the brisket in a Dutch oven; add remaining water and Worcestershire sauce to pan. Cover tightly. Bake at 325° for 1-1/2 hours; drain.

Baste with sauce. Bake, uncovered, 1-2 hours longer or until meat is tender. Let stand for 20 minutes; thinly slice across the grain. **Yield:** 10-12 servings.

Editor's Note: This is a fresh beef brisket, not corned beef. The meat comes from the first cut of the brisket.

BANDANA NAPKINS

FOR a casual outdoor gathering, fashion fun napkins from bandanas! Look for inexpensive, cotton bandanas in a variety of colors at discount department stores. Wash and, if needed, quickly touch up with an iron.

1. With the wrong side up, fold the bandana in half diagonally.

2. Bring the point of the triangle over to the long, folded edge.

3. Scrunch the long edge together at the center and tie the bandana in a loose, overhand knot.

Down-Home Outdoor Dining

(Pictured above)

WHEN entertaining in casual, country style, only an informal, down-home table will do.

Start by setting up two sawhorses a few feet apart. Then set a large barn board or piece of plywood on top. Hay bales covered with cotton throw rugs turn into simple bench seats.

Leave the luxurious linens inside and grab a clean, large wool blanket to use as a comforting tablecloth. Inexpensive bandanas serve as nifty napkins. (See the opposite page for fast folding instructions.) Graniteware dinner plates, mugs and serving pieces add to the rustic charm.

To quickly add color to the table with little fuss, arrange wild flowers in unique vases, like the metal coffeepot and graniteware container pictured above.

A Mad Scientist Halloween Scene

GET in the spine-tingling spirit this Halloween by hosting a hair-raising bash in a spooky science lab that even Dr. Frankenstein would envy.

Go out on a limb and concoct a formula for fun with some revolting recipes.

For an enticing experiment, inject a mouth-watering marinade into drumsticks to create the electrifying Spicy Turkey Legs.

Visitors to your loony lab will bolt for the buffet table to scoop up eye-catching Creepy-Crawly Pasta Salad.

Mad Scientist Punch was developed by doctoring up frozen pineapple-orange juice concentrate with sherbet and soda for a batty brew. (All recipes are shown at right.)

SPINE-TINGLING SUPPER
(Pictured above)

Spicy Turkey Legs (p. 244)

Creep-Crawly Pasta Salad (p. 242)

Mad Scientist Punch (p. 244)

Fried Bolts

(Pictured at far right, bottom)

Our home economists' nuts-and-bolts appetizers feature mushroom caps and zucchini sticks.
Assemble them earlier in the day and chill until ready to deep fry.

16 medium fresh mushrooms
2 small zucchini
2 eggs
2 tablespoons water
1/2 cup all-purpose flour
1/2 teaspoon chili powder
1/4 teaspoon salt
1/4 teaspoon sugar
1/4 teaspoon garlic powder
1/4 teaspoon cayenne pepper
1/4 teaspoon ground cumin
Oil for frying
Sweet-and-sour sauce, optional

Remove stems from mushrooms. Cut a thin layer from the top of mushroom caps; cut mushroom edges, forming a hexagon shape. Cut zucchini lengthwise into quarters, then into 2-in. pieces. Trim one end to fit into mushroom caps.

Insert a toothpick through the top of the mushroom into the zucchini, leaving about 1 in. of toothpick to use as a handle for dipping.

In a small shallow bowl, beat the eggs and water. In another bowl, combine the flour, chili powder, salt, sugar, garlic powder, cayenne and cumin. Dip zucchini-mushroom bolts in egg mixture, then coat with flour mixture.

In an electric skillet, heat 1 in. of oil to 375°. Fry bolts in batches for 2-3 minutes or until golden brown on all sides. Drain on paper towels. Serve warm with sweet-and-sour sauce if desired. **Yield:** 16 appetizers.

Buggy Snack Mix

Chocolate-covered raisin "bugs" are a tasty surprise in this sweet and crunchy
snack mix from our Test Kitchen. Candy corn adds a bit of color.

1 can (3 ounces) chow mein noodles
1 cup unsalted cashews
1 cup salted peanuts
1/2 cup packed brown sugar
1/4 cup butter
2 tablespoons light corn syrup
1/8 teaspoon salt
1/4 teaspoon baking soda
1 cup candy corn
1 cup chocolate-covered raisins

In a large heatproof bowl, combine the chow mein noodles, cashews and peanuts; set aside. In a microwave-safe bowl, combine the brown sugar, butter, corn syrup and salt. Microwave, uncovered, on high for 2 minutes or until sugar is dissolved and syrup is bubbly, stirring frequently. Stir in baking soda; microwave 20 seconds longer or until mixture begins to foam.

Carefully pour over chow mein noodle mixture; stir to coat. Transfer to a greased 15-in. x 10-in. x 1-in. baking pan. Bake at 300° for 25-30 minutes, stirring every 10 minutes. Spread on waxed paper; cool for at least 30 minutes.

Place snack mix in a large bowl. Add candy corn and raisins; gently toss. Store in an airtight container. **Yield:** 6 cups.

Editor's Note: This recipe was tested in a 1,100-watt microwave.

Backbone Roll-Ups

(Pictured at right, top)

These roll-ups from our Test Kitchen are sliced thick, then stacked slightly askew to resemble a backbone. Feel free to use other fillings.

3/4 cup garlic-herb cheese spread
6 flour tortillas (8 inches)
1 cup fresh baby spinach
6 thin slices deli ham
12 thin slices hard salami
6 slices provolone cheese
1/2 cup chopped green pepper
1/2 cup chopped sweet red pepper

Spread 2 tablespoons of cheese spread over each tortilla. Layer with spinach, ham, salami and cheese. Sprinkle with peppers. Roll up tightly and wrap in plastic wrap. Refrigerate for 1 hour or until firm.

Unwrap and cut each into six slices. On a serving plate, stack roll-ups to resemble a spine. **Yield:** 3 dozen.

BODY-PARTS PARTY GAME

HAVE the guests at your Halloween party gather 'round for a fun game that focuses on feeling frightfully fun foods. Place the "body parts" listed here in separate, large resealable plastic bags, then place in paper bags.

Dim the lights and have everyone sit in a circle. Tell guests to pass around the bags one at a time, reach into each bag without looking and guess the body parts. Here's what you need for a howling good time:

- Hot dog chunks (noses)
- Whole cooked, chilled cauliflower (brain)
- Peeled grapes (eyeballs)
- Cooked spaghetti noodles (intestines)
- Latex glove filled with warm water, tied and frozen (hand)
- Dried apple rings, cut in half (ears)
- Slab of gelatin (liver)
- Nut shells (toenails)
- Pieces of chalk (teeth)

Chunky Chili

(Pictured at far right)

My family (especially my dad) loves chili. After experimenting with several recipes, I came up with
my own version that uses ground turkey and is conveniently prepared in a slow cooker.
—Jolene Britten, Gig Harbor, Washington

1 pound ground turkey *or* beef
1 medium onion, chopped
2 medium tomatoes, cut up
1 can (16 ounces) kidney beans,
   rinsed and drained
1 can (15 ounces) chili beans,
   undrained
1 can (15 ounces) tomato sauce
1 cup water
1 can (4 ounces) chopped green
   chilies
1 tablespoon chili powder
2 teaspoons salt
1 teaspoon ground cumin
3/4 teaspoon pepper
Sour cream and sliced jalapenos,
   optional

In a large skillet, cook turkey and onion over medium heat until meat is no longer pink; drain. Transfer to a 3-1/2-qt. slow cooker.

Stir in the tomatoes, beans, tomato sauce, water, chilies, chili powder, salt, cumin and pepper. Cover and cook on low for 5-6 hours or until heated through. Garnish with sour cream and jalapenos if desired. **Yield:** 6-8 servings (about 2 quarts).

Apple Peanut Butter Cookies

These spiced peanut butter cookies are great for fall gatherings. They're crisp outside and soft inside.
—Marjorie Benson, New Castle, Pennsylvania

1/2 cup shortening
1/2 cup chunky peanut butter
1/2 cup sugar
1/2 cup packed brown sugar
1 egg
1/2 teaspoon vanilla extract
1/2 cup grated peeled apple
1-1/2 cups all-purpose flour
1/2 teaspoon baking soda
1/2 teaspoon salt
1/2 teaspoon ground cinnamon

In a large mixing bowl, cream the shortening, peanut butter and sugars. Beat in egg and vanilla. Stir in apple. Combine the dry ingredients; gradually add to creamed mixture.

Drop by rounded tablespoonfuls 2 in. apart onto greased baking sheets. Bake at 375° for 10-12 minutes or until golden brown. Cool for 5 minutes before removing to wire racks. **Yield:** about 2-1/2 dozen.

Editor's Note: Reduced-fat or generic brands of peanut butter are not recommended for this recipe.

Breadstick Bones

(Pictured at right)

Our home economists lightly season refrigerated breadsticks, then tie the ends into knots to create these Breadstick Bones.

1 tube (11 ounces) refrigerated breadsticks
1 tablespoon butter, melted
2 tablespoons grated Parmesan cheese
1/4 teaspoon garlic salt

Unroll and separate breadsticks. Carefully stretch dough and tie the ends of each breadstick into a knot. With a scissors, snip a small notch in the center. Place on an ungreased baking sheet; brush with butter.

Combine Parmesan cheese and garlic salt; sprinkle over dough. Bake at 375° for 10-12 minutes or until golden brown. Serve warm. **Yield:** 1 dozen.

Fruity Eyeball Salad

A light mint dressing nicely coats assorted fruity "eyeballs" in this recipe from our Test Kitchen. Just watch this salad disappear from the buffet table!

2 cups watermelon balls
2 cups cantaloupe balls
2 cups honeydew balls
1 cup seedless red grapes
1 cup seedless green grapes
DRESSING:
1/3 cup unsweetened apple juice
1 tablespoon honey
2 teaspoons minced fresh mint

In a large bowl, combine the melon balls and grapes. In a small bowl, combine the dressing ingredients. Pour over fruit and toss to coat. Cover and refrigerate until chilled. **Yield:** 8 servings.

Creepy-Crawly Pasta Salad

(Pictured on page 237)

*As a change of pace from pasta salads featuring Italian salad dressing or mayonnaise,
our home economists developed a delicious sweet-and-sour dressing.*

8 ounces uncooked fusilli *or*
    tricolor rotini pasta
1 medium zucchini, julienned
1 cup cherry tomatoes
1 cup fresh cauliflowerets
1 cup colossal ripe olives,
    halved
3/4 cup pimiento-stuffed olives
1 small green pepper, chopped
1/2 cup chopped red onion
DRESSING:
  1/4 cup ketchup
  2 tablespoons sugar
  2 tablespoons white vinegar
  1/2 small onion, cut into wedges
  1 garlic clove, peeled
  1 teaspoon paprika
  1/4 teaspoon salt
  1/4 cup vegetable oil

Cook pasta according to package directions; drain and rinse in cold water. Place in a large bowl; add the zucchini, tomatoes, cauliflower, olives, green pepper and red onion.

In a blender, combine the ketchup, sugar, vinegar, onion, garlic, paprika and salt; cover and process until blended. While processing, gradually add oil in a steady stream; process until thickened. Pour over pasta salad and toss to coat. Cover and refrigerate for at least 2 hours before serving. **Yield:** 13 servings.

SPOOKTACULAR SCIENCE LAB

TRY these tricks for creating an eerie lab where Frankenstein would be happy biding his tormented time! For many of these eye-popping props, we headed to a local science and surplus store.

- A spooky sterile environment starts with a simple stainless steel table. Concoct creepy serving containers from stainless steel baking pans and mixing bowls.
- Use stainless steel cooking instruments for serving and a meat cleaver to cut the Frankenstein Cake (see photo above right).

- Spine-tingling table toppers include beakers in various shapes and sizes, tall test tubes to display chocolate candy eyeballs, chains and Shrunken Apple Heads (see page 245).
- Tint water a yellow-green color and pour into assorted test tubes and beakers. Carefully add a little dry ice if desired.
- A white lab coat and skeleton in the background is an alarming addition.
- For a monstrous mood, dim the lights and fire up drippy candles on an inexpensive candelabra.

Frankenstein Cake

(Pictured at right)

Convenience items like a cake mix and canned frosting make this clever dessert a breeze to prepare. It always elicits oohs and ahhs at Halloween parties.
—Nancy Bresler, Kinde, Michigan

1 package (18-1/4 ounces) chocolate cake mix
1 package (8 ounces) cream cheese, softened
1/2 cup sour cream
1/2 cup sugar
1 egg
1/2 teaspoon vanilla extract
1 carton (8 ounces) frozen whipped topping, thawed
Moss green paste food coloring
1 can (16 ounces) chocolate frosting
1 Swiss cake roll *or* Ho Ho

Prepare cake batter according to package directions. Pour into a greased and waxed paper-lined 13-in. x 9-in. x 2-in. baking pan. In a small mixing bowl, beat the cream cheese, sour cream, sugar, egg and vanilla until smooth. Drop by tablespoonfuls about 1 in. apart onto batter.

Bake at 350° for 40-45 minutes or until center is firm when lightly touched. Cool for 10 minutes before removing from pan to a wire rack to cool completely.

To make Frankenstein, cut a piece of cake for the head (about 10 in. x 7-3/4 in.) and neck (about 2-1/2 in. x 4-1/2 in.). Cut two pieces for ears (about 2-3/4 in. x 1/2 in.). Save remaining cake for another use. Position head, neck and ears on a covered board.

Place 1/4 cup whipped topping in a small bowl; tint dark green with moss green food coloring. Cut a small hole in the corner of a small plastic bag; insert round pastry tip #3 and fill with tinted topping. Set aside.

Tint remaining whipped topping moss green. Frost face, neck and ears, building up areas for the forehead, nose and cheeks. With reserved dark green topping, pipe mouth, stitches on neck and forehead, and eyes with pupils.

Cut a hole in the corner of a pastry or plastic bag; insert pastry tip #233. Fill with chocolate frosting; pipe hair 1-1/4 in. from top of head to forehead and about 4 in. down sides of head. Cut cake roll in half widthwise; place on each side of neck for bolts. Store in the refrigerator. **Yield:** 12-15 servings.

Spicy Turkey Legs

(Pictured on page 236)

Guests at your Halloween party will get a kick out of these flavorful turkey legs from our Test Kitchen.
For less spicy flavor, reduce the amount of hot sauce and inject 1/2 ounce into each leg.

2/3 cup Louisiana-style hot sauce
5 tablespoons vegetable oil
1 tablespoon chili powder
1 tablespoon soy sauce
2 teaspoons ground mustard
1 teaspoon garlic powder
1 teaspoon poultry seasoning
1 teaspoon onion powder
1 teaspoon celery salt
1/2 teaspoon white pepper
1/2 teaspoon hot pepper sauce,
   optional
6 turkey drumsticks (1 pound
   each)

In a small bowl, combine the first 11 ingredients; set aside 1/4 cup for basting. Draw remaining marinade into a flavor injector. In several areas of each drumstick, inject a total of 2 tablespoons (or 1 oz.) of marinade into the meat while slowly pulling out the needle.

Place drumsticks on a foil-lined 15-in. x 10-in. x 1-in. baking pan. Cover and bake at 375° for 30 minutes. Uncover; bake 45-55 minutes longer or until a meat thermometer reads 180°, basting occasionally with reserved marinade. **Yield:** 6 servings.

Editor's Note: Flavor injectors can be found in the outdoor cooking section of your favorite home or cooking store or through numerous Internet sources.

Using Flavor Injectors

FILL the flavor injector with the marinade. With one hand holding the turkey leg, inject the marinade into the meat, slowly pull out the needle. Inject into several other areas of the meat.

Mad Scientist Punch

(Pictured on page 236)

Our home economists concocted this "potion" with kitchen staples such as
juice concentrate, soft drink mix, soda and sherbet. It appeals to kids of all ages!

2 cans (12 ounces *each*) frozen
   pineapple-orange juice
   concentrate, thawed
2 cups water
1 envelope unsweetened orange
   soft drink mix

2 liters lemon-lime soda, chilled
1 pint orange sherbet, softened

In a punch bowl, combine the juice concentrate, water and soft drink mix; stir in soda. Top with scoops of sherbet. Serve immediately. **Yield:** 16 servings (4 quarts).

Shrunken Apple Heads

(Pictured at right)

USE your noggin when decorating for your Halloween bash by fashioning foul faces from ordinary apples. Tuck these haunted "heads" around the food on your buffet table or stack them on candleholders.

With a paring knife remove the skin from large, medium and small Golden Delicious apples. (Note that the apples will shrink in size as they dry.)

Immediately dip the peeled apples into lemon juice to prevent browning.

Cut away the bottom of the apple to form a rounded chin. Carve a nose. Hollow out two circles for eyes and a single circle for a mouth.

Dip the carved apple in lemon juice again and sprinkle with non-iodized table salt.

Place the apples on a rack in a low-sided pan. Set aside in a warm, dry place away from direct sunlight until completely dry. (This may take up to three weeks.)

When dry, the apple heads can also be hung up for display. With a long, hand-sewing needle, insert nylon thread through the center of apples and tie a knot at the bottom end.

REFERENCE INDEX

Use this index as a guide to the many helpful hints, food facts, decorating ideas and step-by-step instructions throughout the book.

GENERAL RECIPE INDEX

This handy index lists every recipe by food category, major ingredient and/or cooking method.

ALPHABETICAL INDEX

Refer to this index for a complete alphabetical listing of all recipes in this book.

Here's *Your* Chance To Be Published!

Send us your special-occasion recipes and you could have them featured in a future edition of this classic cookbook.

YEAR AFTER YEAR, the recipe for success at every holiday party or special-occasion celebration is an attractive assortment of flavorful food.

So we're always on the lookout for mouth-watering appetizers, entrees, side dishes, breads, desserts and more...all geared toward the special gatherings you attend or host throughout the year.

Here's how you can enter your family-favorite holiday fare for possible publication in a future *Holiday & Celebrations Cookbook*:

Print or type each recipe on one sheet of 8-1/2" x 11" paper. Please include your name, address and daytime phone number on each page. Be specific with directions, measurements and the sizes of cans, packages and pans.

Please include a few words about yourself, when you serve your dish, reactions it has received from family and friends and the origin of the recipe.

Send to "Celebrations Cookbook," 5925 Country Lane, Greendale WI 53129 or E-mail to *recipes@reimanpub.com*. Write "Celebrations Cookbook" on the subject line of all E-mail entries and *include your full name, postal address and phone number on each entry.*

Contributors whose recipes are printed will receive a complimentary copy of the book...so the more recipes you send, the better your chances of "being published!"